"[An] affecting, illuminating memoir . . . With compassion and grace, Bruni guides us along a literal pilgrimage between light and darkness, a tender meld of science reporting and philosophical investigation."

—*Oprah Daily* Most Anticipated Books of 2022

"Weaving together his own story of diminished eyesight with the stories of many other people, Frank Bruni constructs a philosophical narrative of resilience: how we can discover it in ourselves and how we can recognize and support it in others. His writing is lively and intimate, and his message is powerful and lucid."

—Andrew Solomon

"Frank Bruni lost sight in one eye and turned that experience into a life-changing journey of empathy, discovery and renewal. Once again he has enlightened us all."

—Tom Brokaw

"A masterful storyteller. A wonderful book. Honest. Poetic. Uplifting."

—Lesley Stahl

"In this wonderful book, Frank Bruni offers insight and inspiration as he grapples with a daunting medical crisis. Beautifully written and bracing in its honesty, this book rewards its reader with the precious gift of learning how we all may seek resilience and ultimately recreate a meaningful life."

—Jerome Groopman

"Uplifting and beautiful."

—Katie Couric Media

"With the same precise clarity and melodic wit he layers in his *New York Times* op-eds . . . *The Beauty of Dusk* transcends memoir. Bruni's sharing creates a beacon, reminding us that often in life's cruelties there can be the opportunity to stretch beyond our measure."

—Maria Shriver's *The Sunday Papers* newsletter

"A compassionate take on growing older [that] illustrates Bruni's knack for writing about the unpredictable beauty of the human condition. Smartly mixing memoir and cultural criticism, this movingly speaks to an entire generation."

—*Publishers Weekly*

"In this memoir, Frank Bruni gives an ultimately hopeful account of his sudden illness and confrontation with mortality . . . a welcome reminder, despite the inevitability of dusk in each person's life, of how 'enriching and beautiful that dusk can be' when one examines it closely."

—*Shelf Awareness*

"An uplifting exploration of human potential . . . [A] poignant, often wise look at how nearly everything bad that happens to us can actually be good."

—*Kirkus Reviews*

ALSO BY FRANK BRUNI

Where You Go Is Not Who You'll Be:
An Antidote to the College Admissions Mania

Born Round:
A Story of Family, Food and a Ferocious Appetite

Ambling into History:
The Unlikely Odyssey of George W. Bush

A Meatloaf in Every Oven:
Two Chatty Cooks,
One Iconic Dish and Dozens of Recipes—
From Mom's to Mario Batali's

The Beauty of Dusk

ON VISION LOST AND FOUND

Frank Bruni

AVID READER PRESS

NEW YORK   LONDON   TORONTO   SYDNEY   NEW DELHI

Avid Reader Press
An Imprint of Simon & Schuster, Inc.
1230 Avenue of the Americas
New York, NY 10020

First Avid Reader Press trade paperback edition February 2023

AVID READER PRESS and colophon are trademarks of
Simon & Schuster, Inc.

For information about special discounts for bulk purchases,
please contact Simon & Schuster Special Sales at 1-866-506-1949 or
business@simonandschuster.com.

The Simon & Schuster Speakers Bureau can bring authors
to your live event. For more information or to book an event, contact
the Simon & Schuster Speakers Bureau at 1-866-248-3049 or visit
our website at www.simonspeakers.com.

Interior design by Lexy Alemao

Manufactured in the United States of America

1   3   5   7   9   10   8   6   4   2

Library of Congress Cataloging-in-Publication Data has been applied for.

ISBN 978-1-9821-0857-1
ISBN 978-1-9821-0858-8 (pbk)
ISBN 978-1-9821-0859-5 (ebook)

To Leslie Jane Frier Bruni, 1935–1996.
You remain so very, very near.

Author's Note

Some of the details and language in this book appeared previously in columns and newsletters that I wrote for the *New York Times*. Some quotations are reproduced not from formal interviews but from incidental conversations, recounted to the best of my memory.

The
Beauty
of Dusk

Chapter One
"THIS IS BAD"

They say that death comes like a thief in the night. Lesser vandals have the same MO. The affliction that stole my vision, or at least a big chunk of it, did so as I slept. I went to bed seeing the world one way. I woke up seeing it another.

I went to bed believing that I was more or less in control of my life—that the unfinished business, unrealized dreams and other disappointments were essentially failures of industry and imagination and could probably be redeemed with a fierce enough effort. I woke up to the realization of how ludicrous that was.

I went to bed with more grievances than I could count. I woke up with more gratitude than I can measure. My story is one of loss. It's also one of gain.

It begins in a bumbling fashion, with a baffled protagonist. That first morning, a Saturday, I struggled to figure out what had happened to me. I wasn't sure that anything of significance had happened at all. Several hours would pass before I grew even remotely worried, before curiosity curdled into a vague, tentative concern.

I got out of bed sluggishly, my head full of lead. Bad Frank. Sloppy, undisciplined Frank. On Friday night, I'd had four generous glasses of wine with dinner when two would have sufficed. That had left me with a bit of a hangover, slowing down every part of me: my thoughts, my steps from the bedroom to the kitchen of my apartment on the Upper West Side of Manhattan, my gestures as I went about making coffee. Coffee. That's what I needed. Caffeine would surely jolt everything into working order. It would snap everything into place.

When I poured boiling water from a teakettle into a French press, my aim was off; I watched a puddle spread across the counter. Huh. How did that happen? I chalked it up not to a visual miscalculation but to carelessness, and while I was aware of a slightly hazy, swimmy quality to the space around me, I attributed *that* to the wine, and to what must have been fitful sleep, and to a week that had been more frantic than usual, and to the vagaries of energy and concentration. I was just dragging. This might be one of those days when I needed three or even four mugs of coffee, a brisk run, a cool shower. I'd shift into gear at some point.

There was work to do. I had more than ninety minutes of audio to transcribe from a conversation that I'd had days earlier with George W. Bush's twin daughters, Barbara and Jenna, whose joint memoir, *Sisters First*, was about to be published. They'd granted me one of their first interviews about it, in part because I'd once written a column for the *New York Times* about the importance of siblings and it had touched them. Barbara had told me in an email that it was a small part of what prompted their book. Transcribing the interview wouldn't require any particular mental sharpness—it was a rote exercise, a matter of keystrokes, tedium and time—so I figured that it was the perfect chore for my languid state. I sat down at my computer, created a new file and began. And then, only a minute or two later, I stopped.

Why was I having to try so hard to make out the words on the screen? What explained the dappled fog over some of them? I took off my eyeglasses, reached for some tissue and wiped the lenses clean. I never did that often enough, and that was surely the cause—some random grease, some vagabond grime.

Back to the audio. Back to the typing. But the fog wouldn't lift, and I noticed now that it was heavier toward the right than toward the left. Also, the words occasionally shimmied. Or did they pulse? I couldn't describe it, not even to myself: It was at once subtle and unsubtle and so very, very weird. I doubted what I was seeing—or, rather, *not* seeing.

I cleaned my eyeglasses again, this time with a soft piece of cloth. I used another soft piece of cloth for the computer screen. The problem didn't go away.

Apparently, the grime—the gunk—was *in* my eyes, or at least my right eye, which I determined from shutting one eye and then the other, testing each independently. And it was probably just some phlegmy residue from the night, some goo that I could splash away or flush out with water. I muddled through another hour of transcription, marveling at how the lines of type seemed to be tilted instead of neatly horizontal, then I hopped into the shower and turned my face toward the spray.

That, too, didn't work. Nor did the four-mile run through Riverside Park after it, nor the shower after *that*, and while I know this may be difficult to believe, what I did next wasn't panic or call a doctor or even mention this strangeness with my vision to my longtime romantic partner, Tom, who lived with me and just so happened to be a doctor himself.

What I did next—as I got ready for a dinner party at a friend's apartment, as Tom and I took a cab to get there, as we ate and drank and laughed high above Park Avenue, the lights of Manhattan twinkling around us—was lean on my left eye and put my curious situation as far out of mind as possible. That twinkling was actually prettier than ever because those lights wobbled, just as the words on my computer screen had. I chose to be enchanted. I beat back any inklings of alarm.

I said that my story is one of loss and gain. It's also one of faith, or of different, sequential faiths, beginning with my arrogant, unwarranted and since-abandoned conviction that everything was ultimately fixable, that humans of my place and time had devised ways to transcend the maladies and petty indignities— from soaring blood pressure to sagging jowls—that less invincible humans of less fortunate eras hadn't. I'm a boomer, born in the last of the qualifying years (1946 to 1964), and thus the inheritor of a brand of overconfidence and a kind of defiance that don't make adequate allowances for the wages of aging and inevitability of affliction.

We boomers are the weekend warriors who trade one fitness craze for the next in an insistence on permanent trimness, who try one cosmetic procedure after another in a quest for eternal tautness. And oh the trove of pills at our disposal: statins for out-of-whack cholesterol, selective serotonin reuptake inhibitors for depression, finasteride to keep baldness at bay, Viagra or Cialis for erectile dysfunction, allopurinol for gout.

I was taking a statin, finasteride and allopurinol when the vision in my right eye deteriorated, and I mention that not because those drugs factored into what happened—to the best of anyone's knowledge, they were irrelevant—but because they partly explain my first-blush complacency. I believed in medicine. I believed in remedies.

I was fifty-two then. Over the previous ten years, I'd had one relatively harmless carcinoma surgically excised from my back, another erased from my nose by a chemotherapy cream. Painful inflammation in my shoulder had required an even more painful injection of a steroid, but damned if the injection hadn't done the trick. The sciatic nerve running down my right leg had been screwy for a few months, but a prescription-strength analogue of ibuprofen and an end to jumping rope as part of my gym routine took care of that.

All of these ailments suggested a body in the throes of aging, but none of them broke my stride. I got the right medicine. I contorted or elongated myself into the right stretch. I adjusted my exercises. I did less of this, more of that. I pressed on, in firm possession of the acuity and energy necessary for fifty-

and sixty-hour workweeks, for four to five nights of socializing every week, for summer vacations in Greece that might include steep three-mile hikes to and from remote beaches that Tom and I would sometimes have to ourselves. I clambered across seaside rocks. I swam. I flourished.

So my attitude about my right eye was that there would be a logical explanation and a ready course of treatment, if any treatment were necessary at all. How many ankle strains and neck crimps and headaches and achy feelings fled as suddenly and inexplicably as they'd arrived? I'd woken up to inexplicable blurriness; I'd wake up to inexplicable clarity. That Saturday night, after the dinner with friends, I didn't set an alarm, and I asked Tom to be quiet when he got out of bed the next morning. A few extra hours of sleep would ensure my recovery.

But my vision was no better on Sunday. If anything, it was worse. The problem was still limited to my right eye, and when I tried to use it alone, closing the left one, I saw the shapes of objects but no details. The computer screen was just a wash of white light. The print in newspapers, magazines and books was indecipherable, a sludgy gumbo of fuzzy letters and blotchy word clusters with whole pieces missing. When I used both eyes, I could get by, but the bad one intruded on the good one, throwing a patchy mist over my field of vision, which sometimes seesawed and made me feel woozy.

I finally told Tom. And partly at his urging, I reached out to my ophthalmologist, an approachable man who had at one point shared his mobile phone number. I sent him a text message, telling him about my eyesight and asking if I was OK to wait to see him when his office reopened on Tuesday or if I should go to an emergency room. He responded right away, telling me that he happened to be a few blocks from that office and would meet me there in an hour.

It was just us: no other patients, no receptionists. He arrived so shortly before I did that many of the lights weren't yet turned on. The darkness and the silence amplified how out of the ordinary this visit was and created a sense of foreboding.

We were there for at least ninety minutes, as he went through all the familiar paces of an eye exam plus other, unfamiliar ones. I planted my chin in a hard plastic cup and my forehead against a hard plastic band and held steady, steady, steady as my palms went slick and my heart sort of hiccupped and he positioned one telescope of sorts after another in front of my right eye, as if he were an incredulous astronomer studying some exotic new galaxy. I assumed the "incredulous" part—I couldn't figure out what was taking so long and decided, based on no evidence whatsoever, that he was stumped. When you're sitting that still for that long, you make up stories just to pass the time. You hatch theories. You conjure metaphors, and thus I became an inscrutable cosmos. I became a black hole.

When he finally stepped back and told me that I could remove and relax my head, indicating that the exam was over, I pummeled him with questions: What was wrong with me? If he didn't know, what did he *suspect*? I told him he didn't have to commit to one guess: He could give me a top three, even a top five. I'd been a journalist my whole professional life, so I was practiced at pleas and demands and bartering for information, and I slipped into journalist mode: *What? How? Why? When?* He hemmed and hawed, reluctant to play the game, then acquiesced.

Maybe, he said, I had multiple sclerosis. It sometimes first presented with vision problems. Maybe some other auto-immune disease or systemic disorder was starting to wreak havoc and that havoc had begun like this. Maybe the issue was with my brain, which wasn't accurately processing the information that my eye was sending it. One word dominated his remarks. "Maybe," "maybe," "maybe," "maybe."

"Definitely" I should see a specialist, a "neuro-ophthalmologist," a breed of physician I'd never even heard of. From my eye doctor's cursory exam, he could almost surely conclude that I didn't have corneal or retinal damage. So my right optic nerve was likelier the weak link in my eyesight, and optic nerves were the provinces of medical experts versed in both ophthalmology *and* neurology.

He gave me the name of such an expert. He placed a hand on my shoulder. He wished me luck.

Three days later. A different arsenal of vision-testing machines, in a different part of Manhattan, with a different doctor, but not the one he recommended. When you travel down the road of a complicated, unusual or serious illness, you learn that your ache for answers isn't necessarily anybody else's; that the hurry in you doesn't automatically prompt hurry in others; that while your predicament is front and center for you, it is quite likely back burner for your white-coated saviors, who juggle scores of equally pressing cases and equally needy supplicants. That doesn't fully excuse their aloofness, but it does explain it. And the specialist whose name was given to me? He had room in his schedule—*in a month.*

Tom stepped in. He was affiliated with a local hospital, was acquainted with a neuro-ophthalmologist there and got me in to see her on Wednesday morning. In her teeming waiting room, I was one of the youngest patients—the most outwardly healthy, the most obviously mobile. Someone across from me wore an eye patch. Someone to my left had an eye covered in a thick pad of gauze, with the tape that kept it in place stretching from one side of her forehead to the opposite cheek. I turned from one patient to the other, then back again, seeing if I could catch either's flawed gaze, wanting to offer a smile and a nod, perhaps just to discover whether I could get a smile or a nod back. I had confided to a few friends that I had this appointment, and they'd offered to accompany me, but I'd turned them down. Now I wondered about that decision. I felt profoundly alone.

"Mr. Bruni?"

A nurse or physician's assistant or technician—I didn't know her precise role—was calling my name, summoning me to and through a doorway, the portal to an answer to the riddle of my fog. I got up quickly and buoyantly, which has always been my habit in doctors' offices. It's silly, but it's my way of saying, of showing, of *proving* that I'm unafraid, not so much to the other patients or to the medical workers as to myself.

And I wasn't afraid, not then. Bizarrely, I was excited. That's not precisely the right word for it, but it's not far off, and what I mean isn't that I was looking forward to whatever came next or that I was pleased about it. Hardly. What I mean is that I was in suspense, and there's a crackle to that, an electricity, and by one of those wondrous coping mechanisms that we humans possess, I was able to step somewhat outside of myself, compartmentalize the stakes of what was going on and marvel at the minor melodrama that I was starring in. I was able to ride it.

The neuro-ophthalmologist, Golnaz Moazami, repeated most of the same tests and deployed many of the same machines and instruments that my regular eye doctor had, but added a "visual field" exam, which involves sitting uncomfortably still and staring exceptionally hard into a deep box where pinpricks of light appear at different spots in various quadrants at irregular intervals; you press a button whenever you see one. It charts whether and where you have blind spots and if and how much your peripheral vision is compromised, and it became, over the next two years, the bane of my existence, a sort of psychological torture chamber that, when I was lashed to it, drove me insane. The lashing could last up to thirty minutes. This first time out, though, it was maybe half or even a third that long.

Dr. Moazami reviewed the results of it, reflected on her examination of me and, about two hours after I'd arrived at her offices at NewYork-Presbyterian Columbia, gave me her diagnosis. She cautioned that she wasn't *100 percent* sure: I'd need an array of blood tests and an MRI to rule out scenarios beyond the powers of her immediate observation. But she was confident—based on that observation, on the symptoms that I described and on my account of when and how they'd first appeared—that she understood what had happened.

I'd had a stroke.

Make that a *kind* of stroke or an analogue to a stroke, which is when there's a sudden blockage or cessation of blood flow to the brain. In my case, Dr. Moazami explained, a sudden drop in blood pressure had denied one of my optic nerves—which connect the eyes to the brain and are in fact a part of it—of the blood *it* needed, ravaging the nerve.

What, I asked, triggered this?

Sometimes, she said, it's related to sleep apnea. I told her I didn't have that. There's a suspicion, she said, that use of Viagra or its pharmacological kin can be the culprit. I'd used Viagra only twice, more than a decade earlier, out of curiosity, and never again. She said that people with diabetes or high blood pressure were at elevated risk for this. I didn't have diabetes. I didn't have high blood pressure.

There are instances, exceedingly rare ones, when this just happens, she said. I was apparently such an instance.

One of the big clues to what ailed me was that I had woken up to the blur. Blood pressure falls during sleep, so if it's going to plummet *too* far, that's likely when, and as many as half of the people who suffer the kind of stroke that I'd suffered do so overnight.

All of that fascinated me. But none of it was obviously or immediately relevant to what I most wanted to know: How would we fix it?

"There's no treatment," she said, and what initially impressed me more than those words was the tone—the timbre—of her voice: a finely calibrated amalgam of commiseration and soothing calm, an alarm-purged acknowledgment of awful luck, the aural equivalent of the hand that my usual eye doctor had placed on my shoulder. Her tone was telling me that

I could feel sorry for myself while also encouraging me not to grieve too much, not to panic. It was meticulous. I almost told her so.

She paused. There was something else that she wanted to say—something, I sensed, that she *needed* to say—and to the extent that I could perk up further, I did. And what came next explained the commiseration part of her manner and why, though I was getting by OK with my vision as it was, she projected a considerable measure of worry.

"You should know," she said, "that this could happen in your other eye."

My pulse quickened. "Could?" I asked. "Or will?"

"Could," she answered. "The literature suggests that patients who've had this happen in one eye are at much greater risk than the average person of having it happen in the other."

"How great a risk?" My questions came quickly because they didn't require much thought. They were the obvious ones.

"About a forty percent chance," she said, adding that if my left eye stayed healthy for the next two years, that chance shrank significantly.

By this point her manner had turned professional, clinical, academic. She was a student reporting on her research, a professor imparting her expertise. She had traveled, just like that, from the arbors of sympathy to the antiseptic, harshly lit corridors of science. So it was almost possible not to hear or register fully what she was telling me. And what she was telling me was that there was a very definite chance I'd go blind.

There were asterisks to this projection, qualifications, strands of hope to grab hold of and cling to. In some patients with my condition, vision in the already-affected eye improved slightly over the weeks and months immediately following the stroke, as the injury to the optic nerve receded. Also, the damage from these strokes varied from patient to patient. It was often much subtler than what I was experiencing. So my left eye, if afflicted in the future, could be only minimally compromised.

Could I do anything—extra exercise, better diet, pills—to increase the odds that my damaged eye would improve?

No, she said.

Well, then, could I do anything—extra exercise, better diet, pills, eye drops, eye *calisthenics*, hanging upside down, you name it—to lower the odds that the other eye would be hit?

Not really, she said.

She had minor recommendations, but she was quick to add that they were hardly amulets. I should be careful about not going to bed dehydrated—which meant drinking less alcohol at night or drinking a whole lot more water to counter any booze—because dehydration lowered blood pressure. That *might* matter, but then again might not. I should monitor my blood pressure and cholesterol, but then I should be doing that regardless (and was). High altitudes and long flights: There was some belief that these weren't advisable, because they decreased the level of oxygen in the blood, so some people with my condition avoided both. But it was just that: a belief. A hypothesis. When it came to my inadequately understood condition, knowledge took a back seat to supposition, even superstition.

This was a lot of information, almost too much to take in, and I wondered if perhaps I'd missed or misunderstood something. I didn't think I had, but still I should check, shouldn't I?

"This is bad, isn't it?" I asked Dr. Moazami.

She nodded. "This is bad." For a few seconds, there was silence. She broke it: "I'm sorry. I have nothing to offer you."

Offer you. I almost laughed, because the phrase was so genteel, so benign, as if she were a server in a restaurant or an attendant on a flight that had run out of soda and nuts.

There was, she said, one option of sorts that I should be aware of. She had no strong opinion about it. A clinical trial of a drug to repair some of the optic-nerve damage done by my kind of stroke was in progress, with sites all over the country, including in New York City. The trial had been approved by the US Food and Drug Administration; that meant that its safety had been persuasively established and that experiments prior to it had at least suggested its possible efficacy.

"I want in!" I said, then realized that if the decision were that easy, that clear-cut, she would have pushed this path on me sooner and harder. "Why wouldn't I want in?"

There were several reasons. One: As in any such trial, I could wind up in the placebo group, spending all the time that I'd have to devote to it for no possible personal benefit, at least not right away. I'd be doing something for the greater good, and if the drug worked, it might later be available to everyone with my condition, including me. But that would likely be years down the line, at a point so distant from the stroke that its damage could no longer be undone.

Two: The criteria for admission into the trial included that my diagnosis be definitive and that I get the first dose of the drug no more than fourteen days after my stroke. Five days had already elapsed. So I'd have to be able and willing to dedicate much of the next week to sprinting through the MRI and the blood tests that she had mentioned plus many other medical paces, compressing a sequence of hospital visits that would normally proceed less frantically into a short period of time.

Three: The method of the drug's delivery wasn't any picnic. It was a series of shots straight into the eye.

The trial, in other words, wasn't for pessimists, and I had ample pessimism in me. I was frequently sure that it would rain on the days when I most wanted sunshine, often braced for a desired romantic partner's immediate or eventual rejection, convinced at crucial junctures that a coveted promotion or assignment would go to somebody else, certain at times that I'd be dismissed from any such assignment if, by some fluke, I did get it. My experience didn't support this darkness: The mash of advantages, disadvantages, windfalls and setbacks in my life had plenty of good stuff: a surfeit of it, really. But it was my curious and unflattering nature to prepare for the worst.

The trial also wasn't for cowards, and I considered myself a coward, with plenty of supporting evidence: the marathon I'd never screwed up the grit to train for and run; the men I'd been too timid to ask on dates; the promotions and assignments that I hadn't even put my hand up for; the tough conversations with friends or colleagues or bosses that I'd steadfastly avoided.

Someone so negative, someone so meek: That was someone who wouldn't bother with the trial. But without any hesitation or equivocation, I decided that I wanted to bother. I hustled through the accelerated screening, got a confirmation of Dr. Moazami's diagnosis, joined hundreds of other patients around the country as a test subject and disappeared into an odyssey that was medical, yes, but even more psychological and spiritual, a process of revelation in which I learned either how little I knew of myself or how profoundly a person can change—adjusting as necessary, rising as needed and moving onward, onward, onward. It's the only sensible direction to go.

I grew accustomed, day by disorienting day, to reading and typing with a field of vision that was sometimes off-kilter and always screwy toward the right, as if someone had deposited a blob of jelly in that eye. Meanwhile, I dealt with the much greater challenge of figuring out and then fine-tuning the proper emotional response to what had happened to me. I asked myself questions that each of us must ask sooner or later, when an unexpected limit, a sudden vulnerability, a loss of complete agency inevitably enters the picture: To what extent do I reject it, grasping for fixes and insisting on daily routines, weekly schedules and monthly goals as rigorous as they were before? To what extent do I accept it, recognizing that there comes a time, definitely as we grow older, when we can't do what we once did and must say goodbye to certain aspirations and feats?

Defiance or resignation? It seemed to me that both were in order, but the proportions of each had to be right. The mix—the recipe—had to make sense. The same went for hope and dread. I could wade into but not wallow in either.

A small measure of defiance and a generous splash of hope

propelled me into that trial, and twelve days after my stroke, I took the subway from West Seventy-Second Street and Broadway to East Fourteenth Street and Third Avenue; walked a long, chilly block to the New York Eye and Ear Infirmary of Mount Sinai; slalomed through a thicket of old women hunched over walkers and old men slumped in wheelchairs and tiny children whose smiles were a heartbreaking contradiction of the bandages on their heads; searched in vain for a check-in desk; cursed the labyrinthine layout of this sprawling hospital; took a gamble on a set of elevators in a back hallway; arrived by luck at the suite of rooms on the fifth floor where I was, in fact, supposed to be; felt a flutter of nerves—or was it a fizz of adrenaline?—as someone buzzed me through the glass doors, into a colorless reception area; waited and then waited and then waited some more; was summoned at last to a similarly colorless, even more charmless examining room; listened to a new doctor, Ronald Gentile, describe what he was going to do to me and assure me that it would be bearable or, at the very least, quick; tilted backward in a reclining chair that could have used more padding; let him slather a cold goo of topical anesthetic on the surface of my misbehaving, traitorous eye; let him slather another coat of it when he returned ten minutes later; heard his footsteps approaching the room again ten minutes after that, when I knew we were past the numbing and about to proceed to the piercing; gripped the arms of the inadequately padded chair tight; imagined myself in a movie, my valor saluted with a swell of woodwinds and a surge of violins; turned my face upward, toward Dr. Gentile, willing him to get it over with, willing him to tell me it was all a mistake and we didn't have to do this; felt an unpleasant tug as he used a metal clamp to yank open my right eye and prevent any blinking; and then felt something worse, so very much worse, like a splash of acid delivered with a heavyweight's punch, as he plunged a needle into it.

Chapter Two
WHEN ONE EYE CLOSES ANOTHER OPENS

Nora Ephron, who was a friend of mine during the final decade of her life, had a trademark saying—"Everything is copy"—that one of her two sons even used as the title of his posthumous documentary about her. "Copy" is an old-fashioned newspaper term for material, and Nora's dictum was often treated as an arch defense of writers' oversharing the details of their and their acquaintances' lives. It was a warning: Abandon all privacy, ye who enter here. But it had an additional, less glib meaning. Nora was simply stating that if you were in the words business and something amusing or interesting or maybe even profound happened to you, you used it. You turned it into copy. That was your trade. Maybe it was even your calling.

Well, in October 2017, something interesting happened to me, and while it hardly rose to the level of the traumas and trials that so many other people face, it made me tremble, tested me and forced me to see in a new way. That was true physically. It was even truer philosophically.

Interesting, isn't it, how limber and omnipresent the verb "see" and its variants are, how easily and constantly those variants toggle from referring to the visual processing of objects to the mental processing of reality? "To see" isn't just to lay eyes on the terrain and the people around you. It's to figure out what that terrain and those people mean. It's to recognize something that demands recognition, to have an epiphany that eluded you until that eureka moment of "insight," a word with a telltale second syllable.

"Don't you see?" we ask the ignorant. "You saw the light," we tell the newly informed. "Look," we say at the beginning of a command that someone acknowledge and comprehend our "point of view," an elastic phrase that can refer to a spatial perspective or a spiritual one. And "insight" keeps etymological and linguistic company with "foresight" and "hindsight," our keenest intellectual observations framed in optical, ocular terms. Sure, there's a similar double duty performed by "I hear you" and "I feel you" or "I feel your pain," but those phrases don't get quite as thorough a workout. Your ignorance of a situation can be expressed in terms of your being "deaf to it," but it's more often expressed as your being "blind to it." There are "blind spots" but not "deaf spots." And someone who is attuned to events in a deep and special way has "vision," while someone animated by the grandest of plans has "a vision."

That's consistent with our literary and pictorial fixation on eyes, cast as nothing less than "the mirrors of the soul." "Blindness seems to have nearly irresistible appeal as a literary trope," wrote the blind writer, performer and educator M. Leona Godin in *There Plant Eyes: A Personal and Cultural History of Blindness*. Her book, published in 2021, more than backs up that assertion, producing a compendium of blindness as parable, as metaphor or as plot-convenient conceit in the Bible, in Homer, in short stories, even in George R. R. Martin's multipart epic A Song of Ice and Fire, which became the HBO juggernaut *Game of Thrones*. "The blind seer in particular is so foundational that it's become a cliché: you'll be hard-pressed to read a book of science fiction or fantasy that does not include a blind character," Godin noted.

Eyes are a locus of power, but even more so of vulnerability. From Oedipus in the immortal Sophocles tragedy through the Duke of Gloucester in Shakespeare's *King Lear* and countless victims in serial-killer novels and movies, losing one's eyes is the worst degradation, the ultimate horror. Not having use of them in the first place is the ultimate danger. No random act of narrative whimsy accounts for Audrey Hepburn's blindness in the 1967 thriller *Wait Until Dark* or Uma Thurman's in *Jennifer 8* a quarter century later. Their disability—in particular, *this* disability—identifies them to remorseless predators or squirming audiences as ready prey, theoretically much easier to dupe and to dominate than people who can spot the killer drawing near them. In a game of trust, whether staged in a scientific setting or a fraternity house or two consenting adults' bed, it's not the ears that are covered. It's the eyes.

And for many of the people who haven't experienced blindness or had to contemplate it seriously, it's unthinkable, unbearable, the equivalent of some cosmic hand yanking out the universe's plug. I wasn't quite in that category, but I indeed took in the idea that my vision was at risk in a manner much different, I believe, than I would have registered similar news about my ability to hear, touch, taste or smell. In our minds, in our bones, in our viscera, sight is the unrivaled monarch of the senses. Of course I trembled.

But, as I said, I did more than that. I regrouped. I asked questions that I hadn't asked before, navigating emotional straits unlike any that I'd previously encountered, reassessing my friends and acquaintances and reaching out to strangers who'd lost vision, who'd dealt with the possibility of losing vision or who'd encountered some other disability or illness long before old age, which is when we expect affliction. Ahead of schedule, these people took a crash course in limitations and uncertainty and compromises, and now I was enrolled in it.

That was the lens through which the renowned journalist Michael Kinsley viewed Parkinson's disease, with which he was diagnosed when he was forty-three. He titled his 2016 memoir about it *Old Age*. A little more than a third of the way through the book, he wrote that he sometimes felt "like a scout from my generation, sent out ahead to experience in my fifties what even the healthiest boomers are going to experience in their sixties, seventies, or eighties. There are far worse medical conditions than Parkinson's, and there are far worse cases of Parkinson's than mine. But what I have, at the level I have it, is an interesting foretaste of our shared future—a beginner's guide to old age."

Now came my own foretaste, subtler than his but maybe even more universal and instructive because of that. In my mid-fifties, I was where a great many people find themselves in their midsixties and a great many more do in their midseventies. I was stripped of delusions about my physical indestructibility, and I watched the parameters of possibility shrink. No, scratch that, I watched the parameters of possibility *change*. I was learning the importance of interpreting what had happened to me with that kinder, gentler language. It was not only a valid interpretation. It was also the healthy, happiness-preserving one.

Strangely, I began to feel more alive, more attuned, more appreciative. Did that make me a sort of cliché? You bet, and you should brace yourself for a boatload of clichés and jump ship if they're going to bother you. They shouldn't, because a small part of what I came to appreciate was that clichés are clichés—pervasive, enduring, axiomatic—for a reason: They're kissing cousins with verities, down-market analogues of insights. When you're given lemons, you can indeed make lemonade, and that was a big part of my education, which included the confirmation that the grass is always greener on the other side of the fence, that clouds have silver linings and that the night is darkest before dawn, although my story isn't about dawn. It's about dusk. It's about those first real inklings that the day isn't forever and that light inexorably fades. It's about a rising and then peaking consciousness that you're on borrowed and finite time. It's about a shifting temperature, an altered ambiance.

And it's about how paradoxical, enriching and beautiful that dusk can be. My world blurred, but it also sharpened. I held my breath; I exhaled. I said hello to new worries; I said goodbye to old ones. A clever friend of mine summed up my status wittily and well: "When one eye closes another opens."

With my one good eye, I looked harder and longer and, I hope, more soulfully at everything around me, starting with my acquaintances and friends. I realized that we know too little about the people in our lives, because we inspect them only superficially, ask the easy and polite questions, edit them down to the parts that give us the least complicated and most immediate pleasure. There's heartache in them that we don't adequately recognize, triumph in them that we don't sufficiently venerate. On the morning after my stroke, I woke up to that as well.

To get it out of the way, some grounding. Some basics. The medical nitty-gritty. The formal term for my stroke—for what caused it, what it signified—was non-arteritic anterior ischemic optic neuropathy, a mash of arcane verbiage that tells you why I've been going with the colloquial shorthand that I have. I'm pretty sure that none of the doctors I spoke with ever said all those syllables to me; they referred to the condition by its more popular abbreviation, NAION. Only from my own reading and research did I discover what the initials stood for and also that there was an AION, which was even rarer, along with a slew of other kinds of optic neuropathy. Neuropathy means any injury to, or disease of, the nervous system, so it applies to the whole body, and that's why the "optic" is in there, a crucial modifier. The "ischemic" signals that inadequate blood flow is the culprit in the nerve injury. But now I'm getting into the weeds.

I'll pull out of them to throw some numbers at you, but, first, a caveat: They're all the best guesses of experts who, when talking candidly, admit that. "Let me explain what we know about ischemic optic neuropathy," Mark Kupersmith, arguably the leading neuro-ophthalmologist in New York City, told me when he and I were talking once about the lack of progress in treating it. "Not much!"

The conventional wisdom in the field is that in the months following the ischemic event—the stroke—during which the optic nerve was ravaged, as many as 40 percent of the afflicted experience some cryptic healing of the nerve, some fractional alleviation of the damage to their eyesight. Dr. Kupersmith is skeptical. He thinks it's probable that they compensate for the damage, leaning on and learning to maximize the portions of their field of vision that were unaffected or the least affected. That may be why they do better on eye tests three months after the stroke than three days after. Whatever the case, the majority of people with NAION do *not* get better. Once the nerve damage is done, it's permanent. That was the situation with me.

As for how many people suffer from NAION, the figure usually cited is one in ten thousand, though some specialists, Dr. Kupersmith among them, think that that's an undercount and that many subtle cases, especially in very old people who are declining on a range of anatomical fronts, go undiagnosed or misdiagnosed. Regardless, NAION is unusual, a tremendously unlucky roll of the dice. It's far down the list of diseases and conditions that significantly diminish or rob people of their sight, though all of those diseases and conditions together add up to more visually impaired people than you'd guess. An estimated one million Americans (or about one in 320) are legally blind, meaning that their corrected vision is no better than 20/200. A few million more have life-altering vision impairment, and that group expands if you include people with "low vision," meaning that their corrected vision is no better than 20/40.

Blindness, by the way, isn't blackness or blankness or nothingness, not for most people. That's a common myth. "Blindness is often perceived by the sighted as an either/or condition: one sees or does not see," the blind writer Stephen Kuusisto explained in *Planet of the Blind*. Not so in his case: "I stare at the world through smeared and broken windowpanes." The smear and the breakage are enough to constitute a major deficiency and mammoth challenge. "Smear": When I read that word, I found myself nodding without having made the decision to nod, so perfectly did it describe the bedevilment of my right eye. Smear, I thought, comes in gradations, and mine is mercifully thinner and more uneven than his—and has confined itself to just part of my field of vision. But my window, like his, is defective. And like his, it cannot be wiped clean.

The overwhelming majority of blind and visually impaired people saw serviceably well at birth and as children. They knew the visual splendor of the world before it was veiled, and it was usually veiled in the second half of life, by cataracts or glaucoma or macular degeneration or diabetic retinopathy. And most people who go blind get some advance inkling about what's happening, followed by a period of waiting and gradual vision loss and dread.

NAION also strikes late, almost always after the age of fifty and usually much later than that. I got in on the action early. Its severity and impact vary greatly from person to person. Just as it can move on to the second eye or be sated with the first, it can leave minor or major damage or something in between. That damage is usually to peripheral vision, making it harder for people with NAION to see objects above them or below them or to the side. But my *central* vision was affected, making it harder for me to read, to write, to look at a computer screen, which, if I shut my left eye and used only my right, was a wash of smudged white light, the smudges being the indecipherable letters and words. With just my right eye, the page of a book looked much the same. I could tell that there were paragraphs there, and I could even, with concentration, divine where they began and ended. I just had no idea at all what they said. A fog enveloped them. They existed, wanly, on the far side of a smear.

The obscurity of NAION is a principal reason for the absence of any effective treatment for it. Drug companies logically care about the potential profitability of what they develop, and we NAION sufferers are a puny, unmotivating market. But even if we weren't, we'd still be in a bad spot, because of the anatomical source of our fog.

"I consider optic nerve damage the holy grail of solving blindness," Neil Miller, a professor of ophthalmology, neurology and neurosurgery at Johns Hopkins University's medical school, told me. "If you have somebody who's virtually completely blind from cataracts, we can cure that. Corneal damage? We can cure those patients. We can help a lot of patients with retinal disease. But there is really very little that we can do to restore vision that's damaged from optic nerve disease."

Rudrani Banik, one of the neuro-ophthalmologists who monitored me and other people with NAION in that first clinical trial and then in a second one in which I participated later on, told me to think of the nerve and its surrounding sheath as "a cable within a pipe." Extensive and sophisticated examinations of my eyes had revealed that my pipe was about a quarter of the normal size, so if the nerve swelled—as nerves do when bereft of oxygen—it was more likely to bang against the pipe and be hurt. "Everything is congested," she said. "Anatomically, we call it a disc at risk. I hate to use that term because it scares patients."

It scared the hell out of me. I now knew about my left optic nerve what I hadn't known about my right before it fizzled or frizzed (or whatever the right word was) and became a disc in disarray. I now knew that it carried a potential for grave trouble that other people's optic nerves didn't. It was like a bomb that could go off at any moment. Tick, tick, tick.

Where I was lucky—very, very lucky—was that with my glasses on, my left eye still clocked in at 20/25 on a bad day, 20/20 on a good one. But my right eye got in its way and dragged it down. I could have patched that derelict eye, and I considered doing that, but if I had, I would likely have slowed or prevented my brain's eventual performance of that same phenomenon. And I wanted to prod and train my brain. More than four years later, I'm still prodding and training it—hence the "eventual." Its progress has been constant. It has also been tediously, maddeningly incremental.

For the first few months after my diagnosis, I worried less about my sluggish, recalcitrant brain doing a better job of coordinating my eyes than about that my one good eye hanging in there. I came to regard it as my body's Fabergé egg. Ever checked out pictures of an optic nerve? After my stroke, I appraised a Louvre's worth of them. And I couldn't get over how fragile it seemed, this slender thread, fed by about a dozen minuscule blood vessels, that tethers the back of the eye to the brain and alone decides whether you get to see the setting of the sun or the rising of a soufflé.

The whole of the human body is like that: millions of contours and connections, at once unthinkably delicate and unimaginably durable, with so much that can go wrong. That more *doesn't* is a wonder, even a miracle. That so many of us skate across long expanses of our lives in an unbroken glide and a straight line defies logic. But the glide eventually ends. The line at some point—at multiple points—jags. These bodies of ours *are* time bombs, but each detonates in a different way.

I'd catch myself absentmindedly rubbing my eyes, as everyone does, and terror would sizzle through me. Had I been too rough? Was the congested nerve behind my left eye still OK? During a run through the park, a gust of wind blew dirt into my left eye, and I panicked: I couldn't allow any injury to it. I no longer had a spare.

Nights were worst. If the left eye were going to quit on me, it would probably do so then. I quaffed two, three, four glasses of water just before my head hit the pillow. Superstitiously, that was also when I took a daily baby aspirin: something Dr. Banik had recommended, a method for promoting blood flow, in case that mattered. If I somehow forgot either the water or the aspirin, I bolted out of bed, no matter how close I was to sleep, and made amends.

Then, in the middle of the night, when my bladder screamed, I hesitated before opening my eyes. What if I'd had another stroke? It was the same every morning: a stab of suspense, then a gale-force sigh of relief when I had confirmation that I could still see out of my left eye.

Although my story is, I hope, about getting wiser, it's also the testimony of a damned fool. I'm referring to my path to the point at which my eyesight faltered, to all the mental and emotional energy I wasted. I'm referring to all the good stuff—no, *great* stuff—that I took for granted. From the vantage point of a legitimate misfortune, my past looked shameful to me, because it was riddled with stupid resentments and pocked with pointless grudges. I had squandered so much time on mapping the roads closed off to me rather than the roads wide open, on tallying what I perversely considered slights: Why did I gain weight so easily and lose it so glacially? Why did I burn so quickly in the sun? Why didn't I have my older brother's gregariousness and social ease, my younger brother's ability to lose himself elatedly in elaborate projects and the mythology of Star Trek, my younger sister's wicked, wicked wit? Why were so many interactions with my father strained? Why were so many interactions with my mother layered and fraught? I had countless complaints, when, really, I had none at all.

That father? He was a model of generosity and grace in dealing with other people. He made sure that I never wanted for anything important and that I got a good education, three years of it at a private secondary school that was the on-ramp to a special merit scholarship at the University of North Carolina at Chapel Hill.

That mother? Her demands paled beside her cheerleading, and her moods couldn't compete with her love, as fortifying as love can be. She modeled excellence, throwing herself into any endeavor she pursued. And she passed down to me her reverence of words, giving me a life in language that no affliction could ever steal.

There *was* one indisputable complication in my childhood, one tricky negotiation: By the age of twelve, if not much earlier, I knew beyond any doubt that I was gay, and the culture back then—the late 1970s—was much less accepting than it is now. If you were gay, you almost certainly went through a period when you wondered if, or concluded that, you were defective. You feared how the world might treat you and weren't sure you were up to that. I remember a span of days during my senior year of high school when I thought obsessively about suicide because my unspeakable and unreciprocated crush on one of my classmates seemed to me a harbinger of everlasting alienation, of not being able to live the lovestruck lyrics of three-quarters of the songs on the radio the way my straight peers could and would and already did. I don't remember what broke that despair and kept me alive.

But when I "came out" at eighteen, in 1982, no one in my family rejected me, none of my friends spurned me and I figured out how to meet and date other gay men with relatively little difficulty or drama. My journey into adulthood coincided with America's journey toward greater recognition of, and respect for, gay Americans, and the pace of progress was fleeter than I'd expected. On that score, if not on others, I appreciated my excellent fortune. I felt appropriate thanks.

By the time my stroke happened, I'd belatedly reached a juncture where I felt more thanks across the board. I had it good, and I knew that. Tom and I had been in a committed relationship for about nine years and had lived together, in our Upper West Side apartment, for the last three of them. We almost never quarreled. We frequently laughed.

Our weeks had a rhythm: On Friday nights, we'd almost always have dinner out alone, just the two of us, and we'd use conversation and wine to slough off the irritations and frustrations of the just-finished workweek. On Saturday nights, we'd socialize, just as we had with the friends whose home we went to on the first day of my blurry future. On Sunday nights, I'd make an enormous salad with plenty of protein in it—usually slivers of skinless chicken thigh, glistening in a tangle of arugula, tomatoes, cucumber, blue cheese and olive oil—and Tom would do the cleanup after dinner. Our dining room table had acres of space, and the festive red chairs around it were cushiony and comfy. Tom's face, on the other side of that table, was as handsome to me almost a decade into our relationship as it had been during the first weeks.

Professionally, I was successful, even if certain grander ambitions weren't realized, even if I didn't make the kind of crazy money that my siblings and some of my friends did and couldn't purchase the second homes and top-of-the-line cars that they had. In my thirty-year journalism career to that point, more than twenty of those years at the *New York Times*, I'd seen much of the world and I'd had some extravagant adventures, including a long, heady stint as the newspaper's chief restaurant critic. In my current post, as an opinion columnist, I made regular television appearances and gave occasional speeches on the side. People in the neighborhood grocery store approached me with compliments. These encounters made me self-conscious about the baggy T-shirt and baggier sweatpants that I was invariably wearing and the extra fifteen pounds I was usually carrying. But mostly they made me proud.

I had been given many advantages, and I had worked hard, and while I was still plugging away and putting in some days as long as fourteen or even sixteen hours and many weeks longer than sixty, I was also reaping considerable rewards, savoring the payoff in terms of material comfort, financial independence, a certain standing in the world, a security. I suppose I realized that this could be threatened in an instant, even taken away. We all do. There were bumps that made me think "cancer," twinges that whispered "heart attack," strains and pulls that told me that I wouldn't be able to run forever. But before my stroke, these threats were theoretical and my awareness of them fleeting. When I surveyed the days, weeks and even years ahead and adjusted for my pessimism, I wasn't worried, and I definitely wasn't scared.

A little more than two years after my stroke shattered my calm, a worldwide pandemic shattered everyone's. The coronavirus, which emerged and spread with breathtaking swiftness, was a once-in-a-generation catastrophe that changed how most of us processed time and regarded mortality. It was its own parable of affliction and aging, an unimaginably grand and cruel reminder that our fates are unguessable and our worlds can be transformed in an instant, compelling us to fulfill our obligations and seize our pleasures in a more tightly circumscribed and improvisatory fashion, from a shorter menu of options, with fear gnawing at us all the while. It made my personal drama seem puny, which is to say that it put it in the right perspective. There were circumstances infinitely more daunting than the tilt and blur and potential fade of my vision. A pathogen poised to kill millions of people—including, in just a year's time, more than 500,000 Americans—was at the top of that long list.

There was America before Covid-19 and America after, and while the coronavirus arrived here earlier than March 6, 2020, that date was my personal dividing line, separating one reality and the next. The lockdowns and the social distancing had not yet begun. Almost no one I knew was seriously worried about infection, and the acquaintances stocking up on toilet paper and bottled water looked nutty. That night I was staying with my father in the Westchester County suburbs of New York, taking care of him, because he and his wife were apart for a few months, cooling off from one of their many periods of conflict, and Dad, then eighty-four and struggling with Alzheimer's disease, couldn't be left alone. I took him to a movie, a new, feminist update of *The Invisible Man*. Our hours in that theater stayed with me afterward and stood out forevermore as some innocent, lost "before" period because my worry during them wasn't about the physical proximity of other people and how that might endanger Dad's very life. It was whether I'd chosen something too dark and violent for him and whether he was following the plot. Also, whether we ate too much popcorn. All that salt couldn't be good for him.

Just five days later, President Trump made a prime-time television address about the coronavirus. Just five days after that, New York closed schools. In short order, indoor dining in New York went away, offices shuttered, public gatherings were banned and going to a theater—for a movie, for a play, for a musical performance—wasn't possible. Daily life bore scant resemblance to what it had been just weeks earlier, and our *Invisible Man* outing was like some falsely planted memory, some hallucination.

That spring, that summer, I spent almost every day missing. Missing the smiles of officemates who—because of some spark they possessed or some chemistry we had—lifted my mood several notches every time they walked by. Missing the way this one neighbor of mine and I always hugged hello, a tender and nurturing act that was now dangerous and forbidden. Missing the subway at rush hour (and I didn't think it was possible to miss the subway at rush hour). Missing the huffing, preening and vacuously peppy music in gyms.

That summer, that fall, I spent every day enraged, because America and Americans were making so many mistakes, with fatal consequences, and the devastation was so much greater than it had to be. But I also spent every day awestruck at how nimble and resourceful my neighbors and countrymates were. In lockdown, people might well have shut down, stunned into numbness, frightened into paralysis. But most people didn't.

They lined up, six feet apart, outside the supermarket, as if that had always been the drill. They did push-ups and planks on the bedroom floor. They moved not only their conferences but also their cocktail parties to Zoom. They celebrated virtual birthdays. They held digital funerals. They learned to cook. They fussed over sourdough cultures. There was a run on fire-pits and heat lamps and outdoor furniture, as patios became the new living rooms. They guided their children through online education and into social pods that gave them some degree of companionship without an excessive degree of risk. They made scores of little and big tweaks, and then they woke up the next day and made scores more.

In the blocks right around my apartment, I watched restaurateurs pivot to stave off financial ruin, turning the sidewalks and parking lanes outside their establishments into makeshift, miniature gardens with trellises, shrubs, tenting and drapery. They reflected a can-do, entrepreneurial spirit that kept a battered economy from collapsing and that was just as visible beyond my immediate surroundings, wherever I looked. Hotels changed their way of checking people in and cleaning rooms. Airlines revised seating plans in planes and rethought interactions between their personnel and their passengers. In seemingly every area of commerce, there were contactless exchanges where such a scenario would have seemed undoable or unacceptable before. It was done. It was accepted. After a month or two of scattershot shortages, food was still being produced in bounty and distributed with efficiency. Mail arrived slowly but surely. Packages were delivered, sometimes even faster than before.

Most important and most heroic, legions of health-care workers at every level worked longer hours at greater risk than should be expected of anyone; stretched finite supplies beyond what seemed possible; muddled through initial guesswork about the precise nature and threat of the virus; and kept going, with no clear end point in sight. We in the media wrote stories about how many of them were teetering on the brink and about which of them broke, and we were right to do so, as their desperation spoke to the ordeals that people in their professions were enduring. But it had a way of distracting from their endurance, which was the more prevalent reality, the more salient takeaway.

If you subtracted government failures—and government didn't fail entirely, certainly not many state and municipal governments—you saw a response to the pandemic that was a testament to finding work-arounds when the usual regimens and routes were closed off, to cultivating new sources of comfort and pleasure when old ones were no longer available, to doing what afflicted and aging people are called to do. It underscored the human talent for adjusting and optimizing. For all the flaws in America that it exposed and all the reality checks it presented, it was in large measure a tribute to resilience.

—

I took just one psychology course in college, and I'm not sure why I chose it. I don't think I ever flirted with a major or minor in psychology—maybe the course met some distribution requirement. I remember little about it apart from the word "introduction" in its title, the presence of about eighty students in the lecture hall, the professor's graying beard and, most of all, his refrain, maybe even his mantra, a sentence that he must have uttered between a half dozen and a dozen times over the course of the semester. It made an impression on me then and an even bigger one across the years, as I kept hearing it and kept turning it around in my brain: True or false? Profound or banal? Instructive or just plain depressing?

"Life," he would say, "is about adjusting to loss." I think I have the words right, though I can't swear he didn't say "dealing with loss" or "learning to live with loss." The idea was the same in any of those iterations. And I sometimes quibbled with it, getting all Talmudic: Wasn't *life* too broad and sloppy a designation? Wasn't a child in the first ten years of life adjusting only to gains: new information, new skills, new friends, new horizons? Didn't such gains carry forward beyond ten years, maybe all the way to the finish? I wondered about the professor's balance sheet. I dinged him for overgeneralization.

But I think, from my perch here in my sixth decade of life, that he was more right than wrong, and if the economy of his expression is taken into account—if he's given allowance and forgiveness for the imprecision that comes with that—he was telegraphing something essential.

The *challenge* of life, present for most of it but more dominant in the second half, is adjusting to loss or, more specifically, developing the judgment and grace not only to accept its inevitability but also to recognize that it's not the only trajectory, that there are many ways to meet and measure it and that there are consolations, including all that remains. Cherishing those leftovers—those *holdovers*—is the key to thriving, and sometimes even to surviving.

Chapter Three
THE DONKEY KICKS

I had many terrific friends in college, all of them sources of joy and comfort in their own ways, but only one was pure sunshine: Dorrie. I'd never met anybody with a readier smile. I'd never met anybody with a bigger one. A dedicated runner, she was skinny, and I often thought that if a smile could be put on a scale, hers would account for half her body weight. *Dorrie, Dorrie, hallelujah* was what I sometimes called her in my head, making a rhyme with the *glory, glory, hallelujah* lyric that I recalled from church services in my youth. She was a godsend, as quick with her laughter as with that smile, someone who always lifted my mood with the impossible buoyancy of her own.

We kept in touch after graduation—I attended her wedding, to another college friend of mine—but as the years went by, we reached out to each other less and less. There was no rift, just drift. I usually knew where she was living and what she was doing for work, and she told me when her marriage collapsed and also when she met someone new and married again. But I didn't attend that second wedding, if there was any full-fledged celebration. I can't remember. By 1995, when she and her second husband had a child, I hadn't seen Dorrie in years. A decade or so later, when she got in touch to say that she'd be in New York City for a few days and would love to get together, I hadn't seen her in what felt like forever.

We met for lunch. Right away I knew something was wrong. She smiled at me, only it wasn't the smile from college. It had boundaries. By the standard of her college smile, it was crimped and cinched and maybe even slightly crooked. I could tell that this wasn't an emotional shift but instead something physical. Then I noticed a difference in the angle of her head—in the way she carried it—and in the cadence of her speech and movements of her left arm. Both were less fluid. A few minutes into our meal, she revealed that she had Parkinson's disease and that she'd been diagnosed with it about five years earlier, at thirty-six.

I was taken by surprise, and I was overcome with sadness. I was also panicked. I wanted to ask the right questions, but I didn't want to ask too many. I wanted to express concern, but I didn't want to express too much of it. She wasn't treating or talking of her disease as some tragedy, so I didn't want to, either. Mostly I just wanted to hug her—which I did, tightly, when we parted, after a long conversation that moved on from Parkinson's to her life in Madison, Wisconsin, with her husband, Eric, and their daughter, Madelyn, then ten. Dorrie was clearly besotted with Madelyn, and vice versa.

I was better about keeping in touch with Dorrie from then

on. Not great, but better. I saw both her and Eric when they swept through New York more than five years after that lunch. Dorrie was a big Facebook user, so we traded messages that way, and sometimes I'd spot one of her Facebook posts. I didn't tell her, in late 2017, about my stroke, but about five months after the *Times* published a long column of mine about it in February 2018, she emailed me.

"I haven't seen any of your writing lately—granted, we were in Germany for two weeks," she wrote. "How are your eyes? I cried when I read about what you are going through. You said it, my friend, when you essentially said you never know what life is going to deal you. With Parkinson's I feel like that every day. I have been doing really well; we walked seven to ten miles just about every day in Berlin."

Dorrie crying for *me*, after what she had been through? Completely ridiculous and completely Dorrie. I choked up as I read her message. I also keyed in on her ready mention of Parkinson's—of what it had taught her and how it had changed her. Why hadn't I asked her more about that or invited her to tell me as full a version of her experience with it as she cared to? She had never declared it off-limits; if anything, she'd given the opposite signal. So I asked, and she began to write me long, detailed, beautiful reflections and recollections.

Her Parkinson's story had actually begun twenty-three years earlier, in 1995, when she was four months pregnant, living in Virginia and working as the marketing manager for several shopping centers and malls. One day, a guy on the maintenance crew at one of them said, "Hey, Dorrie, what did you do to your arm?"

"Huh?" she answered. She had no idea what he was talking about. Then she looked down and saw that her left arm was twisted strangely behind her back. She hadn't put it there. Or, rather, she hadn't meant to.

Over the following months, her left hand became unusable. It wouldn't do what she commanded it to. Doctors didn't want to submit her to an X-ray or MRI because of her pregnancy and told her she might just have a pinched nerve, anyway. Pinched nerves often vanish on their own. But her left hand remained immobile after Madelyn's birth in October. There was no un-pinching going on. Dorrie had to figure out how to dress and diaper her wriggling infant with just her right hand.

Meanwhile, something strange began happening when she ran. Her left leg jerked backward, in a manner that kept happening and that she came to jokingly label her "donkey kick." Then she couldn't get the leg to lift off the ground. It just dragged behind her.

One doctor said she had a "drop foot," whatever that was. Another doctor recommended knee replacement. A third doctor told her she had "dyskinesia," a highfalutin term for her symptoms, not an explanation of why they were occurring. Dyskinesia means the involuntary movement or disobedience of body parts, and it can be caused by muscle problems, by medicines, by brain injury, by stroke. There's a whole big buffet of possibilities. Dorrie wasn't told which one applied to her.

"My foot dragged so badly," she remembered, "that my left shoe would wear down unevenly. My sister said that I needed to find a shoe store that sold just left shoes. Maybe for pirates?" At least in lore, many of them had one peg leg, leaving only the other to be shod. Dorrie kidded that wherever they shopped, she should, too.

She consulted additional specialists, one of whom reclassified her dyskinesia as "dystonia," which refers to uncontrollable muscle contractions and also has multiple possible causes, none of which were pinpointed in Dorrie's case. New *dys-*, same mystery. This latest specialist recommended Botox because it freezes muscle movement, as all those unfurrowing foreheads in Hollywood attest. And so Dorrie experienced a new torture: Over the course of an interminable hour, a medical worker jabbed and rejabbed a needle into her "dystopian foot," rooting around for the right spot for the drug. Finally, the needle stilled. The medical worker pumped in the Botox. And, Dorrie said, "I left with a foot that felt like it was simply asleep."

"Granted," she added, "it did look five years younger."

Humor. It takes the punch and sting out of what's happening, turning scary to silly, and that was a lesson from not only Dorrie's narrative but also my own: I automatically latched on to it during the first months of my medical saga and discovered that it worked wonders, not as an evasion of the truth but as a defanging of it. Screaming wouldn't get you anywhere. Nor would sobbing. But laughing? That was as close to a panacea as anything in anyone's emotional repertoire. It calmed everything somehow. Besides, there was an aesthetic, dramatic logic to it. It suited the eccentricity of the situations that a medically needy, physiologically distressed person meets. It accented donkey kicks and accessorized asymmetrically scuffed footwear.

Dorrie rattled off punch lines and quips. That was crucial, but not as crucial as something else she did—or, rather, *didn't* do: She forbid any excessive or extravagant contemplation about what had happened, was happening and might happen to her. She thought about it only so much. Sure, she appraised it to the extent it demanded appraisal, she adjusted to it as necessary and she attended to it fully, seeking out the right doctors and carefully and often skeptically evaluating what they had to say. But she didn't stare at it. Didn't focus on it. That was a choice, a discipline, one that she mastered when she was dyskinetic and when she was dystonic and when, at long last, in 2000, she got her final and correct diagnosis: Parkinson's.

She took her medications. When those no longer worked as well as doctors had hoped they would, she had brain surgery, terrifying as it was to have her head drilled into and her skull opened. She described for me how her cranium was immobilized in one of those metal halos and how some but not all of her hair was shaved. Afterward, she said, "I looked like the lead singer from a Flock of Seagulls," whose lopsided hair appeared to be the work of a cyclone, not a stylist. "A mullet would have been better."

Doctors threaded cables from her brain to her chest, where a battery placed beneath her skin pumped out currents of stimulation. The outline of those cables was just visible—a long, thin, faint ridge—if you looked closely at the nape of her neck. Doctors adjusted the amount of stimulation, to get it just right. Then they readjusted it. Then they readjusted it again.

But Dorrie never dwelled on all of that. Never obsessed over it. Couldn't see the utility in that.

"Eric used to have a motorcycle," she wrote to me. "When we were first dating, I decided to take a motorcycle instruction course in case he was incapacitated and I had to drive the cycle home. To this day, the only thing I remember from the class is: 'If there's a hole, don't look at the hole. If you look at it, then you will go into it.' I took it as a metaphor for life. If you dwell on the bad (the hole), you'll go into the hole. I don't want to sound like I've always dealt with having a disease in perfect form. I have looked at the hole many times." But whenever she did, she realized that "getting in is shockingly easy. It's the getting back out that's the trick."

So she never got in. When she couldn't run any longer, she cycled. During periods when her limited control over her movements made that too dangerous, she cycled inside, on a stationary bike. And she kept traveling, kept seeing the world, as her message to me in the winter of 2018, when she mentioned the Germany trip, indicated. Maybe she didn't walk through those foreign cities as fleetly as she once might have, but she still covered plenty of ground, and she concentrated on that—on what she could do.

⁓

I had always thought that if a devastating injury or a major illness befell me, I'd lean hard into the dispensation it gave me. I'd seize the excuse to stop working for a while, to climb into bed with a stack of novels and a long list of binge-worthy TV shows. I'd take a pity lap. I'd have a pity party. Sorry, dear editor, I can't write that column *because I might be going blind.* Forgive me, boss, if I'm scarce for the next few days, but *someone just stuck a needle into my eye.* I'd convalesce like no one had ever convalesced. Would you mind fetching me another glass of chardonnay? I'd do it myself but *I might trip on account of my blurry vision.*

And in the first week or two after my right eye failed, I did allow myself some melodrama, though it wasn't exactly melodrama but more a half spoof of it, a mixture of melodrama and comedy. As I said, comedy comes in handy. It did for me.

"Would you still love me with a cane and a bad habit of bumping into things?" I asked Tom. It was one of many questions along those lines. He rolled his eyes at all of them.

"You have to give me one of your dogs," I told my sister, Adelle, who had two flat-coated retrievers, which look like black Irish setters. I called dibs on Marlin, her boy, rather than A.J., her girl, because Marlin was the one who always snuggled close to me on Adelle's couch and tried—I kid you not—to steal little slurps of my martini. "You're going to have to retrain him, though," I said. "He needs to be a companion for the blind."

"If I'm finally going to finish *Middlemarch*, I better do it now, lest I have to scale it in braille," I said in a text message to my friend Jennifer. She got the lion's share—if you can call it that—of such outbursts. I didn't want to lean too hard on Tom, who, beyond those eye rolls, was having a strangely flat reaction, which I took as a sign of worry but learned only later was something else, something worse.

"I'm fat, I'm old and now I'm a Cyclops," I said to several friends, polishing my lines and honing my routine as I went through the list of people I should call and fill in on what was happening. I called them all, although it took many hours, because it was a way of not being alone with my darkest thoughts, of not brooding in silence, of burning off all this strange energy that I had.

And I did have energy. I had adrenaline, so much of it, undammed by the awareness that I was going through something so unusual. There were parts of me—the part that loved stories, the part that *told* stories—that thrilled to it, bizarre as that phrase sounds. In terms of the period immediately after my diagnosis, in terms of the furious rushing-around, in terms of all the new information I had to process, in terms of all the new information I had to recount, it's more accurate than not. What strange magic the mind performs, what acts of salvation: Instead of sinking low in the face of the danger I was in, I soared in some ways. I was high. Buzzed.

Was it compensatory? Prophylactic? Both? I think it was about avoiding what Dorrie called the hole, though I didn't have that metaphor at the time. In its place I had an instinct, an intuition, a sense that I should be sarcastic and cinematic and should keep charging ahead because to indulge a temporary paralysis was a trap. Temporary could become permanent. It's harder to rouse yourself from a standstill than it is to keep moving, to let the velocity you've worked up carry you a bit further, and then another bit beyond that, and then another.

Coping can be incremental and sequential. It's less daunting that way. The writer Anne Lamott made that observation with her usual eloquence in her book *Bird by Bird,* and I can't remember if I read the passages in question before or after my stroke because I had *Bird by Bird* in my iPad and dipped into and out of it over a span of not just months but years, consuming its chapters, many of which worked as stand-alone essays, out of order. I read some parts two, three or even four times, either not remembering right away that I'd already read them or wanting to refamiliarize myself with counsel worth savoring more than once.

Like this bit, which, mirroring the book's subtitle, *Some Instructions on Writing and on Life*, equated wisdom for the wordsmith with wisdom, period: "E. L. Doctorow once said that 'writing a novel is like driving a car at night. You can see only as far as your headlights, but you can make the whole trip that way.' You don't have to see where you're going, you don't have to see your destination or everything you will pass along the way. You just have to see two or three feet ahead of you. This is right up there with the best advice about writing, or life, I have ever heard."

Just a page later, at least in my digital copy of the book, Lamott got at the same general idea with an anecdote about her older brother, at the age of ten, rushing to finish a school report on birds that he'd had months to do but had left to the last minute. It was due the next day. "He was at the kitchen table close to tears, surrounded by binder paper and pencils and unopened books on birds, immobilized by the hugeness of the task ahead," Lamott recalled. "Then my father sat down beside him, put his arm around my brother's shoulder, and said, 'Bird by bird, buddy. Just take it bird by bird.'"

Bird by bird, with only a few feet of the terrain in front of me illuminated, I pressed on.

That column on Jenna and Barbara Bush was due just a week and a half after my stroke—a week and a half during which I easily spent an aggregate thirty hours having my eyes examined and having my blood taken and lying in an MRI machine and pinging from this hospital to that one and submitting to an extra-long physical to be cleared for the needle-in-the-eye trial—and I got it in on time. The *Times* published it on the morning of the first eye injection.

And it was the second of my columns to be published that week. I'd also wedged in a humorous (or so I hoped!) rant about the tyranny of a certain seasonal flavor and fragrance—in coffee, in doughnuts, in cereal, in *pet shampoo*—during October. "Lock the refrigerator, bolt the cupboards and barricade the pantry," I wrote. "Pumpkin spice is here."

I not only had to concentrate harder to write those columns but also had to still the anxious racing of my heart, ignore the way the characters on my computer screen sometimes wouldn't stay fixed in their places, direct my gaze to the left of that screen, away from the encroaching waves and ripples of fog. My brain hadn't done much of the promised adapting yet. My brain wouldn't, in fact, do a lot of the promised adapting for a good long while. But I couldn't give in. I couldn't give up. As depressing as this resistance sometimes felt, how much worse would *that* feel? In slogging through, there was a future.

If anything, I overdid it. As part of my contract with CNN, I usually appeared twice weekly on Don Lemon's 10:00 p.m. show, and I agreed to schedule one of those appearances for the same day I would be getting that first shot in my eye. I knew that there'd be a bandage over my eye for hours after the injection but had been told that I should be able to take it off by dinnertime. As dinnertime approached, though, the stinging in that eye hadn't receded, and I peeked beneath the bandage to find a heavy-lidded, watery, bloodshot mess. I contacted one of the show's producers and apologetically backed out. I told her what was happening with my vision and explained that while I could if necessary do the show, I'd need to cover my eye somehow, lest I frighten viewers who'd braced for nothing more than President Trump's latest antics, and I couldn't imagine any covering that wouldn't raise a whole bunch of questions. The producer implored me to take the evening off, not for the sake of the viewers but for the sake of my own stress and health.

Five days after that, I was due to give a speech at the private New Jersey school where my sister, Adelle, had enrolled her two children, Gavin and Bella. I had written a well-received, bestselling book on college admissions, *Where You Go Is Not Who You'll Be*, and had given presentations about it at dozens of secondary schools, sometimes for a fee, sometimes simply to publicize the book, but in this case I was donating my time as a favor to my sister, niece and nephew. They repeatedly told me how excited they were about it. There was no way on earth I could cancel it.

But I was exhausted. I was petrified. Working through my smudged and swimmy vision to research and write a column was one thing; when I did my book speeches, I glanced repeatedly from the notes on the lectern in front of me to the audience and then from the audience to the screen behind me, which showed slides that I changed with a clicker. There were all these moving parts, all these different fields of vision, and if I lost my place in the notes or found some of them difficult to discern, there would be awkward pauses, a herky-jerky rhythm, and my certain embarrassment would only quicken my pulse and make matters even worse. How to prevent that? *Was* it preventable?

Usually, I printed the notes out in a seventeen- or eighteen-point font size, for ease. This time, I used twenty-two. Fewer words fit on each page, so the stack of pages was that much higher and more unwieldy. So be it. I was no longer living in the land of the perfect, to the extent that I'd ever lived there; I was living in the land of getting by. I worked harder than usual to memorize portions of the presentation, as a fail-safe. I willed myself to relax, telling myself that the world wouldn't end if I wasn't anywhere near my best. The school could hardly contemplate or ask for a refund. Even if I was terrible, at least I was free!

Well, not entirely: They did send a car to Manhattan to get me and then, after the speech, bring me home. On the ninety-minute ride down, I studied my notes, still trying to memorize more of them, even though reading in cars makes me slightly carsick. It started to rain, which made me sicker still. When I arrived, I had to meet and make nice with various school administrators and teachers, not letting on what a crushing headache I had, not showing how worn down I was, how nervous, how much I wished I were somewhere—anywhere—else. I'd made this commitment. I should fulfill it in good humor. In a few hours, it would be over. Who couldn't grit their way through a few bad hours?

I was dizzy at the lectern: There really was something over-whelming, vision-wise, about this particular arrangement, this panorama. I could feel the back of my shirt growing damp with my perspiration. I wondered if I'd sweat not only through my T-shirt and dress shirt but also through my sport jacket. Looking out in the crowd, I saw my nephew, smiling. I saw my niece, also smiling. I could do this. I *would* do this. And I did, not as fluidly as in the past, but fluidly enough.

In the car back to the city, I conducted telephone interviews with two different psychiatrists for a column I was writing about Harvey Weinstein's abuse of women over many years. Then I wrote the beginning of the column right there in the back seat, in a shirt now sopping wet. I had a 6:00 p.m. deadline, and I didn't want to blow it because there might be deadlines I had to blow in the future, columns that I needed to skip more than I needed to skip this one, and because I had this in me. Dammit, *I had this in me*. I got back to my apartment just before 4:00 p.m., submitted the column, dealt with my editor and finished the day's obligations by six thirty. I was done, period.

I showered, put on sweatpants and a fresh T-shirt and poured myself a glass—more like a fishbowl—of white wine. I sunk into the living-room couch. The sky outside had darkened. I could hear the faint, staggered beeping of car horns over on Amsterdam Avenue; I could hear a dog bark in the opposite direction, on Columbus. It took all the oomph I had left just to lift the glass to my lips. My body was a boulder.

But my mind whirred and whirled. Not even three weeks had gone by since my overnight transformation, and I felt like I'd been on a yearslong odyssey already. And it wasn't over. Not even close. I'd be back at the hospital for another injection in less than a month's time, then for a last one a month after that.

In between those shots there would be additional visits to that same hospital, an annoying forty minutes by subway and foot away: Now that I'd offered myself up as an ophthalmological guinea pig, I'd be poked and prodded and studied to a fare-thee-well.

I was supposed to return to the New York Eye and Ear In-firmary in exactly one week for *four hours* of eye examinations that were part of the constant charting of progress (or its ab-sence) during the drug trial and then, from there, I was due up-town, on the Upper East Side, for an additional examination by Dr. Banik at her office. So I was looking at maybe seven hours in all, counting travel time. This would be on Halloween, when I turned fifty-three. Happy birthday to me.

I took another gulp of wine. My heart lightened, but not from that. Waves of satisfaction and consolation moved through me. So, astonishingly, did a ripple of optimism. Look at how I was holding it together. Look at the statement I'd made—not to the world, but to myself—about how well I could handle this freaky eye condition, this looming threat to my independence. Look at how little in my life had to be sacrificed to it. Look at this show of force.

Look only at this very day and my arrival on the far side of it.

Chapter Four
FLYING SOLO

Being able to keep much of my life as it was didn't mean that nothing would change. On that first day when Dr. Moazami gave me her tentative (and, in the end, correct) diagnosis, she told me that I should be careful about flying. What had devastated my optic nerve was inadequate oxygen, due to diminished blood flow. To protect my other optic nerve, she said, I should avoid or compensate for situations in which the oxygen in the air I was breathing might be thinner than usual. The passenger cabins of airplanes represented one of those situations.

Over the next month, I had round-trip flights scheduled between New York and Chicago and between New York and Austin. She suggested canceling the latter if it wasn't mandatory, given that it involved considerably more time in a passenger cabin. But for the former trip and for all trips of all lengths in my future, "I'll have you fly with oxygen," she said. "I have all my patients do this." She meant patients with NAION, and she made it sound like a common, easy-peasy arrangement.

Would I actually carry an oxygen tank on the plane? Have those little plastic bulbs in my nose? She nodded. The following week, when I saw her for a second time—which would also be the last time, because entering the clinical trial meant being monitored by Dr. Banik and the neuro-ophthalmologists affiliated with it—I circled back to the matter of flying and oxygen. I was, understandably, anxious about it: She'd issued her decree, making the oxygen sound paramount, but still hadn't provided me with any concrete details about how to execute her orders.

"I just give you a letter," she said, again making it sound like a breeze. "Then the airline arranges it." Great, I said. But about the letter: Would I get it on the way out of the office today? How would that work? Her vagueness and nonchalance frustrated me.

She said that her office would get the letter to me the next day. She didn't say how, but she and her staff had my email address, my snail mail address, my phone number. I told myself to calm down and let them do their jobs.

A week later: no letter. And the Chicago flight was just six days away. I called Dr. Moazami's office, identified myself to the woman who answered the phone and asked about the "letter I need for the airlines, the one about traveling with supplemental oxygen."

"I've never heard of that," she said brusquely.

Never heard that such a letter was being prepared for me? Or never heard of a letter in this genre, period? I couldn't tell; I just knew that I was following Dr. Moazami's instructions. I just knew that I needed this letter. I urged the woman to ask Dr. Moazami about it.

A few hours after that, I got an email from Dr. Moazami's office with a scanned copy of the letter, printed on her letterhead. It was addressed "To Whom It May Concern" and said: "I am writing to you in regards to Mr. Frank Bruni, who is traveling by plane. The pressure of the cabin must be kept steady. If there should be any lowering of cabin pressure he will require oxygen at a rate of 120 liters/hour. Please give us a call if you have any questions." Whew. Under doctor's orders, the airline would take care of me. That settled that.

Except it didn't. My flights to and from Chicago, arranged by the arts festival where I'd agreed to moderate a panel, were on Southwest Airlines, and when I worked my way through the usual hellish voice-mail maze to reach a Southwest representative and ask where I should send Dr. Moazami's letter, I was told: nowhere. Southwest didn't give patients oxygen. The airline didn't get involved in patients' medical care.

The representative explained that I could *bring* oxygen that I myself acquired, provided that I gave Southwest and the Transportation Security Administration a heads-up that I was doing so. But the representative had no information about where I might get an airport-ready, transportable oxygen system, tank or whatever for air travel.

Maybe Delta did? That was the airline I usually flew, and I had several upcoming Delta flights, so I figured I'd ask someone there for guidance. A representative for Delta told me that it also didn't provide oxygen but that I could reach out to a service named Oxygen To Go. I did, and Oxygen To Go informed me that I had to order the oxygen tank and apparatus at least two weeks before traveling—the Chicago trip was less than a week away—and that it cost $325 for a week's use. A week's use was the minimum, and the $325 didn't include what I'd owe them to ship it to me and what I'd have to pay to ship it back.

Dear God. If I were to fly this way forevermore, I'd spend thousands of extra dollars a year, I'd be receiving and mailing back cumbersome packages, and I'd have to be super coordinated so that I never failed to request the oxygen in time. And that's not to mention what a conspicuous figure I'd be on the plane, a scuba diver who'd taken a wrong turn on his way to the ocean.

I felt defeated. But, wait, did I have 100 percent or even 50 percent confidence that this new rigmarole was necessary? I was bowing to Dr. Moazami's counsel even as I was gathering evidence that she'd given me incorrect information, in terms of how easily a person arranged to fly with oxygen, so I thought that maybe I should double-check on the counsel itself.

I scoured the internet—which, yes, can be dangerous if you're indiscriminate, but I wasn't—and found no consensus that patients with optic neuropathies were at significant risk in airplanes. Because of my participation in the clinical trial, I was being introduced to, and interacting with, neuro-ophthalmologists besides Dr. Moazami, and while it wasn't technically their job to treat me beyond the parameters of the trial, I figured it couldn't hurt to ask one of them about flying and oxygen. I put the question to Dr. Banik, who volunteered to share it on a digital chat board of neuro-ophthalmologists in which she participated. The next day, she called me with the verdict: She and most of her colleagues didn't think I should bother with, or worry about, supplemental oxygen when flying, the risk of which was ambiguous and, if it existed, minimal.

So Dr. Moazami was an outlier on that—and, it turned out, on something else, something fundamental. As I read more and more about NAION and as I spoke with Dr. Banik and other prominent neuro-ophthalmologists, I learned that the prevailing thinking on how likely NAION was to occur in a person's second eye was 20 percent, not 40. That was still a plenty frightening sword hanging over me, but appreciably duller than I'd been led to believe.

I mention Dr. Moazami's misdirection not to disparage her: She nailed what was wrong with my vision. She was thorough and perceptive in that regard. She also knew about the one clinical trial underway for my condition. She steered me into it with the necessary dispatch. But my experience with her underscored something that must be understood by people who, because of affliction or aging, begin to have more and more medical care in their lives: Doctors are flawed. They're human. We want them to be gods, because we want that certainty, that salvation. We want clear roles: The doctor commands; the patient obeys. But, at times, in their imperfection and arrogance and haste, they make assumptions and mistakes. So it's crucial to approach a relationship with a doctor, any doctor, as a partnership and to consider yourself an equal partner, respectful but not obsequious, receptive but skeptical.

Within a few months of my stroke, I had been examined or put through tests by more than a dozen doctors or medical technicians, and while I was impressed by the patience and kindness of many of them, I was also struck by their oversights. Not one of them ever asked me how I was faring psychologically and emotionally and whether I needed any assistance in that regard. They knew that, overnight, I'd gone from someone who never thought about blindness to someone presented with that as a distinct future possibility. But not one of them brought up counseling, if only to note that I should keep it in mind if I felt that anxiety or fear was getting the best of me. Not one of them mentioned mental health at all.

Not one of them mentioned that there's a whole field called low-vision therapy or low-vision rehabilitation that's essentially occupational therapy for people learning to make the most of impaired eyesight. It may be that they didn't regard me as someone who had to worry about that yet: With my glasses on, I could still see 20/20 from my undamaged eye. But I'd told the doctors and the technicians about my slowed-down reading. I'd told them about occasional visual disorientation. And if that undamaged eye *did* get damaged, I might be an ideal candidate for low-vision therapy.

It became clear to me that most medical professionals, no matter how conscientious, are managing the task at hand, by which I mean the specific affliction that you present with, the pain or discomfort that you're trying to rid yourself of, the immediate juncture that you have to move past. They're not managing *you*—certainly not *all* of you. That larger, longer, more panoramic task can be outsourced to exactly no one.

For as long as your mind remains intact and your energy endures, you are your own best case manager. You hold the levers for your moods, the switches for your feelings. You alone have all the information. You alone can update it by the second. You alone have no priority more urgent. You alone live fully with the consequences. Others may want or mean to come to the rescue and, in discrete instances, may try to. But they're the guests, not the homeowner. They don't stay forever or know how to work the thermostat.

Alone. Maybe because that word was so front-of-brain and top-of-heart, I found myself doing something that I'd done irregularly and infrequently before. I was surprised by it. I didn't tell my family or friends about it, lest they deem me melodramatic. I also knew that they'd find it so out of character that they'd seek an explanation, and I wasn't sure I understood it myself. What I was doing was praying.

Not so much to God as to—well, I'm not sure. To the universe? To the serenest place inside me? To my better angels, which weren't crowned with halos but cloaked in prudence, humility, hope? I'm struggling with this because I struggle with religion, the organized forms of which have so often been agents of division, sources of bigotry, destructive political forces. I ascribe to no formal dogma and have zero patience for zealots, be they hypocrites (as many are) or not. And I don't believe in some bearded celestial being who set this universe in motion, sculpted the human creatures who inhabit it, entertains their pleas and doles out mercies in accordance with where they're needed most. The mess of the world—the rampant suffering, the runaway cruelty—just doesn't support that. And our aching need for such explanation and reassurance undercuts their validity. God as conceptualized by most creeds is suspiciously convenient.

But I've never been able to say that I *don't* believe in God, at least God in the sense of an organizing principle to things, a transcendent spirit, a code of conduct to which we're all called, a good and pure voice that's both within and without us. If that sounds like gobbledygook, well, my God *is* gobbledygook, almost by necessity: How could anything so omniscient and ambient not be? I'm not remotely sure that this God exists but I'm not wholly sure that this God doesn't: I have long called myself an agnostic but have never been able to take the plunge and declare myself an atheist. Something has always held me back. Is that something merely superstition? Am I taking out an insurance policy against the .000001 percent chance that hellfire awaits the heretic? Or is this thing called God holding me back? Is my pause divine proof?

I just know that in my head during the weeks and months after my stroke there was a monologue that sometimes morphed into a dialogue, and the script fit the definition of prayer.

I asked if there was a reason for what was happening to me: Was it punishment for past misdeeds, penance for my errors? Was it part of some lesson I had to learn, some deficiency I had to answer for?

A second voice—also mine, but calmer and wiser—told me that such questions smacked of arrogance and immaturity, inasmuch as they failed to take into account all the random occurrences and ordeals in every person's existence.

I asked that I not be saddled with more than I could bear and that my back prove sturdy enough to be saddled with a lot.

That second voice told me that I shouldn't think in terms of burdens and setbacks but should hold tight to the knowledge that during previous chapters and moments of fear and distress, I'd discovered the necessary stillness and constructed the requisite sense of security. Why shouldn't I trust that I'd discover and construct them now?

I was talking to myself and responsible for both halves of the conversation, but it seemed to be infused with and even guided by something larger than the sum of those halves, and it brought me a peace much like the one that so many religions describe. It gave me a kind of companionship that was crucial.

As I moved on from my stroke, as I went through the clinical trials, as I gritted my teeth and commanded my occasionally screaming brain to quiet itself, I was unprepared for how private and invisible all of this was and by how quickly almost everyone around me forgot what had happened to me. Stupidly, I hadn't foreseen that one of the fruits of coping reasonably well was that people didn't spot your efforts to do just that. And my efforts weren't spotted easily.

They occurred when I was reading, which I loved to do, which I needed to do and which I did more of after my stroke, as a talismanic way to make sure that it didn't exit my life or, conversely, as an indulgence of it before it did. But I had to be more deliberate in my concentration. I had to pause whenever the lines went from neat rows to crosshatches or I got stuck, like a boxed-in bumper car, between words. Sometimes that was just once an hour, sometimes every ten minutes.

Writing, too, was more complicated. I'd always been someone who didn't commit many typos, but now I did, so I was constantly circling back to previous sentences and paragraphs to check and correct. Still, errors slipped through. In the span of five paragraphs in one of the weekly newsletters that I wrote for the *Times*, I referred to a "sliver lining" instead of a "silver" one and to my walk down a "nature trial" that was obviously supposed to be a "trail." There was something weirdly scrambled and swirled about the bastard teamwork of one eye doing its job correctly and another eye that insisted on meddling despite its incompetence.

My depth perception was sometimes slightly out of whack, along with my sense of objects' exact positioning in relation to one another. Writing text messages with my iPhone, I "loved" when I should have "lived" and "lived" when I should have "loved" because the "i" and "o" are side by side on the keypad, scrunched close together, and my vision routinely guided my thumb to the wrong vowel. I was often stymied when buying or refilling a MetroCard for the New York City subways, because I only thought I was pressing the inside of the correct rectangle on the electronic screen when my index finger had actually fallen outside of it. My eyes told me different.

They made me a worse host, one who might well pour wine on you, so you were better off drinking white than red around me. I'd extend the bottle toward a visiting friend's glass, begin to refill it and hear a scream of "Stop!" because I'd either come up short of the glass, and the wine would cascade to the table or the floor, or I'd overshoot it, and the wine would slosh onto the friend's lap. I'm a quick(-ish) learner, so I started to listen for the clink of the bottle's neck against the rim of the glass for confirmation of its precise location. Only then would I pour.

While I could still legally drive and driving wasn't any problem during the day, it could be stressful at night. It was terrifying on a particular night in Texas. I had traveled there to interview one female military veteran in San Antonio who was the Democratic Party's choice to try to wrest a House seat from a Republican incumbent and another female military veteran near Austin to whom the party had assigned the same task. I had scheduled a flight into San Antonio but out of Austin and rented a car so I could drive the roughly eighty minutes between the two cities. But that road trip occurred long after sunset, during a heavy downpour, and what would have not been ideal even before NAION was now grueling. Although there was no traffic, the trip took me nearly four hours: I not only poked along at about forty-five miles an hour but also exited the highway repeatedly to give my eyes and brain a break and to wait out the most furious bursts of rain. I was behind the wheel because I was intent on being self-sufficient, on letting go of as little of my pre-stroke life as possible. But I didn't want to kill myself—or, worse, someone else.

No one was with me to witness my distress. My labored reading and farcical texting weren't obvious to anyone around me. My affliction didn't announce itself with braces or bandages or a limp or a stutter. My appearance was unchanged—the bad eye looked the same on the surface as it always had—and the few friends who *did* remember and continue to remark on what had happened to me routinely said, "You can't even tell that anything is wrong." The statement was meant as a reassurance or compliment. But it sometimes felt like a reprimand.

"It's weird, I know," I typically answered. That was my way of simply moving the conversation along. It was also the truth. Debilitation-wise, I was in a halfway house, a limbo that defied easy labeling, a circumstance that was daunting but manageable. And it was a lonely place, in part because of the camouflage of normalcy that it wore.

But I felt adrift and alone for an additional reason. My stroke, with its exquisite timing, had occurred as one of the two most important men in my life faded away—and as the other was about to.

Like many people in their early fifties, I no longer had two living parents. My mother had died some two decades earlier, when she was just sixty-one, from a rare form of uterine cancer. That forced Dad, who had always been the more introverted and aloof parent, to step up.

He couldn't replace her. He wasn't built that way. But he understood that he had to start asking me and my three siblings some of the touchy-feely questions that he hadn't asked before. He understood that he had to be more demonstrative, more open. So he was. Bit by bit, he and I talked more and more, and it turned out that he needed those conversations as much as I did—to confess his regret that he hadn't been as strong for Mom as he could have been, to wrestle with his awful awkwardness when he went on a few dates, to figure out whether he should marry the woman he'd ended up dating most steadily.

Until then I'd seen him as a kind of hyperconfident superman. He'd grown up in humble circumstances, to Italian-immigrant parents who didn't speak serviceable English for much of his childhood, and he'd worked up to four hours a day in the family's bodega of sorts from the eighth through twelfth grades. Without the sorts of advantages that he would later give me, he'd managed to excel in his classes and be elected president of his high school during his senior year, after which he attended an Ivy League college on a full scholarship. From there: an MBA and a distinguished, lucrative career at one of the world's biggest accounting firms, where he was a senior partner by the time he retired. I didn't just love him. I was in awe of him.

But with Mom gone, I also grew to *like* him in a whole new way. And I saw, maybe for the first time, that he liked me—beyond any paternal obligation. Better yet, he thought well of me. He did marry that woman, but when, more than ten years into their often turbulent union, he refined and updated various legal documents, it was me whom he named his health-care surrogate, me whom he gave a broad power of attorney that not only authorized but also invited my help in managing his affairs if that ever became necessary or appropriate.

Manage *his* affairs? Back *him* up? Those notions were surreal. I wasn't his rock. He, for all his reticence and remove, was mine: there to celebrate any big milestone or advance in my life with an indulgent, expensive restaurant meal; there with his business acumen to talk me through the intricacies of mortgages and taxes; there to tell me—and he always did tell me—

that he could be my bank if I were ever in financial trouble and my hotel if I were ever roofless; there to make the world several critical degrees less terrifying.

But over the year or so before my stroke, he went through a marked, obvious cognitive decline. He would ask the same question or tell the same story three times in a span of twenty minutes. He would freeze as he played his usual scorekeeper role in a beloved family card game called "oh, hell!," unable to fill in the right numbers. To a degree and with a frequency far beyond the norm, he would forget where he had put his shoes, belt or wallet and whether he had paid a bill or written out a check.

Around the time my vision deteriorated, Dad, then eighty-two, was diagnosed with age-related dementia—one doctor, in short order, specified that Alzheimer's was a principal culprit—and while there was no way to predict how fast he would deteriorate, there was only one trajectory. One month, he couldn't keep track of where his various financial accounts were and what was in them. The next, he was briefly and wrongly convinced that his investment adviser had stolen all of his money. During group meals, he'd sometimes go silent, a clear sign that he had lost the thread, or he'd pipe up with some story from the distant past, because memories from decades ago were more complete and available to him than any recall of what had been said just minutes earlier.

He was too flustered by email to use it anymore. He stepped away from computers altogether. He struggled with his smartphone, not noticing voice mails for days or even weeks and then not remembering how to retrieve them. When he returned my calls, it was always long after the fact, usually irrelevant by that point and seldom because he'd listened to the message I had left. We'd exchange a few rote sentences. Then he'd hurry off the phone before the conversation moved beyond pleasantries, into territory that was now so difficult for him to navigate.

This was what age had in store for some of us. Dad was a reminder of how vulnerable we all are, no matter how powerful we may feel at a given moment, and of the future's unpredictability. My mother's family, not my father's, was the one with a medical history of Alzheimer's, so she'd been the one to express worry about it, until something that she couldn't have foreseen, something deadlier, came along. And yet here Dad was, losing track of names, losing track of time, in a cognitive fog much thicker than my visual one. There were twists of fate infinitely crueler than what I'd encountered.

Dad could no longer be my rock. He couldn't even absorb what had happened to me. When I told him about my right eye, he shook his head and asked maybe two marginally relevant questions, then changed the topic. I don't think he ever brought up my vision again, so I didn't, either. What I owed him at this point was sturdiness, not neediness.

What did Tom owe me? He was the other important man I referred to, the person with whom I shared my home, my bed, my vacations and, of course, my confidences. He was, essentially, my spouse—my husband. That we hadn't actually married seemed irrelevant: a bit of complicated, time-intensive business that we simply hadn't gotten around to; an unnecessary provocation for some members of his family, who were extremely conservative Christians; a mere formalization of a commitment that we'd adequately established by combining our households and that was evident in calls and text messages almost every hour—every half hour at times.

Or at least that's what we'd always told ourselves, and I usually believed it. But there was an occasional gnawing: Was he so verbally undemonstrative and unromantic only as a function of his personality, as he claimed whenever I raised the subject, or did he not feel all that he was supposed to feel? Did I refrain from probing further because, at some level, I didn't care enough and didn't expect our relationship to go the distance?

Before my stroke, I didn't have the answers. About seven months afterward, I got some of them.

But first, those seven months: Tom finagled that rushed initial appointment with Dr. Moazami. He used his inside connections to make sure that all the NAION-confirming tests that I needed were done in time for me to begin the clinical trial. He did some reading, asked around, added the knowledge that he was accruing to the knowledge that I was rounding up. We talked through the science of what was happening to me.

But the idea that I might go blind and the fear that inevitably went along with that? If I broached it, he batted it away, telling me not to be an alarmist and assuring me that this wouldn't be any big deal in the end. The dread of having a needle stuck in my eye? He also downplayed that—maybe, to be fair, to calm me—by noting that many patients with other conditions received similar treatments and endured them just fine.

My first shot was scheduled smack in the middle of a work-day for him and, because of the preparations for the shot, would consume several hours, certainly if you added travel time to and from the hospital. I knew how intricate and packed his office schedule could be, so I didn't ask him to accompany me. I had my friend Elli join me instead. For the second shot, a month later, my friend Alessandra came along. For the third shot, two months after that, I went alone.

More unusual was that every few weeks, there'd be a three-hour or four-hour span of time when he didn't respond instantly to texts the way he usually did. And on one or two of my out-of-town trips, when I called home in the usual fashion, well before his typical bedtime, to say good night, I didn't find him and he didn't return the message. I pressed him just a bit on why. He said he'd fallen asleep super early and saw that I'd called only when he woke up the following morning.

I remember asking at one point: "Are you having an affair?" I cringed as I said it: how unoriginal. I was my own bad television movie.

"You're crazy," he told me—do these conversations ever leave the realm of terrible screenwriting?—and sounded not just annoyed but offended, making me feel foolish. I let it go. I put it out of my mind.

But I guess I didn't succeed in getting it *all* the way out of my mind because, months later, on a Sunday night, as he cleaned the dinner dishes because I'd made the dinner, he asked me if I was happy with our relationship. The question was a complete non sequitur. We'd been talking seconds earlier about, I think, blue cheese. It was also entirely out of character. Discussing *feelings* typically made him squirm. That's how I knew. That was the tell.

"You're involved with someone else?" I asked. Or at least it should have been a question. But it came out more like a statement, a declaration—and, in fact, was. Because I was that sure of it.

"Yes," he said.

"And it's serious enough that you're thinking maybe you want to be with him—live with him," I said. I was sure of this, too, because it was the only explanation for Tom's initiation of this conversation. It hit me that he'd never wade into words this messy unless there was no avoiding them, unless things had gone that far.

Again: "Yes."

"How long has this been going on?" An actual question this time—and yet *more* triteness.

"Since September," he said.

I took that in. I riffled through the calendar in my brain. So he'd been involved with this man for just one month when my stroke happened in October. Still he didn't end it. He'd watched me over those crazy two weeks after the stroke, when I was zipping in and out of doctors' offices, when I was being plopped down in front of one machine and then pinned below another. Still he didn't end it. Shouldn't the usual guilt of doing what he was doing double, triple? Shouldn't that have derailed the affair?

Or was I just that trivial in the end? That easily disregarded and discarded?

"I think you should go to him tonight," I said. "I think you should leave now. You want to be with him—be with him." And

I moved from the kitchen to the living room, where I sat in silence as he packed a bag and walked out the door.

That wasn't the end of it, not just then. Less than a week later, he moved back in, swearing that he wanted to make this right. I didn't know what to think or exactly how I felt: My emotions since the stroke had been so varied, so messy. Especially in light of that, I worried about rushing the decision whether to end a nearly decade-long relationship and disentangle two lives that were so tightly entwined. This was no ordinary crossroads. I shouldn't speed through it.

Besides, Tom and I had a problem. It was May now, and in July we were scheduled to spend a week and a half in Greece with my younger brother, Harry, his wife, Sylvia, and their four children, who were so excited to be introduced to this gorgeous, fabled country by Uncle Frank and Uncle Tom. If one or both of those uncles were no-shows, it would cast a pall over the trip, maybe even prompt its cancellation. I didn't want that. Couldn't bear it. I asked Tom if we could just keep our troubles to ourselves for a little while, put on the faces of a happy couple, show them some of our favorite places, as we'd promised we would, and have a good time. I asked him if we could delay any determination about our future until after Greece. He agreed. And so, as the eight of us hiked down rocky slopes to hidden coves, swam in water the color of gemstones and sipped wine as the sun set over the Aegean, there was no talk of bittersweet endings, broken promises and bruised hearts. Tom and I fooled them, no doubt because for those nine days, we fooled ourselves. In the land of myths, we wrote and acted our own.

August returned us to reality. Well, it returned me; Tom, strangely, never said a word about what had happened between us, where that left us and what we should do. It was as if he'd washed the memory from his mind. I hadn't. I couldn't. And I edged closer to, then arrived at, my answer to the question of our future. That answer was that we didn't have one.

My stroke—my vision—drove that determination.

A part of me was pulled the opposite way. I wondered how I could choose to be alone during this chapter of all chapters, when my future was so uncertain and might leave me less independent than ever. At such a juncture, who threw away a second set of hands? A second set of eyes?

But a much bigger part of me overrode that impulse, which was born of insecurity and timidity and trepidation, of the sorts of currents that should never govern a life and that I didn't want to govern mine. That bigger part of me listened to different considerations and calculations: What if I did lose my eyesight, and Tom and I were indeed together, and it became clear around or after that point that he didn't want to be there, or that he was again dividing his affection and attention, but because of my disability, he and I both felt trapped? What kind of hell would that be? I had to imagine it, because I knew now that there was a real cap on Tom's reliability and love. I couldn't ignore it.

I couldn't ignore my new acceptance of uncertainty: how it's the given in all our lives—the default setting—and might as well be embraced. What awaited me after Tom? I could only guess.

But I could control how I approached that mystery. I could walk tall toward it, not shuffle or slouch or cower.

Tom and I set Labor Day weekend for when movers would come and take away the furniture in our apartment that belonged to him, which was about a third of it, and deliver it to an apartment he'd rented. He asked me if maybe that was a time when it made sense for me to be away—to visit one of my siblings or out-of-state friends or such—because, he said, the sadness of leaving our home for good would be amplified if I were there when he left. I made arrangements for a three-day trip to Santa Fe, where there was material for a column about higher education that I'd wanted to write. I invited my friend Barbara, who lives in Austin, to meet me there. I'd do some work, have some fun, have a few drinks. I'd lose myself in adobe and agave.

En route to the airport, I thought: Now *this* is a movie. I could almost hear the soundtrack—a thicket of violins, with a flute peeking out tentatively from behind the trees. Our hero clenches his jaw as his eyes tear up and his taxi presses on and the longest, most significant romantic partnership of his life recedes, like the Manhattan skyline, farther and farther in the rearview mirror.

But I could reject that music. I could rewrite that script. That was my next thought, the one I dwelled on. I could insist on the bright side or at least on the brightest side possible. I imagined—then experienced—my heart as a clumsy, crotchety old car. It could be moved, with enough effort, in alternate directions, down one of two forking roads: toward an inventory of all that had gone wrong and the sorrow of that tally, or toward a recognition of how much good remained, how much happiness was still within reach.

I took the latter route. I embraced my good fortune: The breakup wasn't forcing me to move, because I'd had the resources to buy the apartment on my own, in my name only, and I still had enough resources to live there alone. Amid the other disruptions in my life, I could stay put, and I could also afford to replace the furniture that had been taken away, to fill those empty spaces.

More good fortune: I had friends, like Barbara, who would fill the empty *emotional* spaces that Tom had left, and I had a job that involved adventures, travel. I was not only getting away, I was also getting away to a storied city with its own distinctive architecture, its own special light, a setting in the mountains . . .

Mountains. The realization came to me only after the plane had taken off, and it stopped me short. Somehow, amid all the upset, I had completely overlooked that part of the lure of Santa Fe, New Mexico, was its elevation. Its *altitude.*

I had sworn off future trips to Aspen, where I had sometimes attended—and spoken at—an annual conference. I had deleted Machu Picchu from my bucket list. But I'd made these arrangements for Santa Fe—and was now halfway there—without putting it in the company of those places. What a dunce I could be.

I was using the airplane's Wi-Fi, so I did a Google search for exactly how high Santa Fe was: just over seven thousand feet. Not great, but not awful. Surely, I—or, rather, my optic nerve—

could survive seven thousand feet. That was thousands lower than Aspen, thousands lower than some spots in Bogotá, Colombia, another city I'd visited several times pre-stroke. Maybe my body wouldn't even notice seven thousand feet. Just a big hill, really.

Chapter Five
HOPE IS GNARLY AND EVERGREEN

I met and got to know Juan Jose not because he's blind but because he's a close friend of two close friends of mine, Joel and Nicole. Not long after my stroke, we all had dinner together in a restaurant on the Upper East Side of Manhattan. Juan Jose—a career diplomat from Mexico City, who was then Mexico's permanent representative to the United Nations—came with his romantic partner, Mariangela, an Italian diplomat who also worked at the UN. They're a great-looking, globe-trotting, multilingual couple, and that's probably what most people's first and most lasting impression of them is. But what intrigued me that night were the whispered directions that he was getting from Nicole.

"Asparagus at two o'clock," she would say, a reference that had nothing to do with the hour. "Beef at six o'clock." This was information that recast the plate in front of him as a giant timepiece. Nicole was telling him where to steer his fork to connect with the various components of his meal.

That was pretty much the only evidence that he couldn't see—that and the fact that when he and Mariangela arrived, they maintained physical contact for most of their approach to the table, a gesture that was one part display of affection, one part navigational assistance. When you spoke with Juan Jose, he looked you straight in the eye and held your gaze. When someone else spoke, his head turned that way as quickly and confidently as anyone else's. Once he'd figured out, via those verbal cues and the subtle movements of his fingers, where everything in front of him was, he didn't fumble for objects or seek additional help. Many months later I was at a dinner party with him and about twelve other people, including my friend Alessandra. When she and I discussed him afterward and I referred offhandedly to his blindness, she had no idea what I was talking about. She had sat mere feet from him for about four hours and never picked up on it.

That's not because he hid his disability. It's because he had adapted to it so fluidly and fluently and didn't go out of his way to mention it. But when I asked him how he lost his sight, how he adjusted to that and how it affected him now, he answered me in great detail. He's proud of his route from there to here. That's a major reason that he traveled it so successfully: He regarded it not as a burden but as a distinction.

He grew up in the 1960s and '70s in an upper-middle-class neighborhood of Mexico City, to parents who provided well for him and his siblings. And he was unremarkable, or at least that's how he remembers it. He was bad at baseball. Bad at basketball.

Soccer flummoxed him: His leg-eye coordination didn't match his peers', and if he were playing late in the day, as the light faded, he'd lose track of the ball and even bump into people. He didn't do particularly well on his schoolwork. At times, he recalled, "I thought I was officially stupid."

His eyesight was never good. He wore glasses from an early age. But in his late teens, as his vision became almost useless in darkness and semidarkness, his eye doctor realized that Juan Jose didn't have anything as run-of-the-mill as nearsightedness or farsightedness or astigmatism. "The guy started to become excited," Juan told me. "*Excited.* He was a small neighborhood doctor. He went and picked up a book and said, 'You have *retinitis pigmentosa.*' I was his first case ever. He said, 'You are going to lose your sight.' Just like that. 'By forty, you will be blind, more or less.' My mother was collapsing. She was in shock. Me? I was not. It's funny, but I was experiencing some kind of fascination."

If the doctor's manner was off-key, his conclusion was on target: Juan Jose indeed had retinitis pigmentosa, a rare retinal disorder that often asserts itself around the age that he was at that time, is more common among men than women and routinely leads to blindness within ten to twenty-five years. It didn't have a cure then and still doesn't have a cure now, but his mother, desperate, toted him to specialist after specialist, not just in Mexico but also in nearby countries.

"She was ready to turn the world upside down," Juan Jose said. "I was enjoying the ride, really enjoying the ride. It was awful to go to doctor after doctor. But it was fun to go to Colombia. It was an adventure." It was also an explanation. Of course he hadn't been an athletic god or scholastic genius: He was putting in much more effort than his schoolmates did to see the words on a page or the ball on a field much less well. Now he understood why, and now there was a novel dimension of his life that set him apart. He even thought to himself, "I'm special."

Maybe that was a form of denial, which gets a bad rap. Denial comes in handy up to a point. Maybe time has warped his memory. But the response he remembers having in the months and years following his diagnosis was consistent with his responses to blindness in the decades to come. He never freaked out, never gave up, never even brooded, as best I can tell.

He had serious difficulties, physical and emotional, and was at times painfully aware of what he was missing out on. Although his diagnosis absolved him of the conviction that he lacked smarts and, in that fashion, provided motivation to apply himself in college in Mexico and then in graduate school at Georgetown University, those studies required a real force of will. He wasn't blind yet, but he was on that path, and he had to use particular software and devices to get all of his reading done. He had to push himself.

That was true, too, as he began his career with the Mexican Foreign Service in his midtwenties and rose in the ranks. During that period, he did conceal his vision troubles, an exhausting charade that required a layer of energy on top of all the other layers. He didn't tell his boss about his looming blindness until he was around thirty and working in London, and he made the admission then only because he needed time off to go to Cuba for a sequence of experimental procedures, including an intricate surgery involving, as best he recalls, an implant and extensive stitching. When he woke from it, he said, he was in agony. For days afterward, he felt as if he had a beach's worth of sand in his eyes.

And yet the surgery didn't work. By his midthirties, his vision was effectively gone. Blindness strained and eventually ended his marriage, in part because it introduced all sorts of logistical complications and changed the dynamics between him and his wife. It also filled him with worry about being a good father to their two little girls, Sofia and Paloma. He didn't want them to consider him frail and dependent or to be self-conscious about him.

He told me: "When Paloma was five years of age, one of her favorite jokes was when we both were walking on the street holding hands, she would say 'Careful of this step!' when there was none."

"That's mean," I said playfully. We were talking, after all, about a five-year-old.

"No," Juan Jose corrected me. "That's beautiful."

"Why beautiful?" I asked.

"Because it meant that I'd succeeded."

"Because she could be light about it? Jocular?"

"Yes," Juan Jose said. "Exactly."

He said he knows what Sofia and Paloma look like as young women and he knows—or feels he knows—what Mariangela, whom he met long after he went blind, looks like as well. His world isn't a complete blur: He catches small patches of objects, of faces, depending on how near they are and how much light is falling on them. He spots contours. They're like pieces of a jigsaw puzzle that he can build over time in his brain. He does the same with places, especially if he's been somewhere before. He retrieves images from memory and grafts on the few details from the present that he can gather and assemble.

The faces that are wholly inscrutable are the ones of strangers he passes on the street. They're there too briefly and move too quickly for him to put together his Picasso of them. That bothers him. People with good vision, he told me, underestimate the diversion, the solace, the company of those faces. "You make eye contact," he said. "You read expressions. You're more or less communicating with those who are walking past you. You connect just by seeing." He paused. "It's a lonely world, this one of *not* seeing."

But he described many more satisfactions than regrets. And he is convinced that he wouldn't have had his exciting diplomatic career and attained his altitude of success without the prospect of blindness and then blindness itself. "I am completely grateful," he said, quickly adding that he knows, when he expresses that sentiment, that people think he has "brainwashed" himself.

But going blind and then being blind steeled his will and concentrated his energy, because he approached his vision impairment as a test that made him and his life that much more interesting. That viewpoint was made possible in part by his parents' support, the safety net that they provided and his access to an excellent education. But it was still a mental discipline. A decision. And it was the path and precursor to a confidence that he feels certain he wouldn't possess otherwise. He isn't just a high achiever; he's a high achiever who could so easily have been marginalized, including by himself.

Additionally, he said, losing vision "gave me skills, tools, a way of thinking, a brain that brought me here. For any person with a disability, from the moment you wake up until the moment you are back in bed, you are facing all kinds of challenges, all kinds of obstacles that you have to sort out. In New York, getting to my office, getting out of the car, going through the building, getting to the elevator—the things that you do, automatically, without thinking, require strategy and problem-solving for me." And that's just a half hour in the morning. The rest of the day has many more half hours like that.

His temperament, too, has been forged by not seeing. "I became patient," he told me. "I think patience is one of the biggest attributes I may have. In all my defects, patience is one of the good things. Because you *have* to become patient. And you have to become resilient. Why? Because you will need to be with all kinds of little problems all the time or you may get into trouble, and you need to pause and think and be careful." Otherwise, he said, you walk through the wrong door, down the wrong hall, to the wrong departure gate. You stray into a physically dangerous place or space. The care that he takes to avoid that is a care that informs and improves the rest of his life. Blindness, he said, gets the credit.

"I never saw it as a burden," he said. "I saw it as a characteristic. You might or might not be happy with how you look. You might wish to be taller or thinner. But you are what you are. To me it was exactly that."

"Honestly," he told me, "I have taken full advantage of not seeing."

⌒

Juan Jose's story doesn't suggest that people with disabilities or diseases can just whistle their way through them. It doesn't insinuate that they're secretly blessed, and I have no reason to believe that he'd say anything like that. Also, he was speaking for himself, and his circumstances—his family, his talent for optimism, decades of vision before he lost it, aptitude for a job in which eyesight wasn't essential—gave him a better chance at flourishing than many people have. In addition, he may well be sugarcoating both his past and his present. Many of us do that when it serves us. It can be an effective and prudent method of getting by.

But even if that's the case with Juan Jose, the narrative that he tells the world and, more important, himself is a valid one, a cup-half-full version that's absolutely workable and totally plausible. It's also an example. It has a moral: While we have minimal control over the events that befall us, we have the final say over how we regard and react to them. Juan Jose can't fix his eyesight, but he can shape his story. He can underscore the themes that he wants to in the cause of contentment, fulfillment and self-esteem. Shouldn't he—shouldn't all of us—do exactly that?

Two aspects of his response to his circumstances had special resonance for me after my stroke. They played a particularly helpful role in my very pale echo of his experience. One was the repurposing of trauma or upset as a badge of honor, the turning of the statement "I can't believe what I'm going through" from a complaint to a boast, from "I can't believe what I'm being *put* through" to "I can't believe what I'm managing to *get* through." The other, which had some Venn diagram overlap with that, was the reframing of difficulty as dare, the conversion of a predicament into a puzzle that you're solving, a seminar that you're mastering, a curriculum of new information and new skills. Juan Jose saw an "adventure"—his exact word for it—where he could have seen an ordeal. I had instinctively begun to do the same before I met him. Our conversations bolstered that effort, especially in regard to the second clinical trial I enrolled in.

I've already mentioned the first, the one that I joined immediately and that involved monthly injections in my right eye. I've made clear that it wasn't much fun. But I should back up and explain a bit more about it. What was being injected was an engineered molecule that—if it worked—was supposed to halt the post-stroke chain reaction by which cells die. In doing so, it might restore some pre-stroke function. But it apparently didn't work: The pharmaceutical company conducting the trial ended up halting it before it reached full enrollment because the patients who had already completed their participation, including me, weren't showing a promising degree of improvement. I may not have actually received injections on the second and third months, when I felt mere discomfort instead of intense pain. I subsequently learned that there was one cohort of patients who got the drug once and then a placebo twice. Getting a placebo, in this case, meant getting nothing: The doctor went through the whole eye-numbing and eyelid-clamping ritual—

and lavishly bandaged the eye afterward—but a blunt-tipped needle was pressed against the eye's surface and didn't actually puncture it. The idea was that patients might not figure out that they weren't being administered any treatment and would thus remain an acceptable control group to measure against patients who were.

The second clinical trial was a much more protracted affair. It began enrolling NAION patients about a year after I'd completed the first one. I became, I think, the second patient enrolled in Manhattan, one of about twelve sites around North America. The trial was gauging whether a liquid compound made from the resin of mastic trees, which are gnarly evergreens found mainly in the Mediterranean, could repair ravaged nerves. Those of us with NAION were ideal test subjects because any restored function in our optic nerves was easy to detect and quantify via our performance on good old-fashioned eye charts: Either we read more letters or we didn't. But we weren't the real targets of the Israeli biotech start-up that had patented the compound. If it worked, it could be used for people who had suffered other kinds of strokes, people with spinal-cord injuries, people with Alzheimer's disease, people with an array of neurological or neurodegenerative disorders. There was a potentially enormous market of patients beyond me and my kind.

Both of the trials meant that over the course of the treatments and long after they were finished, I had to march down at regular intervals—every month, every two months—to the New York Eye and Ear Infirmary of Mount Sinai for tests, and while that may sound humdrum, trust me, it wasn't. The tests could span three hours and involve more than eye charts. Even the eye-chart part wasn't as straightforward as the usual visit to the optometrist.

Before I was shown the chart, I had to submit to that tedium of having pair after pair of infinitesimally different corrective lenses put sequentially before each of my eyes so that I could say which one worked better. No biggie, really, except that this drill extended well beyond the usual five minutes, recurred in precisely the same painstaking fashion month after month after month and was a joke when it came to my right eye, for which no lens produced anything in the same hemisphere as clarity. Having a profusion of lenses layered over it only hammered home that point. It was like a person repeatedly screaming "You're unfixable!" long after you'd gotten the point.

Once the technician had chosen the best lenses, I'd do the chart. For the left eye, it was an uneventful process. I reliably got down to the 20/20 line; once or twice, I got to 20/15. But for the right eye, the whole exercise seemed to me a farce, and a cruel one at that. Yes, a comparison of how I did with my right eye on one visit versus another visit was a trustworthy indication of whether the experimental treatment was succeeding and my vision was getting any better. And, yes, I could make out some of the letters on the 20/100 and even the 20/80 line.

But it was how I made them out that, to me, nullified that supposed achievement. I had to stare at each letter for up to ten, fifteen, twenty seconds as different curves or angles of it appeared and disappeared. It existed behind a mist that thinned and thickened and shifted, and as I tried to make the letter out (*"Maybe it's a C . . . No, a D . . . Wait, wait, I just saw more of it, it's an O!"*), I was reminded of one of those movies in which a pirate's ship or hit man's car or knife-wielding psychopath emerges from the gloom, telltale detail by telltale detail. If, after twenty seconds, I settled on the right guess, it was counted as a correct answer, so when I say that I could still score a 20/80, I mean I could do it in that glacial manner, which bears no relationship whatsoever to functional vision in the real world. Imagine reading even something as concise as *Pride and Prejudice* and having to linger over and solve the mystery of each letter in each word in each sentence in each paragraph. I love Jane Austen, but still. Elizabeth Bennet would never marry Fitzwilliam Darcy at that rate. The romance would be triply constipated and never consummated.

I was even more frustrated, if that's possible, by what usually came next, that torturous "visual field" test. It's like a video game that no one would ever elect to play, a punishment in a diversion's drag, the kind of contraption the Marquis de Sade would come up with if he trained his energies on ophthalmology. I would put my chin in a cold plastic divot, press my forehead against a cold plastic band, hold my head very still and keep whichever eye was being evaluated focused on a midpoint on the screen while, in the quadrants around that midpoint, fleeting pulses of light appeared at irregular intervals. With each pulse, I was supposed to click, and the accuracy of my clicks would yield a map of where the blind spots in my vision were. But this artificial cosmos of random meteor showers dazed me, then hypnotized me, then drove me mad: I couldn't tell what was really happening and what I was just imagining, and I would begin to click nervously, erratically, spasmodically, my itchy and twitchy finger taking on an indecisive life of its own. During a given visit to the hospital I'd do this test twice, once for each eye, and at the end of one such session, I was told we'd do it all over again because I hadn't held sufficiently still and my clicking hadn't been garden-variety erroneous but singularly incoherent.

"Please," I said, "just shoot me in the head instead." I meant it.

You're perhaps catching on to my congenital quickness to exasperation and my awful fine-motor skills. Keep those in mind as I tell you what I had to do for the second clinical trial. The mastic resin, like the engineered molecule in the first trial, was injected—but not, thank God, in the eye. It went into one of the upper arms, one of the thighs or the stomach. That was the good news. The bad news? The person who prepared the syringe, attached the needle, got the air bubbles out and pierced the flesh was . . . me. And I was to do this twice a week. For six months.

Self-administered injections aren't unusual. Diabetics have long done them. Women trying to get pregnant pump hormones into themselves. But I'm betting that the overwhelming majority of those diabetics and women have more dexterity than I do, because I have less dexterity than a Slinky. When I was a boy, my father gave up trying to guide me through the tying of a necktie and outsourced the task to my uncle Jim, a trained teacher, who succeeded only in guiding me toward some bastard analogue of a half Windsor that, from then on, drew snarky and barbed comments from friends, boyfriends and the occasional CNN watcher. There is not a knot in this world that I can fashion or unfashion. There is not a needle in this world that I can thread. The one time that it fell to me to transfer a SIM card from an old smartphone of mine to a new one, I dropped it on the floor twice, lost sight of it for fifteen minutes and never could position it correctly in its new home. After an hour of fumbling and failures, I walked to the nearest electronics store and paid the guy at the counter ten dollars to do it. It took him thirty seconds.

At Mount Sinai, Dr. Banik and a technician gave me a fifteen-minute tutorial and helped me with the first injection, then sent me home with an instruction booklet, an instruction video and a month's worth of syringes, needles and glass vials containing the compound, plus a whole bunch of alcohol wipes. The vials had to be kept in the refrigerator—I tucked them between two horizontal bottles of chardonnay, figuring that was the most charmed spot—and each was to be taken out one hour before an injection so it could come to room temperature and change from cloudy to clear. Transferring the compound from vial to syringe involved a long needle that was swapped out for a shorter needle for transferring the compound from syringe to the inside of me. There were tiny lines on the syringe to show me how much liquid to use; I had to squint to see them. This struck me as a rather significant design flaw. The trial expected people with vision problems to heed minuscule visual markers.

I suspect that many people in the trial who lived with

spouses or romantic partners trained them to do the injecting. I didn't have that option. For my first solo injection, I read the instruction booklet two times, watched the video three times, laid out all the instruments on a clean washcloth on a table in front of me and imagined the process repeatedly before performing it in comically slow motion. All of this consumed forty-five minutes in addition to the hour of post-refrigerator vial warming, when there was nothing for me to do but wait. By the time needle penetrated flesh, I worried that the liquid in the vial had now been unrefrigerated too long. What happened in that case? Did the drug become ineffective? Or toxic? I assumed that if the margin of error were that slim and the potential consequences that grave, the doctors and technicians supervising this trial would never trust patients to administer the drug on their own.

I used my right thigh that time. The needle was so thin that I barely felt it. I grimaced when I pressed the syringe's plunger and watched the liquid disappear from it into my body—I saw myself as some lab experiment—and I braced for some kind of burn. But there was just a minor sting, followed by a subtle pinch as I removed the needle and then the blooming of a dot, really a seed, of blood where it had been. That was it.

Three days later I used my left thigh and four days after that the right side of my stomach, which stung a little more, so from then on, I pretty much just alternated thighs. (I was told never to use the same injection site twice in a row.) Within two weeks, the forty-five minutes had shrunk to five. Within a few weeks after that, it was down to two, even one. I did it in an instant, I did it on autopilot, I did it with all the forethought of flossing my teeth but in a fraction of the time. Behold! The sultan of self-injection.

I allowed myself to crow a little inside, and that was where and how I dovetailed with Juan Jose. In a strange way, I came to look forward to the injections: They were my conquered fear. My prowess. They gave my life its own signature rhythm, its own particular grit. Friends of mine had their mastery of Soul-Cycle. I had my mastery of syringes, and I had a bulky red plastic sharps container that I didn't bother to tuck away in a closet but left out on the kitchen counter, where I could see and revel in it and where anyone visiting me might see it as well. I could tell them, when they asked, why it was there. I could brag about my magical, miraculous transformation into a human pincushion. When God gives you lemons, take a bow.

And when God gives you lemons, try, as best possible, to summon an intellectual curiosity about the bitter bequest and to find some fascination in the science and mystery of what you're going through. Juan Jose did that. It was also the perspective that a few of my friends with cancer had taken: They became students, investigators, explorers. They were purposely and purposefully riveted. That didn't and doesn't cure disease, arrest decline, banish pain or dam sadness, and it's little to no help at all in the direst situations. But in others, it just may sand down a few or more of the edges. It may redirect the mind, or a fraction of it, from anxiety and despair. And if it doesn't fall quite into the category of taking action, it doesn't fall outside of it, either.

I took action in a manner that reflected the particular resources and options that I had. I took action journalistically. My casual, superficial googling about the compound I was injecting had introduced me to a long history and rich culture of mastic that were easily material for an extra-long column. I sold the idea to my editors—man goes to meet the medicine that he's pumping into his body—and then set out for Chios, a Greek island whose identity is inseparable from mastic, which is produced in singularly enormous quantities there.

"Resin" is a fancy word, I suppose, so I'll unfancy it: It's the goo that oozes out when a tree's bark is gashed, at least if a tree is inclined to ooze, and mastic resin has been reputed for millenniums to have powerful curative properties. Ancient Greeks chewed it for oral hygiene. Some biblical scholars think the phrase "balm of Gilead" refers to it. It has been used in creams to reduce inflammation and heal wounds, as a powder to treat irritable bowels and ulcers, as a smoke to manage asthma.

And it belongs to a broader tradition of indispensable medicines that can be traced to the earth's forests and fields. Although we now use a synthetic version of aspirin, it was originally made from a substance found in the bark of the willow tree and its kin. Hippocrates reputedly prescribed chewing such bark or drinking tea brewed with it for pain. The cancer drug Taxol, the malaria drug artemisinin, the opiate morphine and much more are the derivatives of bark, leaves, flowers, berries, herbs or roots that captured modern scientists' attention precisely because they were venerated by ancient folk healers. There's even a formal name for the quest to find more drugs like these—bioprospecting—and scientists involved in it frequently pore through old tomes for clues to where in nature they should look. We've only scratched the surface of what's out there.

Chios, which lies in the northeastern Aegean within sight of western Turkey, has just fifty thousand or so year-round residents, and forty-five hundred of them work in some way in its mastic industry, which goes back centuries. In the 1300s and 1400s, when the island was governed by the Republic of Genoa, the punishment for stealing up to ten pounds of mastic resin was the loss of an ear; for more than two hundred pounds, you were hanged. The stone villages in the southern part of the island, near the mastic groves, were built in the manner of fortresses—with high exterior walls, only a few entrances and labyrinthine layouts—to foil any attempts by invaders to steal the resin stored there.

Portions of a few of those villages are well preserved, as I learned when I arrived in Chios for a three-day stay during which the subtle, evanescent perfume of mastic—which is like a suggestion of pine, a hint of vanilla and a rumor of seawater, but a confirmation of none of the above—kept wafting my way. I spent several hours in the relatively new mastic museum, a glass showpiece high on a hill with a panoramic view of the island's tawny and pale green slopes. In the museum's coffee shop, I had espresso laced with mastic, which tastes like it smells. Over time Chios entrepreneurs have infused it into more and more foods, broadening its gastronomic portfolio.

"Cereal, pasta, tomato sauce, *eggplant* sauce, olive oil, salt, jams," Mairi Giannakaki, a senior official with a Chios food company, ticked off as she and I slalomed around conveyor belts bearing these items. "We put mastic in *everything*." They sure did, though it remained most popular, culinarily speaking, in traditional vessels such as gum, gumdrops and liqueur.

I went to a separate production site to watch dozens of women in sterile garb wash and buff pebbles of mastic, which turns the color of ivory as the drops of it dry and harden. And I pulled my car to the side of the road and walked among the fabled mastic trees. Fabled but frumpy, to be honest. Although they cover much of the island's southern slopes, they're overshadowed by the silver-leaved olive trees that grow taller, fuller and more flamboyant around them. They look like they're slouching next to these divas.

I fingered the brittle leaves of one mastic tree. I ran my right hand along the forked trunk of another. The gestures were knowingly overwrought, as was what I whispered to one of the trees: "I'm counting on you." I really did say that, but to amuse myself, and that seemed an important enough purpose to justify it.

On the long flight home, to read more attentively and ideally sleep a bit, I put on a bulky pair of noise-canceling headphones, trying to shut out the world and shut off my hearing. I laughed inwardly: Yet again, I was a loopy literary creation. Meet the man who fears blindness but willfully renders himself deaf.

Deafness. Blindness. They're companion afflictions, dreaded and described in some of the same ways, along some of the same lines, each a cruel amputation of the senses that places simple pleasures off-limits and simple tasks out-of-bounds.

They're competitors: Would you rather go deaf or go blind? Be born without hearing or without sight? I've overheard such conversations—maybe, at some point, I even participated in one—and I've seen long threads about the matter online. It's a parlor game about disability that's played by the fully abled, who speak in theoretical terms.

And when the terms are no longer theoretical? I was now playing this game myself, inside my head, although it wasn't a game anymore. It was a measurement of my misfortune. An assessment of my lot. A wondering about where I fell along the spectrum of deprivation.

The massively popular, widely read advice columnist Ann Landers at one point weighed in on the blind-versus-deaf question, taking issue with an assertion by Helen Keller, who was blind *and* deaf, that "the problems of deafness are deeper and more complex, if not more important, than those of blindness. Deafness is a much worse misfortune. For it means the loss of the most vital stimulus—the sound of the voice that brings language, sets thoughts astir and keeps us in the intellectual company of men." Keller's assessment was sometimes boiled down to the idea that deafness was the greater social obstacle, striking at our primary means of spontaneous communication and thus erecting a barrier between the deaf person and everyone else, while blindness put a barrier between the person without sight and objects or *things*. Landers rejected that take, writing: "Speaking strictly for myself, I would still choose to see rather than to hear if I had to make a choice. The safety element would be the deciding factor for me, although I am well aware that guide dogs can be extremely helpful." She made the case that deaf people needn't be cut off from the hearing world by mentioning a deaf Miss America, Heather Whitestone, and a deaf Oscar-winning actress, Marlee Matlin.

Of course, Landers could have made the opposite argument, for blindness, by evoking two of the most beloved musical performers of the twentieth century, Ray Charles and Stevie Wonder—both blind. There is deaf and blind and even deaf-blind accomplishment galore, proving that regardless of the disability, there is—for many if not all the people who have it—the possibility of transcendence. In that regard, deafness and blindness are more alike than they are different.

I didn't want to be blind. When I let the dread of that seep in, which I seldom did, it threatened to overwhelm me, and I flushed it away as fast as I could. I took a run, I took a drink, I took willful and forceful leave of whatever mood or milieu had permitted this dark presence across my rampart and through my door. I couldn't imagine a life without movies, without Netflix binges, without trips taken for the purpose of *seeing* the coastline around the Cape of Good Hope, *seeing* the Maya temples in Guatemala, *seeing* the Winter Palace in Saint Petersburg. I couldn't let go of color. My living room had a chartreuse love seat, a teal couch, a purple armchair with a matching purple ottoman. My dining room chairs were ruby red. None of that was accidental. It was my way of reveling in the kaleidoscope of life and a testament to the joy that that kaleidoscope gave me.

What's more, I was a reader. A writer. I regarded both of those occupations—narrowly and wrongly—as visual endeavors, and I was indeed having minor, occasional trouble with each because of my visual impairment. Wouldn't a loss of hearing be easier, better? The movies and binges would simply require subtitles. I could behold coasts and museums all the same.

But if the kaleidoscope of life gave me joy, so did the symphony and even cacophony of it. I thrilled to the sight of lightning, but I thrilled even more to the sound of thunder. Of the facets of a man that could most easily attract or repel me, his voice ranked near or at the top of the list, right up there with, well, his eyes. And music: How could I ever part ways with that? Up until the end of Tom and me, we traveled yearly to Austin in October to attend the Austin City Limits Music Festival and listen to five or six hours of live music every day for three to four days. At home, I almost always played music. On runs, it dulled the pain, heightened the high and kept me going, my heartbeat hammering to "Heartbreak Beat" by the Psychedelic Furs. Deafness would mean never again hearing Mary J. Blige's "No More Drama," the Church's "Under the Milky Way," Van Morrison's "Sweet Thing." It, too, was unthinkable.

And it was stupid—not deafness, but this contest and contemplation. I could play a million different iterations of it, positioning blindness against the loss of smell, blindness against the loss of touch, blindness against epilepsy, blindness against lupus, blindness against an alphabet's soup of psychiatric disorders. No matter the matchup, I'd be dabbling in fantasy instead of reality, in "what if" instead of what's what, and that's a waste of emotion. We don't get to choose what we're given in the way of hardship, and each of us—every last one of us—is given something.

Chapter Six
THE SANDWICH-BOARD THEORY OF LIFE

If hope is the thing with feathers, as Emily Dickinson famously wrote, envy is the thing with tentacles. It grabbed hold of me whenever I saw Anthony Bourdain on television or spotted him in the news.

What a swagger he had, an honest-to-goodness, physical swagger, those long legs of his powering a long, thin torso that, unlike mine, seemed impervious to the wages of appetite. And his was a prodigious, glorious appetite: for food, for travel, for language, for life. He was, by all appearances, a fearless man, one who zigged from an elite college (Vassar, in his case) into the rough-and-tumble of restaurant kitchens, then zagged into the writing business, then morphed into a sort of all-purpose culinary legend. He was given his own show, *No Reservations*, on the Travel Channel before being lured by CNN for an even more elaborate production, *Parts Unknown*, whose stature and popularity were illustrated by the guest who agreed, for a 2016 episode, to talk with Bourdain about fatherhood, fame and Vietnamese-American relations while eating noodles in a Hanoi restaurant. That noodle-mate was President Barack Obama.

To say that Bourdain devoured the world is neither hyperbole nor even metaphor, as I noted in a June 2018 essay about him in the *New York Times*: There was no place that he wasn't curious to explore, no food that he wasn't determined to try, no cap on his hunger and no ceiling—or so it always seemed—on his joy. "Seemed" is critical. The occasion of that essay was his suicide that month. While shooting a new episode of *Parts Unknown* in the Alsace region of France, Bourdain hung himself in his hotel room. He was sixty-one.

And everyone was stunned. By "everyone," I mean all the readers and viewers who thrilled to his culinary exploits and came to regard him as the quintessential confluence of swashbuckler and sybarite, who saw him as wanderlust incarnate. But I specifically mean people in and around the restaurant industry, to which I remained tightly connected from my five and a half years as the *Times*'s restaurant critic. They, like me, had intersected with him over the years, and most of them, like me, had no idea, no intimation, that he was vulnerable to such intense pain. We were too busy wishing that we possessed a fraction of his talent, an iota of his outward confidence.

Bourdain loomed large for me. After I was chosen to be the *Times*'s new restaurant critic in 2004, as I prepared to move from Italy—where I was finishing a stint as the newspaper's Rome bureau chief—to New York, one of the many books I barreled through was Bourdain's beloved bestseller *Kitchen*

Confidential. I'd read it before but wanted to reacquaint myself with it. It recounted his sweaty, salty, drug-fueled days as a professional cook, and I turned to it for the way in which it simultaneously and paradoxically mythologized and demythologized restaurants, which seemed to me the right perspective. But I was even more impressed, all over again, by its wit and profane poetry. "Vegetarians are the enemy of everything good and decent in the human spirit," he wrote, and while that was wrong and cruel, it was also the necessary setup to the subsequent punch line, in which he described vegans as vegetarians' "Hezbollah-like splinter faction."

When I moved on from the restaurant-critic job in late 2009 and no longer had to try for an undercover operative's physical anonymity by turning down any and all requests to be photographed or appear on television, many exciting invitations poured in, partly because my exit coincided with the release of my eating-focused memoir, *Born Round*, about my profoundly conflicted relationship with food. I was the subject of a feature on ABC News's *Nightline*. Stephen Colbert had me on *The Colbert Report*. *Top Chef* made me a guest judge for an episode. But none of those opportunities pleased me any more than Bourdain's request that I join him for a segment on *No Reservations*. I met him in downtown Manhattan one afternoon at the chef Daniel Boulud's former restaurant DBGB, and we drank beer and ate a smorgasbord of sausages on camera. He sauntered or maybe swaggered away afterward, as full of energy and as forward-charging as he'd been before all the booze and fat that we'd consumed. I poured myself into a taxi and went home to nap.

Around that same time, as part of the TimesTalks series of

onstage conversations with newsmakers and celebrities, I interviewed him before hundreds of his fans in an auditorium adjacent to the *Times*'s midtown Manhattan headquarters. It was the easiest assignment imaginable because all you ever had to do with Bourdain was wind him up and let him loose. He was effortlessly articulate and insanely charming.

That the weather inside of him might not match the sunny brilliance of his public persona was something that we all should have considered. He'd given us plenty of hints. In *Kitchen Confidential*, he wrote about his past addictions to cocaine and heroin and described the kind of drinking and drug binges that frequently have less to do with gilding contentment than with gutting its opposite.

"I should've died in my twenties," he said more than three decades later. "I became successful in my forties. I became a dad in my fifties. I feel like I've stolen a car—a really nice car—and I keep looking in the rearview mirror for flashing lights." You can take that last sentence as just another of the funny, perfectly turned metaphors that rolled off his tongue or you can wonder about the measures of insecurity and foreboding in it, which is something that Bourdain's acquaintances and admirers certainly did after his death. I found myself homing in on a statement that he made in another interview around the same time. "There was some dark genie inside me," he said, referring to his addictions. Such a genie doesn't vanish easily.

That was one of the possible morals of a documentary about Bourdain's life and death, *Roadrunner*, released in July 2021. It traced the genie's nefarious handiwork, suggesting how uncontrollable and destructive his passions—including, during his final months, a tortured romance with the Italian actress and director Asia Argento—could be. At the peak of his fame he found restlessness, longing, regret, and he didn't know where to turn. "I think Tony, at the end, felt alone and felt he couldn't talk to anybody about the pain that was going on inside of him," the director Michael Steed, who worked with him on *Parts Unknown*, says in the documentary.

That statement reminded me of what Ruth Reichl, who was one of my predecessors as the *Times*'s restaurant critic and knew Bourdain well, told the *Times* when it rounded up reactions to his suicide: "Behind that swagger, there was always that tortured shy guy."

"Swagger." I wasn't the only one struck by it, though apparently not everyone was completely fooled by it.

Bourdain's suicide would have received enormous attention on its own, but it happened just three days after the fashion designer Kate Spade killed herself, also by hanging, in her bedroom, using a red scarf. Spade was fifty-five and such a cultural icon by that point that I'd honestly ceased to realize that she was an actual person as opposed to a pair of proper nouns emblazoned on seemingly every third handbag I saw, a brand disconnected from the blood, sweat and tears of everyday striving. If Bourdain had his swagger, she had her chirp, represented by her company's "insistently cheerful and whimsical accessories," as Daphne Merkin wrote in an essay in the *Times* that pondered the jolt of Spade's death.

"Everything about Spade and her designs suggested a sunny temperament, from her candy-colored aesthetic to the perky image she projected," Merkin observed. "We have a hard time squaring a seemingly successful woman—one with a highflying career, a family and heaps of money—with a despondency so insinuating that it led her to end it all." Merkin noted that Fern Mallis, the former director of the Council of Fashion Designers of America and a friend of Spade's, described Spade's death as "so out of character," though the fact of the matter was that the chirpy, perky, bubbly Kate had, according to her husband, fought depression for many years.

"Out of character." What an odd phrase to attach to a death, but it made a perverse sense in this instance. It applied to both Spade and Bourdain, whose ends spoke so powerfully to the discrepancy between what we see of people on the outside and what they experience on the inside; between their public gloss and private mess; between their tote boards of accomplishments—measured in money, rankings, ratings and awards—and a different, hidden, more consequential accounting. Parts unknown: That was true of Bourdain. That was true of Spade. That's true of every one of us.

I'd long known that. We all do. But I'm not sure how keenly we really register it, how steadily we remember it, and in the wake of my stroke, in the midst of my fog, as I sought to manage the weather within *me*, I found myself freshly appreciative of this fundamental truth. It was a guard against anger, an antidote to self-pity, so much of which hinges on the conviction, usually a delusion, that you're grinding out your days while the people around you glide through theirs, that you've landed in the bramble to their clover. To feel sorry for yourself is to ignore that *everyone* is vulnerable to intense pain and that almost everyone has worked or is working through some version of it.

Talk about blindness.

⁓

"Why me?" There's a better question, of course: "Why *not* me?" Why should any of us be spared struggle, when struggle is a condition more universal than comfort, than satiation, than peace, maybe than love? Should we even be calling or thinking of it as struggle, which connotes an exertion beyond the usual, a deviation from the norm?

Again: An estimated one million Americans, or about one in 320, are legally blind, meaning that their corrected vision is no better than 20/200. A few million more have life-altering vision impairment, and more than thirty-five million Americans who are eighteen or older, or close to one in six of them, report some difficulties related to hearing. By some estimates, nearly one in ten adults between fifty-five and sixty-four—my age cohort—have a disabling degree of hearing loss, a fraction that rises to one in four adults between sixty-five and seventy-four and one in two who are seventy-five or older. That's a lot of physical diminishment, accelerating with age. That's what it means to be alive—and to be fortunate enough to be alive a good long while.

Vision, hearing: They're just two obvious realms of concern. A 2018 report from the US Centers for Disease Control and Prevention estimated that one in four Americans who are eighteen or older live with some kind of physical or cognitive disability, and even that figure doesn't take into account the many who deal or dealt with prolonged or repeated episodes of mental illness or mood disorders. To me these numbers aren't merely curiosities. They're context. For all our claims and gestures of dominion over this earth, all our gravity-defying explorations beyond it, all our artistic triumphs, all our athletic feats, we are a breakable species, and the fissures are all around us. We just stare through and past them, or at least too many of us do.

I started concentrating on those fissures. I keyed into the signs and outright revelations that the public figures who were supposedly living the dream had many of the same nightmares as the rest of us. I identified the parts of friends and acquaintances that aren't so much unknown as unacknowledged; parts that we sweep aside after murmuring a desultory "I'm sorry" or writing a pro forma sympathy note; parts that make us uncomfortable, because maybe they put us on the hook for more than we can or care to provide; parts that are sometimes scrutable only to the scrutinizing; parts that are often muffled by laughter or powdered over with the rouge of a smile.

Just weeks after my stroke, Ross Douthat, one of my fellow op-ed columnists at the *Times*, wrote a column that intrigued me in the moment but had more and more resonance for me as time went by and my attention to fissures intensified. It was titled "The Misery Filter," and it made reference to the psychiatrist and blogger Scott Alexander's writings about both the prevalence of emotional turmoil among the affluent, seemingly healthy people whom he treated and the invisibility of it. Alexander asserted that in our observations of the world around us, we tend to "filter for misery" so that it fades or disappears.

Ross concurred with that and refined it, saying that the filter is especially strong "for chronic miseries that don't fit an easy-crisis resolution arc. We tend to be aware of other people's suffering when it first descends or when they bottom out—with a grim diagnosis, a sudden realization of addiction, a disastrous public episode. But otherwise a curtain tends to fall, because there isn't a way to integrate private struggle into the realm of health and normalcy." That curtain or filter "creates real problems," Ross added, "because it effectively lies about reality to both the healthy and the sick. . . . It lies to the sick about how alone they really are, because when they were healthy that seemed like perfect normalcy, so they must now be outliers, failures, freaks."

Ross mentioned "personal reasons" for his interest in Alexander's perspective but didn't elaborate. In that fashion he kept the curtain over his own life. As I knew then and as he'd later share publicly, Ross was still recovering from a grave case of Lyme disease that, over the course of several years, severely weakened and at times debilitated him. But his prolific output gave no indication of that. With great but inconspicuous effort, he continued to churn out terrific prose, even as he helped his wife care for their three kids. (In mid 2020 they added a fourth.)

What Ross called a misery filter another of my op-ed colleagues at the *Times*, Jennifer Senior, referred to as "the lacquered fakery of our Instagrammed, brand-conscious lives." This description appeared in a column of hers, published about two years later, that approached the matter from a much

different direction: It was essentially a profile of a stand-up co-
median, Gary Gulman, who turned his experience with severe
depression into punch lines. Gulman had a riff, for example,
about his answer to friends who asked if he worried that anti-
depressants would suppress his libido or cause impotence. ("Oh
yes. I was having *so much sex* in the fetal position.") He flashed
back to high school, when he was six foot six and a college football coach who was trying to recruit him told him that he had
"an NFL body." Gulman recalled suppressing his desired retort:
"No more than ten feet from here, I have a blankie."

   "It was thrilling enough," Jennifer wrote, "that Gulman was
calling attention to the depressive's daily charade. But the more
I thought about it, the more I realized he was doing something
else, and it was something quite powerful: He was calling attention to our *culture's* daily charade too." To call further attention to it, Jennifer made an admission of her own. "I know
a thing or two about this," she wrote. "I've always wandered
through the world nerves first. My anxiety can shatter stones,
spook ghosts, freak out a cup of coffee. I jazz-hands my way
through it." Although Jennifer is a friend, I had no idea. I just
knew that she'd done a TED Talk—a TED Talk!—which meant
an eighteen-minute monologue with no lectern, no notes, no
teleprompter. She wore killer boots. She radiated killer poise.
I can attest to that because I watched the video and felt mildly
tortured by it. If only I had her assurance. If only I had her poise.

   Jennifer's anxiety, Ross's Lyme disease: As the shock of my
stroke ebbed and the gruesome novelty of my clinical trial faded,
I did a mental inventory of the people in my life with whom
I frequently crossed paths, examining them afresh for the fis-

sures, the bramble. One friend was recovering from a cerebral hemorrhage though she was under sixty and had been perfectly healthy beforehand. Physicians were so befuddled about its exact cause, its precise implications and how poised she should be for a recurrence that they couldn't provide a whole lot of reliable guidance on what adjustments in her life she should make. For a while she didn't take long flights: What if something happened in the air, halfway across the Atlantic? She cut way back on alcohol, though she'd never been much of a drinker, and she kept a card in her purse with not only her name and address but also her emergency contacts, because what might (or might not) befall her would likely happen instantly, without warning, and she might not be home or near anyone she knew. She had shared some of these details with me only after my affliction with NAION, I guess because it branded me a fellow traveler in a murky and scary land.

Another friend was grieving the death of a *thirty-nine-year-old* spouse. Yet another friend, a mother in her midforties, was questioning whether a rare cancer that had debilitated her on and off for years had really and truly been vanquished, whether she could reasonably hope that she'd be around for her two children's high school graduations. Within a fairly narrow circle of people with whom I routinely communicated, there were infirmed parents requiring extraordinary attention, infirmed children requiring costly care, soul-killing marriages, dream-crushing infertility, ego-shredding jobs, chronic depression, chronic pain, substance abuse and more. But few of these torments were immediately obvious or conspicuous at all. Some were actively and assiduously camouflaged, out of pride or an unspoken pact that you didn't broadcast what could be seen as weakness or advertise your woes.

I did another inventory: of friends who were no longer around because they'd died young. Not one but *three* colleagues from the *New York Times* alone fit that description, and I cringed at how long it had been since I'd thought about them. I'd spent three and a half years in the newspaper's Washington, DC, bureau with two of them: a man who was just sixty-three and less than a month into his retirement when he was murdered with a blow to the head during a mugging on the street near his home, and a woman who was just fifty-four when cancer killed her and she left behind eleven-year-old twins. The third colleague, also afflicted with cancer, died at forty-nine. He was someone I'd dated.

One of my best friends from high school—she was my svelteness-chasing partner in black-market diet pills, liquid fasts and other disordered eating—was long gone, her episodes of depression and anxiety having worsened to a point where, just two years after her graduation from Yale University, she killed herself. One of my best friends from college also more or less killed herself, although many years later, after we'd lost touch, and I learned about it belatedly, when I happened to run into her ex-husband. He told me that her heavy drinking had spiraled out of control, and she was found dead at the bottom of the staircase in the house where she lived alone. She had apparently been drunk and lost her footing at the top.

My God, I thought, I was drawn to both of these women in part because there was a turbulence in them that mirrored my own—that was familiar and thus reassuring. We shared a craving for escape and a neurochemistry that purred, if only at the outset, with the presence of poisons. But I'd been spared because I'd been charmed, in the sense that it had always been my nature to dance along the edge without teetering into the abyss. I always pulled myself back when the dance had gone on too long and grown too dangerous. Within *my* neurochemistry was the ability to put parameters around the drinking, the drugging, the self-destruction. How thankful I should be for that, and how thankful I began to feel.

And then there were the friends who hadn't made it through the worst of the AIDS epidemic, the memory of which had been diluted by subsequent advances in the prevention and treatment of HIV infection. There was Ron, with his acid wit and his attachment to Chanel's Antaeus, a whiff of which always clung to him. There was Max, olive-skinned, raven-haired, impossibly handsome Max. There were Ivan and Joel and Miguel and so many other gay men who, like me, had been young and horny and adventurous and prone to mistakes during a decade, the 1980s, when those mistakes could be lethal. I had behaved cautiously but by no means perfectly. And yet here I was, the undeserving winner of a lottery, my survival attributable in significant measure to dumb luck.

Luck: Around the time when I was reflecting most intensely on all of this, a celebrity with that name disabused the world of its assumptions about how lucky he was. I'm referring to Andrew Luck, the star quarterback for the Indianapolis Colts. He announced his retirement from football at the age of just twenty-nine.

A jock not just hunky but brainy, Luck had attended Stanford on a scholarship and played so brilliantly there that he was twice the runner-up for the Heisman Trophy. In the National Football League's 2012 draft, he was the number one pick. He then led the Colts to the playoffs in each of his first three seasons with the team. His was the definition of a charmed career. Of a charmed *life*.

Except it wasn't, and he made that wrenchingly clear during a news conference in 2019 that he scheduled hastily as word of his decision to quit football leaked out. "For the last four years or so, I've been in this cycle of injury, pain, rehab, injury, pain, rehab, and it's been unceasing," he said, later adding: "The only way I see out is to no longer play football. It has taken my joy of this game away." He stopped talking just then to compose himself, and his silence stretched for more than fifteen seconds, broken only in the middle by a single, strangled word: "Sorry."

I listened to him and, for the millionth time, cursed the physical cruelty of football, a sport I love to watch but have huge moral qualms about. For him that cruelty meant torn cartilage in two ribs, a partially torn abdomen, a lacerated kidney, a torn labrum in his throwing shoulder and at least one concussion. A fresh ankle injury was threatening his participation and performance in a new NFL season set to begin the following month.

But my main takeaway wasn't the brutality of football but rather the riddle of happiness. His talent had become his torment, and there was no untangling the two. For him athletic glory had an exorbitant price unknown to his envious admirers. The ranks of men who wished they were Andrew Luck, marquee quarterback, were legion. They just didn't include Mr. Luck himself.

⌒

Imagine that our hardships, our hurdles, our demons, our pain were spelled out for everyone around us to see. Imagine that each of us donned a sandwich board that itemized them.

"Failed marriage, inconstant ex-husband, autistic son who often can't abide babysitters." A woman I know would be wearing that, and her acquaintances would rightly find her ability to hold down a full-time job and her unflagging professionalism in it not just admirable but heroic. They'd instantly forgive her any tiny lapses of memory, any fleeting impatience, because they'd understand what a miracle it was that the lapses were only tiny and the impatience merely fleeting.

"Bicycle accident, shredded face, agonizing pain, a dozen operations, can no longer fully feel a kiss." A man I know well would be wearing that, the shorthand for an ordeal that included an induced coma—necessary for the extensive first surgeries to deal with all the bones that had been broken and all the skin and tissue shorn off—and that left him with a faint asymmetry in his smile and a slight jag in his nose. He'd be the object of wonder at his optimism and cheer. He'd be an example and admonishment to the defeatists in his orbit.

"Plane crash, prosthetic leg, dead eight-year-old son." A fellow writer who used the same Manhattan workout space that I did would be wearing that, the succinct summary of a harrowing story. Flying was a hobby of his, and he was piloting the aircraft when it went down, killing his lone passenger, his only child. He almost lost his second leg and spent the next five months in treatment centers. I learned all of this not from him but from other acquaintances of his and only after many upbeat, spirited chats with him that gave no hint of it. I was stunned and humbled.

"Debilitating headaches, near-constant shrieking in ears, frequent thoughts of suicide." That's what a celebrity who once confided in me would be wearing, and I doubt that anyone who had ever coveted this person's riches and fame would trade places, not on those terms. The revelation left me awestruck, because its revealer just kept pressing on.

I didn't have to think long or hard to come up with these examples. I didn't have to compel the people in question to share what they were going through. It would dribble out in asides and unguarded moments, and I just had to be sensitive enough to hear and hold on to the details. I now was. I picked up on comments that might have whizzed by me before and lingered in conversational spaces that I would have once hurried past or detoured to avoid.

A little more than a year after my stroke, about five months after Bourdain's and Spade's suicides, I visited a southern university that had invited me to address its students. The "speech" was really a university official asking me questions before several hundred students, who would then ask me some questions of their own, so I didn't have to sweat the visual dislocation I still experienced when juggling notes and slides and microphone positioning and rapport-building glances at the blurry faces in the audience. The university official huddled and strategized with me over lunch beforehand, and then, over the ninety minutes leading up to the event, other administrators, faculty members and students dropped by a nearby conference room where I was hanging out to introduce themselves.

Several of them apologized: The university's president was out of town, so he wasn't able to welcome me to campus in person, and while his wife often took his place in such circumstances, she was dealing with a health problem that might prevent her from doing so. We'd just have to see.

She did show up, her hand extended, her handshake firm, her smile bright. There was nothing in her cheerful manner to suggest that she wasn't feeling well. But the fact that someone had mentioned her health to me signaled that it was probably OK for me to bring it up.

"I'm glad you made it tonight," I said, "and I'm sorry to hear that you've been ill. I hope everything's OK."

Right away she seemed more relaxed. She'd been relieved of the duty of a brave face.

She explained that she had cysts along her spine that had already led to two surgeries and might lead to another if she felt up to it. Her doctors decided that the possible benefit warranted the risk. One of the variables was how well she could tolerate the pain that the cysts continued to cause.

"Is it frequent?" I asked.

"It's constant," she said.

"How long has this been an issue?"

"About ten years."

Maybe because my face betrayed my horror, she hastened to add that she grew ever more expert at dealing with it, at figuring out which shoes to wear, what furniture to recline on, how to position her body. She was reassuring me, but I also suspected that she was reassuring herself, that I was hearing a mantra: *I can do this; I can do this; I'm doing this.*

In any case, she said, there were worse days and better days, episodes of pain and spells of mere discomfort, and when going through the former, she just had to keep her faith in the latter. This was a better day, of discomfort. So she was here, with me. Her sandwich board might say: "Faulty spine, no relief, no end in sight." Or it might say more than that. I got to know her only a little. There are few people we really get to know more than a little.

One of the students in the conference room seemed especially eager to talk with me. He was gay and knew that I was the *Times*'s first openly gay op-ed columnist and had written extensively about gay rights. But we were pressed for time, and I got the sense that there was much more that he wanted to say, so I invited him to join me for a quick dinner.

He indeed had a story, and he shared it, telling me that it was important for people like me, from big, cosmopolitan cities like New York, to know how far behind many smaller, less cosmopolitan places were. To wit: When, in his teens, he was honest about his sexual orientation, his parents sent him to conversion therapy, and when he insisted on ending that humiliation, on quitting that farce, they cut him off. He was paying for school himself, and not because his family couldn't afford the tuition. He recounted all of this matter-of-factly, not as a pitiable victim of some singular injustice, and he interspersed it with professions of genuine excitement about how much he was getting out of college and enjoying it. He told me that he was applying for an internship in a US senator's office. I was somewhat familiar with staffers there and volunteered to put in a good word via email, which I did.

His sandwich board might say: "Parents' love was conditional, ran afoul of the conditions."

———

Some of these sandwich boards were legible to me because I was now reading the world differently, and some were presented to me by people who knew what my own sandwich board said. ("Eyesight compromised, could go blind.") A manager in a Las Vegas restaurant that I visited in late 2018 was one of those people.

I have a soft spot for Vegas's unabashed kitsch and unfettered sparkle, and I went there for a brief change of scenery. My friend Kerry joined me for a few days. One of our dinners, far away from the Strip, was at the kind of small but ambitious restaurant where my name might ring a bell from my restaurant-critic days, and that bell must indeed have rung when I made my reservation, because soon into the meal, one of the restaurant's managers appeared at the side of our table and said a special hello to me.

"I know you're a food genius," he joked, "but the piece you wrote that really meant a lot to me was the one about your vision." He explained that his own eyes "shook" all the time

because of a lifelong condition that would get worse, at an unpredictable pace, over the years to come. He spoke quickly, nervously, so I couldn't follow everything he said. But I thanked
him for sharing it and told him that I was sorry for what he was
going through.

The exchange stayed with me. I thought about it later that
night. I thought about it the next morning. I wanted to hear
more of his story, at least if he wanted to tell it, and so I called
the restaurant. He wasn't there. But another manager who was
gave me the young man's email. I reached out to him that way
and arranged a phone call.

His name is Danny. He's from Scotland. And he's remarkable, though you have to poke and dig a bit to discover that. His
mother's pregnancy with him was troubled, and he was born so
prematurely, he said, that his eyes weren't finished developing.
As a result, he told me, they "rotate from side to side in a sort
of circular motion. A normal person can focus their eyes on
something. I can never do that, because mine are always rotating. It gets worse if I'm tired." The world jitters and skitters, to a
degree that sometimes forces him to shut down for a bit, to give
his eyes and his brain a rest.

Surgery when he was young improved the situation some
but not all that much, and there was nothing more to be done.
He could read if he sat right near the chalkboard, if he put his
nose all the way into a book, if he pushed his face extra close to
the computer screen. So that's what he did, though other kids
teased him about it. He got used to the teasing. There was no
other choice. He had to read because he had to learn because if
he didn't, then what?

And while he had trouble reading—at fast-food restaurants, he would order whatever he'd had before and knew was available, because he couldn't make out the words on menus posted so high above the counter—he didn't have trouble *thinking*. He could take in plenty of information, especially if it was spoken, and store it. "If you're bad at one thing, you become good at another, I guess," he said. "I have a really good memory."

He finished high school. He finished college. And then, interested in a career in the hospitality industry, he resolved to go for it in a big way and make a real adventure of it by enrolling in a graduate program in hotel management at a school in the American city that arguably revolved around hospitality more than any other. Off to the University of Nevada, Las Vegas, he went.

His compromised, vulnerable eyesight factored hugely in that decision, he told me: "I just thought, 'I can live in fear of this and be miserable and live some sort of sheltered half-life, but then I'll never be happy. Or I can just grab life. Why not move to America and try to make a career as best I can, because I might not have the luxury of thirty years to reach whatever goal I set."

He was thirty when we crossed paths, and he was grateful for the way things had turned out. He'd done well in school—so well that he spoke at his commencement. The restaurant he was helping to manage, the Black Sheep, had an excellent reputation. He worried that he'd have to leave restaurants behind when—not if—his eyes gave out, so he had made some adjustments for that, interning for free at a few law firms as a way of potentially setting up a next act. He couldn't imagine being a blind restaurant manager or owner, but a blind law student and lawyer? Maybe. Just maybe.

If anything gets him down, he told me, it's his inability to drive. He's utterly reliant on public transportation in a city with too little of it, on the kindness of friends or on the occasional Uber or Lyft, if it fits into his budget. There were jobs that he'd had to pass on because they were longer commutes than his ninety minutes on public transportation to and from the Black Sheep. There were social invitations that he had to turn down. He noted that he had never had that archetypal experience—not in high school, not in college, not ever—of arriving in a car to pick up a girl for a date. He remembered that when he was growing up, he played with model cars and had posters of cars on his bedroom walls, and was told, when he asked if he could drive someday, "Small chance. Small chance." He grabbed hold of the "chance" rather than the "small" and, when he turned old enough to get a driver's license, went to the optometrist to gauge his eligibility. No, he was told. His vision wasn't nearly good enough.

It was the lowest of lows, but not the last of them. The difficulties in his life do get to him, and he has strategies for coping, one of which he shared. "This sounds corny," he said, "but I'll look through pictures that I've taken on my phone." There he is speaking at commencement. There he is in Hawaii, a magical trip he got to take. There he is, younger, with his mother, whom he loves so much. He studies these pictures and tells himself to "stop being a crybaby."

He trusts that he will catch a few breaks. Shortly before the start of the pandemic, which put so many people in the restaurant business out of work, he got a better, bigger job as director of service for a quickly growing restaurant group in Las Vegas that not only weathered the shutdowns and lockdowns of 2020 but also, in late 2021, continued to expand. It enabled him to move to a new apartment, which was walking distance from two of the restaurants. No more ninety-minute commutes.

"I have stuff to appreciate," he told me. "My dog! My dog's a big one. What would he do without me?" Danny said that he'd always wanted not just a dog but a particular kind of dog, a pug, and one day about four years before we met, someone to whom he was connected on Facebook posted that her sister's pug had just had puppies.

"It's a sign!" Danny thought. He got one.

"It was the dumbest and the best thing I've ever done," he said. "All my money goes to him. But any time I'm upset, he's the thing that gets me out of it.

"Wee Man," Danny said. "His name is Wee Man."

⌣

I got a call when I was in Vegas. My dad had fallen. Not once but twice: He'd lost his balance, lost his bearings, crumpled to the ground and had difficulty righting himself, both physically and mentally. He was in the hospital. They were doing tests. He was stable, his wife said; the doctors didn't think he was in any immediate, serious danger. But she was worried. He was worried.

I canceled my plans to spend the days around the New Year with friends on eastern Long Island and made arrangements to fly to Atlanta, where his wife was living when they met and where the two of them spent the cold half of the year before returning to his longtime home in the suburbs of New York City around Easter. He was out of the hospital by the time I arrived, but he was still headed back there for consultations, and I accompanied him, giving his doctors information that he was hazy about or had forgotten, asking questions that he would no longer think to ask, marveling at the almost inevitable way in which parent and child reverse roles over time. *This was my dad?*

Yes, this was my dad, and that scared me, because I'd never been confident in my ability to take good care of myself, let alone anyone else. But it also filled me with a powerful and particular warmth, generated by the sense that I was repaying a debt, making good on an unspoken promise, showing him with my actions what words can never say powerfully enough: I'm here for you. I appreciate you. I love you. I've got your back.

Weeks later, his doctors would decide that he needed a pacemaker, and he would get one, and his seven-day pillbox, with compartments for morning and night, would grow more crowded and colorful and geometrically diverse: the white circle, the white diamond, the blue egg. But that was after I left.

I was still there, though, for New Year's Eve, when he and his wife were dining with two other couples at an exclusive, expensive Atlanta country club. They insisted that I tag along, a fifty-four-year-old spring chicken among the septuagenarians and octogenarians. The three of us arrived at the club first and were directed into a sumptuous lounge with lofty ceilings, ornate woodwork, enormous Oriental rugs and paintings with rococo frames. It didn't so much drip as ooze wealth. Our cocktails came in thick, heavy glasses. Too eagerly, I lifted my gin martini to my lips, felt the blessed burn of that gateway sip and thought that this place, this moment, this gin was what it meant not to have a care in the world.

But, of course, there's no such place, no such state. The other couples arrived, we were moved to the formal dining room and I dutifully made conversation, politely inquiring about their lives. But here, as in that conference room at the southern university, I was different than I'd been in the past: more attuned, bolder. I asked better questions, and I took in more of the answers.

One of the women said that she and her husband had "seven kids between us." *Between us?* It turned out that they, like my widowed dad and his divorced wife, were on their second marriages, though *both* of them had lost their spouses. The woman told me that her husband had died from melanoma when he was in his midthirties and their one child, a daughter, was merely a year old. The man's wife had died at forty-four. He didn't say the cause. It made him the single parent of *six* kids.

I mentioned my sandwich-board theory of life, my belief that we'd all be a whole lot less consumed with our own misfortunes and slights—and a whole lot more understanding of other people's moods and misdeeds—if each of us had just a glimpse of the burdens that people were shouldering, the fears that they were strangling, the scars that they were concealing. All around the table, there were nods.

The woman recalled that just the other day, she was in a

store where a frustrated customer lost his cool and began screaming at the clerks. People nearby gaped and, after he left, held forth on what a jerk he'd been. But a person who happened to know the man didn't join in and explained to the others that the man's daughter had recently been killed in a car accident. The screaming man wasn't some bully, some hothead. He was unhinged by grief.

"A microchip," said one of the other members of our New Year's Eve dinner party. "Not a sandwich board but a microchip. It's embedded in each of us, and you hold your smartphone over it and it downloads the information." Here you have a shattered father. Here you have a devastated widow. Here are the hurts, the fears, the confusion. Factor them in, not only as you take the measure of this person but also as you take the measure of yourself.

I'll tell you a secret about my journalism career, one that hints at the self-doubt and timidity that has also colored the rest of my life: Before I pick up the phone to call someone I'm about to interview, I have to steady myself. I have to take a few breaths. I'm afraid that I'll ask the wrong questions or at least won't ask the right ones. Or that I'll ask them in a fumbling, embarrassing fashion. If the person with whom I'm about to speak has a well-known name or august credentials, I'm intimidated. Many of my 11:00 a.m. interviews began at 11:02, and many of my 3:00 p.m. interviews began at 3:03. That's not because I'm sloppy or run late. It's because I need and use those extra minutes for those breaths, which are valuable enough to be worth the price of apologizing for my slight tardiness.

But I think I called Alan Krueger on time. We'd emailed back and forth just a bit before our call, and his manner—amiable, approachable—put me at ease. An economist then teaching at Princeton University, Krueger had previously been the chairman of the Council of Economic Advisers under President Obama. He'd done pioneering work on the effects of minimum-wage increases, determining that they did *not* lead to decreased hiring and employment.

He'd also, fascinatingly, used data to come to conclusions about pain and happiness. Unemployment, he'd found, caused more than just emotional distress. Men looking for jobs reported physical pain and took more painkillers. As for happiness, one of the best ways to increase it, according to his analysis of survey data, was to spend time with friends. He often pushed past his end-of-week fatigue to attend social gatherings that he was tempted to skip.

I approached him in late 2014 as I worked on a book about Americans' obsession with admission to elite colleges like Princeton, where, as it happened, I'd been a visiting professor that spring. Krueger and the mathematician Stacy Dale had crunched numbers on the economic benefit of having attended such a college, and they had determined that it was overrated. Krueger's email address was public, so I wrote to him to ask if he'd chat with me on the phone about that research. I mentioned, as an icebreaker and a means of persuasion, my fleeting Princeton professorship.

He wrote back promptly, saying: "You can lecture in my class any time!" He would be happy to discuss his research, he said, but apologized that he couldn't do so just then because he was in Italy and, after Italy, he'd be tied up for a few days with events surrounding his daughter's college graduation. "Can we talk on Wednesday or Thursday next week?" he asked. "Or is that too late?" I got the distinct impression that if I'd said I couldn't wait, he'd have found a way to accommodate me sooner, never mind Italy, never mind the graduation.

The following Wednesday was fine with me. We talked then, and he could not have been more polite, more pleasant, more patient, more wonderful. His words went into my book, and the book was published the following year, and whenever I saw Krueger's name in the news—which I frequently did because he was so generous with journalists—I had a warm feeling; I even had a bit of a crush on him. The photographs that sometimes accompanied mentions of him revealed that he was handsome in addition to brilliant and kind. Some people had it all.

Less than three months after my New Year's Eve dinner in Atlanta, on March 16, 2019, Krueger died. He was fifty-eight. Like Bourdain and Spade, he killed himself, though how he did so was never disclosed.

Obama released a statement, remembering him as a man with "a perpetual smile and a gentle spirit—even when he was correcting you." My fellow *Times* op-ed columnist Paul Krugman, a Nobel Prize–winning economist who taught with Krueger at Princeton, wrote: "I knew Alan reasonably well and never saw a hint that something like this might be coming."

And in a sequence of tweets, Betsey Stevenson, who rotated onto the Council of Economic Advisers just as Krueger rotated off, referred to his research into pain. "Now I know that he was also in pain, perhaps channeling his own pain into thinking about the pain of others," she wrote.

"The truth," she added, "is that we all have more pain than the world typically knows."

Chapter Seven
MATISSE ABOVE MELANCHOLY

There are different responses to unexpected hardship. When Marion Sheppard began to go blind, she cycled through many of them. She pitied herself and cried long and hard, because this wasn't right—this wasn't fair. Her hearing had been impaired since early childhood and she'd endured schoolyard teasing about that. Hadn't she paid her dues? Done her time? She raged, feeling that she'd been unfairly singled out. She trembled. This was the end, wasn't it? Not of life, but of independence. Of freedom. That, at least, was her fear.

She spent months wrestling with those emotions, until she realized that they had pinned her in place. Time was marching on and she wasn't moving at all. Her choice was clear: She could surrender to the darkness, or she could dance. She danced.

That's what she was doing on a Monday morning when I stopped by a Manhattan community center for blind people that's run by Visions, a nonprofit social services agency. Marion, then seventy-three, was leading her weekly line-dancing class. She was teaching about a dozen students the steps to the Electric Slide and similar favorites. But, really, she was teaching them delight. She was teaching them not to shut down when life gives you cause to, not to underestimate yourself, not to retreat. She had briefly done all of that, and it was a waste.

"Ladies and gentlemen, I need your attention, please!" she shouted over the music. Most of her students were people over sixty whose eyesight deteriorated when they were already adults and who could remember different, easier times. She told them: "Just because we can't see well, we can still do things, and one of those things is dance." Her chin was high, her shoulders pulled back and her chest pushed forward.

"We've got to *keep moving*," she continued. "You know why? Because we're alive! As long as we're alive, we have to keep moving."

I met Marion through the executive director of Visions, Nancy Miller. One day, over breakfast in a restaurant a few blocks from my apartment, I asked Nancy if she had any particular programs that—or people who—stood out for the way in which they exploded stereotypes about people with disabilities.

"My dance instructor is deaf and blind and in her seventies," Nancy said.

"Your *dance instructor*?" I responded. That didn't fit my ignorant vision of Visions.

I dropped in on Marion's class to interact with her and her students, who are devoted regulars. I could sense that in the ease with which they joked around with one another. Marion, a short, fit Black woman with close-cropped hair that had grayed along her temples, couldn't make out their faces—just as they couldn't make out hers—but they all knew each other by their shapes, gaits and voices. Marion's hearing aids made it just possible to catch the gist of what someone not too far from her was saying. She did a lot with a little information.

And what she lacked in sensory perception she more than made up for in charm and bravado. She called many of her students "baby" or "sweetheart," a tic in tension with her big, brassy voice, which she used in class to trumpet orders: "To the right! To the left! Back it up! Tuuuuuuuurn!" Cross a drill sergeant with a life coach, add a vocabulary heavy on the sorts of endearments stamped on heart-shaped candies and you got Marion.

She and her students had memorized the layout of the unadorned basement room in which the class was held, and she figured out which of her discs of music to load into the boom box by placing them under a machine, the Aladdin Ultra, that functioned as a gigantic magnifying glass. It enlarged the letters on a disc's case to a point where Marion could make them out. Blindness is a spectrum, and for many blind people, like Marion, the world isn't all cloud; it's just very, very foggy, to a degree that poses formidable challenges and forces clever and sometimes awkward work-arounds.

Marion used her fingers to "read" the controls of the boom box. She used her hands to determine if her students were moving as instructed, coming up right beside them to feel how much they were bending, how wide they were kicking, how

fully they were rotating and precisely how they were positioning their arms and legs. The students with slightly more sight
automatically helped the ones with less, in accordance with an
unspoken covenant.

Sometimes, though, someone asked for assistance, as Marion did when fiddling with an attendance sheet. "I need you for
a second," she told a student standing nearby. "I need your eyes.
Can I borrow your eyes?"

In her forties, Marion began to experience episodes of scar-
ily compromised vision. She got a diagnosis of retinitis pigmentosa, which usually shows up at an earlier age, as it did with
Juan Jose. For her, blindness was delayed, but it was coming all
the same. And it was hardly the first test of her strength. Marion
didn't tally her misfortunes for me, but her daughter, Kokeda
Sheppard, filled me in, to communicate how tough her mom is.
Marion, who had lived most of her life in the Bronx borough of
New York City and still resided there, never really knew her father and was just fourteen when her mother died, according to
Kokeda. While relatives stepped in to help, Marion functioned
as a sort of parent to her younger siblings.

She got a college degree and, as it happened, worked for
decades at the *Times*, though we didn't know each other there.
She was first a key-punch operator and then a library clerk. She
left when she was in her early fifties. By then, her vision had
degenerated badly.

It was partly because Marion had always been so active, so
independent and so prone to helping others rather than needing help herself that her failing vision devastated her at first. She
felt a powerlessness that was unfamiliar and a vulnerability that

she thought she'd put to rest long ago, after the taunting from classmates.

"I was really terrified," she told me, and that terror was distilled into a recurring thought: Unable to see a stranger's approach, she'd be mugged. She was also sure that "people were going to look at me differently, act differently toward me," and she couldn't abide that. So for many months, as her vision faded, she rarely left her apartment. That wasn't a lull that she'd deliberately created, a period of regrouping that she had resolved to end before it went on too long. It was an unplanned, full-scale retreat. It was a rut, deep and immobilizing.

But then, on one of the rare occasions when she was coaxed from her apartment, she attended a social event where, as it happened, there were a few blind people in the mix. But they weren't really *in* the mix. She could see that much. These particular people were quiet, physically withdrawn, an air of timidity around them. They'd ceded the stage and consigned themselves to the wings, in a manner that didn't seem to Marion like the effective establishment of safety and peace. It seemed like a self-imposed exile. Looking at them, she realized that she was looking at herself, and that epiphany chilled her more than the challenges and risks of venturing out into the world again. "I said, 'Oh no,' " she recalled. " 'This is the way my life is going to be? Oh no.' "

As long as we're alive, we have to keep moving. Marion got moving, and she got moving in a big way. Shelving her self-consciousness about her blindness, she didn't merely accept the need to use a cane that announced her disability to the world; she made friends with it. "I always said if I ever had a boy, I'd name him Tyreek, and I never had a boy, so Tyreek is my cane," she told me. "Tyreek is my best friend."

As long as we're alive, we have to keep moving. Line dancing had long been a hobby of hers, and after she started going to events run by Visions and met Nancy, she proposed a line-dancing class. Nancy was agreeable, provided that Marion could attract a following. Marion quickly did, and she maintained it over more than a decade. She attributed that less to her music ("Hot Hot Hot," "Cupid Shuffle," "Blurred Lines") than to her mission: She was creating a rare environment outside their own homes where blind people could be physically uninhibited, where they could move through space not with caution but with joy.

I watched two of Marion's classes, and in both there was a moment when she instructed all the participants, who were arranged in parallel lines, to form a circle instead. One by one, each of them took a turn in the center, busting moves as the others clapped, hooted or stomped their approval.

Marion took a turn, too. She corkscrewed from a standing position to a crouch. She twisted this way and that. She was moving, all right, and not in accordance with any choreography, not in obeisance to any script. She was letting her impulses guide her. She was following her bliss.

⸻

There comes a fork. A decision. It's one of the details of Marion's story that grabbed and made a special impression on me because it so closely paralleled the stories of other people whose lives met new boundaries. It reminded me of the fork that I'd encountered after Tom and I broke up. Marion reached a juncture where she could give in to her sadness and scaredness or she could take deliberate, concrete steps to move beyond them. She took those steps.

Of course, some people, confronting hardship, don't have that agency: The circumstances are so overwhelming or their internal coping mechanisms so compromised that their lots hinge on the interventions or generosity of those around them. But it's my educated guess that more people have sway over the direction they turn in. And it's my observation that there's a crucial period, a discrete phase, when they summon the will to steer toward a sunny horizon or they don't.

Let me amend that: There can be a few such make-or-break passages. A series of forks. They can be the products of unusual hardship, physical or psychological; they can be the wages of normal aging. When they happen, you're tested, and you can either determine that as long as you're alive, you have to keep moving, or you can be so thrown by how much less easily you move that you go nowhere at all. My friend Dorrie exemplifies that. The credo that she adopted—"Don't look at the hole"— was a resolve to march forward, even though her legs didn't cooperate the way they once had.

I thought of Dorrie and of Marion when I read a book about aging by a colleague of mine at the *Times*, John Leland. Both women are proof of its boldly declarative title: *Happiness Is a Choice You Make.* John spent a year interviewing and getting to know a group of people who were eighty-five or older and who, like anybody and everybody at that late stage, had experienced pronounced physical deterioration, profound grief or both. "All had lost something: mobility, vision, hearing, spouses, children, peers, memory," John wrote, going on to cast their responses to that as something of a decision—a choice. "Take the blue pill and you're bemoaning life without the sharp memory or the job that once made you special; take the red pill and you're giving thanks for a life that still includes people you love. You can go to a museum and think, I'm confined to a wheelchair in a group of half-deaf old people. Or you can think, Matisse!"

John was describing a fork, from which you could travel toward engagement or disengagement, positivity or negativity. And he was reminding me of someone in addition to Dorrie and Marion: my mother, Leslie Frier Bruni, who died in 1996, at the age of sixty-one, after living with cancer for at least twice as long as her doctors thought anyone with her particular illness would be able to.

Even before Mom's cancer diagnosis, going all the way back to when my siblings and I were children, she would challenge doomsaying, defeatism and dark moods, and she would do it in a way that—forgive me, Mom—I found irritating. She favored cornball sayings and cheesy songs. She had no patience for highfalutin philosophy, and she had a weakness for life instructions that could be delivered epigrammatically or melodically or maybe even in rhyme. Her commands that we not worry needlessly and not mope too much were perfect examples of that.

She would recite the first stanza of the 1899 William Hughes Mearns poem "Antigonish," taking it out of context in order to repurpose it as a cloying, grating reprimand not to invent or exaggerate problems:

> *Yesterday, upon the stair,*
> *I met a man who wasn't there!*
> *He wasn't there again today,*
> *I wish he'd go away!*

Mom had an even *more* cloying, *more* grating chastisement for pessimism. It was the opening lines of an ineluctable, insidiously catchy 1944 song, which she sang a cappella, about accentuating the positive, eliminating the negative and not messing with "Mister In-Between." All of that was covered in the first stanza, after which, blessedly, she'd stop.

Many years after her death, I went in hunt of the complete lyrics and learned that, had she gone on, the next two lines were about spreading joy "up to the maximum" and bringing gloom "down to the minimum." How fitting: Her dopey bromides notwithstanding, Mom spread joy. She banished gloom. That was true before she was given a death sentence. It was even truer after.

In a macabre coincidence, she and a family friend, a woman of almost her same age, got similar cancer diagnoses and identically grim forecasts around the same time. Mom decided that she'd beat the odds and that, in the meantime, she'd summon what strength she must to keep her life as full as possible. Her friend crumbled—and was gone years earlier than Mom was. There were probably medical reasons for that contrast, but I don't think that's all that was going on. Mom persevered, God love her, because she accentuated that damned positive. She latched on to that hokey affirmative.

When one of her many rounds of chemotherapy started to thin her hair, she turned wig shopping into a lark. When the treatments weakened her or upset her stomach, she hit pause for a few hours, maybe took a nap, and then, at the earliest feasible moment, moved on with her day, her week, her month. She reasoned that if she let cancer debilitate her when she still possessed even the slightest ability to rally, it would win twice— by abbreviating her life and by spoiling the portion of it that nonetheless remained. She was adamant about not granting it that double victory.

She continued to golf. She continued to cook. I'd come home for an extended visit and, as ever, she'd cycle through all my favorite meals, punctuated with all my favorite restaurants. I was hardly demanding that, but I could depend on it. Whether she was wigged or not, whether her natural hair was straight or chemo-kinky, her lasagna was meaty and supple and cooked in quantities that allowed for seconds, thirds, fourths *and* leftovers. As cancer emaciated her, she fattened the rest of us.

A few years after her diagnosis, Dad was transferred by the accounting firm where he was a senior partner from the San Diego office to the one in New York City, and though Mom loved Southern California and her doctors there, she got on a plane to find a new house, and she sprang into action to sell the old one. She sometimes had to go slower than she once would have, so she decelerated, slightly and grudgingly. But life went on. Life had to go on. She and Dad moved across the country and into the Westchester County neighborhood where I would later, toward the start of the coronavirus pandemic, stay with and care for him. She redid the kitchen and several of the bathrooms. She insisted on hosting Christmas Eve dinner for the extended Bruni family, more than twenty champion eaters in all, and went fancier than usual, supplementing the pasta with beef Wellington, each slice of it ringed by a ribbon of foie gras. Dad wondered aloud if they should hire someone—a cater waiter—to help with the serving and the cleanup. Mom wouldn't hear of it.

I lost track of how much chemotherapy she survived. There were just two surgeries. The second came near the end, and she emerged from it weaker than she'd ever been before. She'd stop halfway up a flight of stairs, out of breath. She'd fall asleep on the couch in the first third of *Law & Order*, not able to hang on for the big reveal and final verdict. She'd—gasp!—let Dad bring take-out food home. But having lasted long enough to see the birth of her first grandchild, a baby girl who was named after her, she was determined to stick around for the second.

And she made it, just barely, dying less than a week after that baby boy, named after my father, was born. She hung around long enough to press her lips against his forehead, to breathe in that inimitably powdery newborn scent just one last time, to hold him in her winnowed, frail arms.

⁓

I thought of Mom every day after her death, for many years to come. I thought of her every hour after my stroke, for months.

I put the measly challenge that I was confronting next to the one that she had faced, and I vowed to measure how I rose to it with the yardstick of her optimism and endurance. She hadn't brooded, so why and how could I? I took the fork that she had, having been shown how.

I took every fork that she would have. That first clinical trial? She would have said yes to that—and to the second one, too. And she would have been a trouper, so I tried to be. The emphasis in that last sentence is on "tried." There were many times when I failed, many times when I thought I had turned with great valor in the more upbeat, more determined direction only to find myself traveling down an unsmooth path in unsteady steps. There were many times when I stumbled and more than a few when I fell.

If I've created the impression that I avoided self-pity, that's not quite right. What I really did—and what, I believe, lies closer to the truth for almost everyone—is learn how to sift through a mix of constructive and destructive impulses inside me, of buoyant resolve and leaden sorrow, and to accept that there was no predicting or controlling which took precedence at a given moment. But the severity of the sorrow could be minimized. The frequency, too. The hole was there, but I could will myself not to look too long or too hard at it. I could train myself to lift Matisse above melancholy. Losing the fight against sorrow in one instance didn't mean losing the campaign against sorrow overall.

The second summer after my stroke, I took a trip to Italy, for a work-related conference in Venice of all places. Italy, like Greece, was a country that Tom and I had repeatedly visited together. My patchwork of Italian memories was dominated by meals and drives with him. We loved the same things about the country: its veneration of beauty, the feistiness of its people. We mocked the same things about the country: its proneness to nonsense, the flightiness of its people. Our long walks through Italian cities were a running commentary on all of this, with regular stops for espresso and Nebbiolo. They were some of my happiest times ever, and they were gone.

The summer trip came in the middle of the second clinical trial, so I had to bring two vials of the mastic-derived medicine to keep to my injecting schedule. From the moment I plucked them from my refrigerator to one hour before they went into a syringe, they had to be kept cold. So, in addition to traveling with a small stash of syringes and needles, I had this thick-walled, ice-packed, cylindrical tin—the Klean Kanteen, it was called—for the vials.

To get through airport security, I had to explain myself at length, and I kept a doctor's note in my shoulder bag, just in case. On the plane, I had to ask a flight attendant to put my Klean Kanteen in a refrigerator somewhere. In the hotel, I had to hope for a minibar with enough space for it or make regular ice runs to keep the tin's interior cold. And I couldn't help feeling put out. I had always liked to travel light, to savor the sense that I was whirling weightlessly through the world. But I was traveling heavy, with precious cargo that I couldn't neglect. It was a constant reminder and an undeniable drag.

After Venice I went for just two days to Milan, which was a quick train ride away and got me to a bigger airport for a cheaper flight home. Because this was late August, when Italy shuts down—anyone who can afford to flee to the shore does exactly that—I had to hunt for somewhere, anywhere, to buy a morning espresso within a ten-minute walk of the unexpectedly cramped, dark apartment that I'd rented through Airbnb. The stillness of the streets had a melancholy edge. It rattled me, probably because of the contrast with all the movement and chatter at the Venice conference.

When I found a coffee shop, I noticed two big signs on the wall and thought about how they would have tickled Tom for the precise reasons that they amused me. One announced in big, proudly cursive letters that the place was open for *tutto*—or all—of August. That this was a boast-worthy rarity captured something essential about Italy, as did the longer message spelled out on the other sign, which was an equally Italian defense of not becoming an ambition-driven workaholic and saving ample time for relaxation and diversion. It said that the next time anyone accused you of lacking professionalism, point out that Noah's ark was constructed by dilettantes and the *Titanic* by professionals.

I laughed inwardly at the cleverness of that—and at the use of fable to joust with fact—but I had no one with whom to share it. On the plane to New York from Milan, I had no one beside me to marvel, as I did, at the pilot's explanation of why we were making an emergency landing in Paris. (One of the engines, he said, had "ingested" a bird.) I had no one to pass the six hours in Charles de Gaulle Airport with me. I had no one present to defuse my anxiety when, as I returned to my apartment, the elevator got stuck and I was trapped there for nearly an hour before help arrived. The temperature inside rose higher and higher. I began to sweat profusely. I had no water. And I thought, with a mix of panic and gallows humor: This is where, when and how my medical odyssey ends. My body's dehydration will cause my blood pressure to plunge and—*snap!*—there goes my other optic nerve.

I had no one waiting for me at home when, two months later, I visited the New York Eye and Ear Infirmary of Mount Sinai yet again, this time upon the conclusion of my half year of twice-weekly injections, and I learned that there was no discernible improvement in my right eye—not in the size and number of letters on a chart that it could make out, not in its ability to register those erratic bursts of light on that insufferable visual field test. I spent the initial hours absorbing that alone, and I was alone as well two months after *that*, when I got an email telling me that the clinical trial itself had been stopped prematurely because the drug seemed not to be doing much good for anyone else, either. We'd all been keeping our vials refrigerated and our sharps containers at the ready for naught. We'd all been injecting in vain. We'd all had this sliver of hope snatched from us, and there were no other slivers, no new clinical trials in which we could try to be enrolled, awaiting us. That was that.

And I was fine. I was calm. It had always been possible—no, probable—that the experiment would end this way; that's why words like "experimental" and "trial" were attached to it. It was theoretical, not definitive, and my expectations and even mood had contoured themselves to that. I'd taken a chance, for sound reasons. It hadn't panned out. I'd move on.

The funny thing about sadness—what I was finally learning and wished I'd understood so much earlier in life—was its undependability, the merciful fact that if you rode it out during one period, it might well let you be during the next. While I'd felt sorry for myself in that coffee shop in Milan and while I'd felt like some kind of martyr—like Mel Gibson in eviscerated extremis in *Braveheart*—while marinating in my own perspiration in between floors of my own building, I felt in this instance merely like one of the countless people pressing through difficulty and plodding along admirably. I felt sturdy, and I felt that way in part because I'd seen that while the roller coaster of my emotions would drag me downward, fast, with little or no advance notice, it would rocket me upward with no more warning or sense. I had to have faith in that. I had to have patience. And I did, for the very first time.

People who flourish make a decision to flourish. They point themselves toward joy.

Miguel Neri is a lawyer in San Francisco. More than a decade ago, when he was around fifty, he went blind in his left eye. Around the same time, he began gradually to lose substantial hearing in both ears so that, even with hearing aids, he sometimes had difficulty making out what people were saying. He wasn't happy about that, but he also wasn't sad. His disabilities had prompted a greater degree of reflection about his life—about the whole of it—and the fruit of that reflection was the conviction that it was enchanted. "A fairy tale," he told me.

He and six siblings grew up in southern Texas, near the Mexican border, to Spanish-speaking Mexican American parents with little money. His father was a self-employed carpenter.

His mother was a cook, but not in restaurants—in institutions like nursing homes. She donated her services to a local Roman Catholic school to get enough of a break on the modest tuition to be able to send Miguel there. She hoped that he would go on to the seminary and become a priest.

He disappointed her. He went to Harvard Law. There he met his wife, the daughter of Chinese immigrants, who, like him, pursued and established a successful legal career. They had a son and, three years later, a daughter.

One morning in his midforties, he said, "I was getting dressed to go to work and it looked like a black ghost had appeared in front of me. I reached out to touch it. But it wasn't real—it was in my eye. It was blood." He'd suffered a kind of retinal tear, and doctors determined that there were grave, vision-threatening issues with the retinas in both of his eyes. "I had maybe five or six operations," he explained. "It involved a lot of needles in the eyes as they did the prep work."

Having experienced the shocking pain of such a shot, I told him that sounded nightmarish.

"Well," Miguel responded, "there's not much you can do."

He lost the vision in his left eye, anyway—a preview, possibly, of what would happen in his right eye, too. He couldn't ignore that. He *didn't* ignore that. But this was where he came upon his fork: He could dwell on the prospect, brace for it, let the dread wash over him and risk drowning in it. Or he could use all of his emotional and psychological muscles to wrestle his thoughts to a healthier place.

"I realized early what we should all already know," he wrote to me at one point. "Life is very short, and one day we will grow old and weak, and our world will necessarily shrink. I worry about the present and things I can control. One can go crazy thinking about 'what ifs.'"

And "worry" isn't quite the right word. At least it's not the complete picture. Miguel celebrates and revels in the present by pushing himself and not putting off endeavors that he'd postponed before. He'd long wondered about learning Italian, so he enrolled in night classes to study the language and, when he and his family planned a trip to Italy, he went there ahead of them so that he could do a brief sink-or-swim immersion in this new tongue. He traveled with increased frequency and new purpose. He took up the cello. He'd never learned to read music or play an instrument before and figured it was now or never, "and I thought a cello was good because it plays at low notes that weren't affected by my hearing problem," he said. Although he had been a fly fisherman for many years, he ratcheted up the difficulty—and thus the adventure—of some of the settings in which he took part in the sport. He also added an accessory to his fishing outfit.

"Safety goggles," he said.

"It still scares me to think about being blind and deaf," he said. "But right now it looks like I'm going to be able to slouch my way across the finish line. I've been to Nepal, South America. If my body is completely broken down, right before my eyes close for the last time, I think I will say, 'I led a good life. I wore this body out. I did not give up. I got my money's worth. I used every ounce of my body as hard as I could as long as I could.'

"In the end," Miguel concluded, "we all have very few options. We go forward or we don't. And I think most people elect to go forward."

Chapter Eight
STARFISH AND TWIGGY

Not long after my stroke, I developed a strange habit: When my apartment intercom buzzed, I would press the button that allowed someone entry into the ten-story building's lobby and walk to the foyer of my apartment to wait impatiently for the food deliverer or friend to reach my floor (the seventh). I'd stare through my front door's peephole to watch for the opening of the elevator and the appearance of that person, whom I wanted to greet before he or she pressed the doorbell. I liked the surprise and friendliness of my promptness. Also, the doorbell didn't work.

But it wasn't until one day long after my stroke that I realized that I could tell when the elevator was about to open. I could anticipate it by a second or two. This was a feat not of intuition or extra-sensory perception but of a sort of eye-brain teamwork that I hadn't previously done and maybe hadn't been able to do. Because of this teamwork, I was reading something that I'd never been able to read before. What's more, I was doing it without my glasses on.

What I was reading was the numerical display just outside the elevator: the glowing digits, under a small panel of glass, that tracked its ascent or descent floor by floor. That may not sound like such a big and magical deal, but the display window didn't face my front door. It faced a wall perpendicular to it and was far enough away that the digits it flashed weren't fully visible. They weren't even half visible. But from my terrible angle and my imperfect distance, through the tiny aperture of the peephole, there was just enough gleanable information about the presence or absence of the vertical or horizontal lines that made up different digits to provide clues and permit guesses.

All those horizontal lines: That must be a three. The elevator is on three. Now there has been a change, with a new vertical line appearing: The elevator has ascended to four. The interval of time in which three became four lets me know that the next discernible shift in the digits must be from four to five, and the one after that from five to six. And seven, well, that's an unusually spare digit, that one vertical line meeting that one horizontal line.

While I couldn't see much of those lines, I could deduce their angle to one another and their spareness, and I'd internalized the timing, the rhythm, the velocity of the elevator's rise. "The doors will now open," I said to myself. And the doors indeed did.

Obviously, I could have learned or trained myself to perform this junior-league parlor trick before my stroke, and there was nothing about my diminished state that necessitated it. But its emergence only after my stroke suggested that parts of my brain had clicked into overdrive—as an adaption to, and compensation for, the injury to my vision. They were exercising and honing efficiencies that hadn't been necessary. I'm not saying that it was necessary to soothsay the sliding of elevator doors, but as a general rule, it was helpful to make better use of the visual information that my diminished eyes still received, and my experience with the elevator illustrated my brain's progress along those lines.

I also noticed this enhanced perception or refined deduction—I'm not sure what to call it—on those occasions when I ran after dark. I tried *not* to run after dark, for the obvious safety reasons, but night fell early during certain stretches of the year and sometimes my schedule didn't allow for exercise until late in the day. I'd chart a route that didn't take me too far into Riverside Park or Central Park for too long, but on occasion I'd feel and indulge the desire to head up toward Central Park's reservoir and run on the dirt bridle path that encircled it. The path's lure was its relative roughness, its unadornment, the absence of benches alongside it, the paucity of streetlamps skirting it. But that was also a challenge, even a peril. It lacked illumination and definition and wasn't smooth and flat; stretches of it were a sort of moonscape of subtle craters. It was a sprained ankle waiting to happen.

And it was somehow less treacherous to navigate after my stroke. In a fashion I can't fully and accurately describe, I could translate the faintest shadows and barest ridges into a topographical map in my mind, and so I sidestepped what needed to be sidestepped, swerved when I needed to swerve, picked my feet up a bit higher than usual when that was in order, tacked gently leftward or slightly rightward in perfect accordance with the path's bends. When I realized that I was doing this with fewer mistakes and greater ease than in the past, I was mystified, then exhilarated. The exhilaration wasn't about my vision but about my potential. Even in the later innings of our lives, we have unplumbed abilities, untaxed muscles, flexibility, growth. That made the prospect of further deterioration of my vision less scary. That made *everything* less scary.

Over the past few decades, scientists have revised their thinking about the organ in charge of thinking, which is to say that they have a new understanding of the brain. What they now believe is that it reorganizes and reinvigorates itself over a much greater span of human life, and to a much greater degree, than was long assumed. What they now see in it is an elasticity—"plasticity" is their preferred word, "neuroplasticity" to be precise—that they hadn't appreciated before. This is encouraging news for anyone trying to recover from, or adapt to, an injury or affliction. It's inspiring news for everyone because it means that aging, which we all do, isn't an arc of pure enfeeblement, at least not where our minds are concerned. It's an act of transformation.

Sanjay Gupta, the physician made famous by his daily and sometimes hourly appearances on CNN during the coronavirus pandemic, is actually a neurosurgeon, not an infectious disease specialist, and smack in the middle of the pandemic, he came out with a new book not about the plague but about a subject in which he was even more deeply versed: the brain. He explained the revolutionary reappraisal of it by mentioning the abrupt shift in how he himself was educated about it.

"When I was in medical school in the early 1990s, conventional wisdom was that brain cells, such as neurons, were incapable of regenerating," he wrote in *Keep Sharp*. "We were born with a fixed set and that was it; throughout life, we'd slowly drain the cache." But, he added, "I never believed that our brain cells simply stopped growing and regenerating. After all, we continue to have novel thoughts, deep experiences, vivid memories, and new learning throughout our lives. It seemed to me that the brain wouldn't just wither away unless it was no longer being used. By the time I finished my neurosurgery training in 2000, there was plenty of evidence that we could nurture the birth of new brain cells (called neurogenesis) and even increase the size of our brains. It was a staggeringly optimistic change in how we view the master control system of our bodies."

The veteran science writer Sharon Begley, in her book *Train Your Mind, Change Your Brain*, put it this way: "In the last years of the twentieth century, a few iconoclastic neuroscientists challenged the paradigm that the adult brain cannot change and made discovery after discovery that, to the contrary, it retains stunning powers of neuroplasticity." It can, for example, "expand the area that is wired to move the fingers, forging new connections that underpin the dexterity of an accomplished violinist. It can activate long-dormant wires and run new cables like an electrician bringing an old house up to code." Like a child's brain, it can produce new neurons, repair damaged regions, rezone regions that performed one task to take on another and expand or contract different regions of the brain to "pour more juice into quiet circuits and damp down activity in buzzing ones."

Delve into this topic and you trip frequently across two of the terms I introduced before, "neurogenesis" and "neuroplasticity," but they're not interchangeable. There's more disagreement about the former, which essentially refers to the brain's cellular renewal and expansion, than about the latter, which connotes the brain's perpetual adjustment to changing environments, responsibilities and challenges. While some research suggests that adult brains generate new neurons in abundant measure and at a meaningful clip, other research questions that. Because scientists can't perform the sorts of experiments on live, still-functional human brains that they can on the brains of other mammals, certain questions are difficult to answer and certain debates hard to resolve. Some of what's known, or believed, is an extrapolation of observations in laboratory animals.

Where does consensus end and quibbling begin? Moheb Costandi, who is the author of the books *Neuroplasticity* and *50 Human Brain Ideas You Really Need to Know* and writes the *Neurophilosophy* blog for the British newspaper the *Guardian*, told me: "In the 1990s, evidence emerged that the adult human brain contains what we call stem cells: cells that retain a capacity to generate new cells. This is still quite a controversial idea. We know that the adult human brain can generate new cells, and there are several discrete niches of stem cells in our brains, and they do appear to be generating small numbers of new cells.

"What's controversial, or what we still don't know, is: Are these new cells actually *doing* anything in the human brain?"

he continued. "Or is the process an evolutionary relic? That's the question. What's the extent of the functional significance of new cells in the human adult brain?"

The answer matters, but only to a point: Regardless of neurogenesis, neuroplasticity exists. That *is* definitely known, in part because the evidence of it is abundant around us and *inside* us. When you improve at a repeated task, it reflects the way the doing of it affects your brain. When you do something a new way because the old way wasn't working anymore, that swap of one method for another is directed by your ever-clever, ever-plastic brain.

"Let's put aside the question of neurogenesis," Costandi said. "Brain cells can change their physical structure. They can sprout new branches. They can retract old branches. They can strengthen or weaken existing connections. They can form new connections entirely and completely eliminate old ones. The brain retains its capacity for change throughout life."

That capacity does decline, in general, with age. But it doesn't go away. It declines more in some people and less in others. It can be slowed or arrested by the lifestyles we adopt and the decisions we make. That's the thrust of Gupta's book, as its title—*Keep Sharp*—makes clear. That's Costandi's bottom line, too. Referring to the mounting evidence of neuroplasticity, he said: "The one thing it tells us is that it's not inevitable that getting old necessarily entails everything completely falling apart, and there are certain things you can do that seem to protect against aging."

If you maintain a robust agenda of activities, if you nurture a rich network of relationships, if you intellectually challenge yourself, if you pay attention to your diet, if you exercise regularly and vigorously, if you latch on to a sense of purpose—all of this will probably enhance your cognitive fitness, your mental agility. It's an interesting to-do list, because it mirrors the advice often given about a fulfilling life. Well, a fulfilling life is a brain-nurturing one, and vice versa. There's an elegant and irrefutable logic in that.

I met David Tatel on a frigid day in December 2017, about two months after my stroke. He was then seventy-five and a distinguished longtime judge in his final years with the US Court of Appeals for the District of Columbia Circuit. (He ended up retiring in early 2021.) That court is just one tier below the Supreme Court and a training ground for many Supreme Court justices. Tatel had been appointed to it in 1994, when he was in his early fifties. By then he had been blind for nearly two decades.

That wasn't widely known beyond his professional and personal acquaintances. While he didn't hide his blindness, he preferred not to speak about it or draw attention to it. As he told me during one of the many long conversations that we had, "I never wanted to be 'the blind judge.'" I found my way to him not because I'd read or heard about his story in any public venue but because a friend of mine was working as one of his clerks and introduced us. My friend greeted me on the day I first went to visit Judge Tatel in Washington, DC, and brought me into Tatel's courtroom in advance of my lunchtime meeting with him. So I observed Tatel for a while before we were introduced.

He, along with two other judges, was already on the bench, listening to the arguments of a lawyer, when I arrived. The case they were hearing was some complicated telecommunications matter that I couldn't even begin to follow. So I just studied him, this thin, bald, black-robed figure with a kind face and an alert, thoughtful expression. His head turned toward whoever was speaking. My friend whispered to me that many courtroom observers and even many trial participants didn't realize, at least not right away, that Tatel couldn't see them. There certainly wasn't any clue in the confidence of his posture, any tell in the eloquence of his speech.

After about forty-five minutes, court went into recess and then, only because I was watching so closely, did I spot something unusual. As Tatel walked from the bench to a door behind it, he repeatedly extended one of his hands and grazed the curved wall to his right with his fingers. It was the kind of thing a child might do, just for the sensation, just to investigate the texture of his surroundings, but neither of those explanations made sense in terms of Tatel's age or his familiarity with this courtroom, in which he had spent hundreds and hundreds of hours. Tatel was clearly confirming his bearings. He was making sure that he was on the correct path to his chambers.

Like Juan Jose, Tatel lost his sight to retinitis pigmentosa, and like Juan Jose, he got the first warnings that this would happen in his teens—when he was fifteen, to be precise. He was told then that at some point in the next ten to twenty-five years, he'd go blind. He took the news in and then tucked it away, because what else was he to do with it? What purpose was served by worrying about and girding for it? He went to college. He went to law school. He married his wife, Edie, and they started a family. They lived fully, not adjusting their activities or downsizing their dreams because of something that would happen at a time they couldn't choose and at a pace they couldn't predict.

That time turned out to be the age of thirty-one. He recalls that he was skiing—that's what I mean about a full life—and he needed help getting down the mountain. For the next six years, his world darkened and blurred, until he could see just about nothing at all. It was scary and disorienting and so very hard: He had to make peace with a loss of independence that was real and undeniable no matter how positive an outlook he honed, no matter how much gratitude he nurtured for all that he still possessed. He couldn't just walk out the door on an impulse and meander around his neighborhood. He couldn't just pick up a magazine or book and flip through it. He couldn't drive. All of this was gone. None of it would come back.

He would never see his wife and four children again. He had to take his memories of them and, in his imagination, sketch in the advances of age. In a 2016 speech he gave at a private function of the Foundation Fighting Blindness, he noted that while family members had become "true audible artists," describing everything that they pass on nature walks, "I still can't see the clouds and flowers and potholes myself—or my wife's beautiful white hair." He believes that he knows what his eight grandchildren look like, from the sounds of their voices and his recollections of their parents' appearances when they were young, but he can't be sure.

Part of his resilience is the attitude that he adopted toward his blindness and that he maintains to this day: He concentrates on his luck, a word and idea that kept popping up in our conversations. He considers himself lucky, of course, to have such a supportive spouse and family. He considers himself lucky to have had so many years with eyesight that he was left with a mental picture book that he can access when a person or people are telling him about his physical environment at a given moment. And he considers himself lucky to have gone blind at a point in human progress when technology was so sophisticated and could come to the rescue in many situations. Over recent decades, voice-to-text and text-to-voice software have improved enormously. Audiobooks, along with a range of devices for listening to them, have proliferated. Smartphones have incorporated features designed to help people with disabilities.

Of course, none of this technology would matter if the brain in general and his brain in particular weren't capable of stretching in accordance with different systems for acquiring information and whirring in whole new ways. None of it would matter if he didn't have the ability to train himself to retain the words he *heard* as well as he had once retained the words he *saw*. He was arguably still seeing those words, just with his brain rather than his eyes. Examinations of the visual cortexes of blind people's brains have shown that these regions, once thought to be reserved for sight in the literal sense, light up when the person is reading braille, drawing a picture or imagining a physical scene. The brain is malleable that way.

And it can maximize whatever input it does get, so that blind people often have or report better hearing than other people do and deaf people experience better vision, picking up on—and paying heed to—cues that others don't. I've had many blind people tell me that they can discern which family member, friend or colleague is drawing near by the heaviness and rhythm of that person's footfall or by similarly distinguishing sounds. (That was the case, you'll recall, with Marion Sheppard.) Deprived of one bit of evidence, they make use of another.

In their memories they trap details unimportant to other people and perhaps once unimportant to them. Tatel certainly does. One day we met and chatted in his chambers before heading to his apartment about five miles away. While I'd assumed that he we'd take a taxi or an Uber or such, he said that the Metro, which is Washington's name for its subway system, would be faster and suggested that. He had learned the map of the area around the courthouse so well—had imprinted it so solidly in his brain—that he could navigate the five or so blocks from the courthouse to the nearest Metro station alone, with just a white cane, occasionally asking a nearby stranger a question when that was necessary.

He knew from auditory information when he'd reached an intersection. He knew from memory the distances across a given street or through areas of the station and roughly how many steps it took to get from here to there. His paths weren't always perfectly straight lines, and I found myself nervously and timidly saying "To the left a bit" or "To the right a bit" as we walked, never sure if he needed the information but figuring that it couldn't hurt. But he only reached out for my forearm a few times. And he, not me, was the one directing us. I didn't know which of the Metro lines led to his neighborhood, where we got off or how we exited *that* station. I deferred to and, for the most part, followed him.

I told him, as we rode the Metro, that I was impressed. By then we were well enough acquainted with each other that I knew he wouldn't consider the comment to be patronizing and would take it for the heartfelt compliment—and straightforward wonderment at our species' unfathomable nimbleness—that it was. He smiled with his whole face, then said something that echoed in my thoughts for the rest of that evening and echoes there still.

"Starfish can regrow limbs," he said. "But that's nothing compared to what human beings can do."

I became a connoisseur of the unlikely accomplishments of blind people—unlikely in the eyes (forgive me) of people inattentive to the starfish in all of us, by which I mean people like me before my stroke. Without going in search of such feats, I spotted mentions of them here, there and everywhere: the blind dancer, the blind painter, the blind gallerist. I tripped across the name of the mountain climber and adventurer Erik Weihenmayer, who became the first blind person to reach the summit of Mount Everest, then completed ascents of all seven of the world's highest peaks and, for good measure, kayaked the roiling rapids in the Grand Canyon. That information had no doubt been around me all along, but I had been too distracted, too innocent, too smug to pick up on it.

A little more than a year after the damage to my right eye,

on a segment of the popular television news show *60 Minutes*, Lesley Stahl told the story of a San Francisco architect, Chris Downey, who went blind at the age of forty-five following the removal of a brain tumor that was pressing on his optic nerves. The surgery had carried that risk, and Downey had been informed of it, but he had also been told that such an outcome never really, truly, actually came to pass. With him it did.

Downey's version of blindness, an extreme one, was total darkness, and a social worker who counseled him suggested that they discuss career alternatives. But he wanted the career he already had—and felt, deep inside, that he could hold on to it if he were determined and creative enough. Yes, his eyes had failed, but his mind hadn't, and didn't that matter more?

"The creative process is an intellectual process," Downey told Stahl. "It's how you *think*. I just needed new tools."

Walking through buildings and under roofs that he knew, visually, from before his blindness, he came to understand how sounds—of his own movement, of his cane's tapping, of other people's voices and steps—traced the contours of a structure, and that enabled him to turn such auditory clues from unfamiliar structures into knowledge, or at least educated assumptions, about how they were shaped and what they must look like.

"I was hearing the architecture," he told Stahl. "I was feeling the space."

As for drawing and reading construction plans and room layouts, he could do that by using a printer that turned lines into ridges: architectural braille, as it were. "They just came out in tactile form," he explained. As a result, he didn't consider what he was experiencing blindness per se. He described it to Stahl as "a different kind of vision."

For people with seriously compromised eyesight, there are *many* different kinds of vision, and all of them speak to the real center of perception and to its deftness at filling in sensory blanks.

"You don't see with the eyes, you see with the brain," Paul Bach-y-Rita, a renowned American neuroscientist who was known as "the father of sensory substitution," once said. Bach-y-Rita did revolutionary work in figuring how to deliver visual information to blind people, which he did by translating objects of sight into tactile experiences like, well, braille, or like Downey's ridged drawings.

A device that Bach-y-Rita developed in the 1960s fed images from a camera into a computer that converted them into pulses on a grid of vibrating, Teflon-tipped pins on the back of a chair in which the blind user of the device sat. The nature and location of those pulses corresponded to the images in a manner that the user learned.

As Nicola Twilley wrote in a 2017 article in the magazine the *New Yorker*: "The pins vibrated intensely for dark pixels and stayed still for light ones, enabling users to feel the picture pulsing on their backs. After just a few hours' practice, Bach-y-Rita's first six volunteers, all blind from birth, could distinguish between straight lines and curved ones, identify a telephone and a coffee mug, and even recognize a picture of the supermodel Twiggy."

That bulky contraption was the precursor to the much smaller and more portable BrainPort, which attached to blind people's heads and could be used as they moved around a room, plotting their steps and gestures in accordance with information that they were receiving via pulses not on their backs but on their *tongues*. (The headline of Twilley's article was "Seeing with Your Tongue.") The intricacy and expense of the Brain-Port meant that it wasn't and wouldn't replace guide dogs, not anytime soon, but it offered crucial assistance in extraordinary situations. Weihenmayer used it for some of his climbs, though not the history-making ones. He told Twilley "that he wouldn't take the BrainPort up Everest—relying on fallible electronics in such extreme conditions would be foolhardy," she wrote. "But he has used it on challenging outdoor climbs in Utah and around Colorado, and he loves the way that it restores his lost hand-eye coordination."

Twilley's article wasn't ultimately focused on Weihenmayer, the BrainPort or the tests and triumphs of blind people. Her article emphasized the work-arounds made possible by brains more plastic than was long assumed. "The BrainPort, which uses the sense of touch as a substitute for sight, is one of a growing number of so-called sensory-substitution devices," she observed. "Another, the vOICe, turns visual information into sound. Others translate auditory information into tactile sensation for the deaf or use sounds to supply missing haptic information for burn victims and leprosy patients."

These devices, she added, "have begun to revise our understanding of brain organization and development." Although the neuroscientists of yore liked to divide the brain into a "visual cortex," an "auditory cortex" and so on—and assumed that purely visual or auditory stimuli respectively kicked those regions into gear—more and more of them now take a different view and attribute less rigid compartmentalization and greater fluidity to the brain. A given region can color outside the lines of its supposedly discrete duties.

And so, when we come upon a roadblock, we're redirected. When the terrain shifts beneath our newly uncertain feet, we're reoriented. It's the gift of our cerebral circuitry—of more than that, in fact. Our emotional and spiritual circuitry is also at work, drawing forth the extra care and extra cunning that an absence of basic function demands. The tiny victories that I experienced in my own daily life and the titanic ones that I read about in profiles and biographies of more remarkable people usually lay at some confluence of wiring and wiles, synapses and soul. They combined different measures of each.

"Until the invention of the internal combustion engine, the most prolific traveler in history was also the most unlikely. James Holman was in many ways the quintessential world explorer: a dashing mix of discipline, recklessness and accomplishment, a Knight of Windsor, Fellow of the Royal Society, and bestselling author. It was easy to forget that he was intermittently crippled, and permanently blind."

Those three sentences are from the introduction of an excellent book about Holman, *A Sense of the World*, that was written by Jason Roberts, published in 2006 and became a finalist for the National Book Critics Circle Award. And they merely hint at the "unlikely" aspects of Holman's life, from 1786 to 1857. He was a daredevil traveler, often favoring remote and forbidding destinations. He frequently traveled alone. And he recounted these expeditions in popular books that made him somewhat famous in England, where he was one of the most successful practitioners of a kind of journalism as associated with vision as any other. A compound word that we use for people's motivation and behavior when they visit faraway places is a clumsy redundancy that emphasizes the eyes not once but twice. These people are *sightseeing*. Holman did that—and wrote about it—with eyes that didn't work.

Blind writers drew my gaze for obvious reasons. I wanted to know what, in a worst-case scenario, to expect. I wanted the reassurance that others had navigated it, and with much more distinction than would ever be expected of me. I wanted tips. I wanted promises.

And I discovered a robust, fascinating tradition of writers with little or no eyesight that goes well beyond Helen Keller and all the way back to Homer, who was sometimes referred to as "the blind poet," though there's an asterisk attached to that: Scholars have never settled the question of whether Homer was a single poet or a team of poets. John Milton produced *Paradise Lost* and *Paradise Regained* more than a decade after his eyes failed around 1652. "A good argument can be made that he was able to render these masterpieces not in spite of his blindness but because of it," John Rumrich, who teaches Milton at the University of Texas, told me. "He himself thought as much."

Milton chose to regard blindness as the price he was paying for "inner illumination," Rumrich said. It bolstered his sense of mission.

Perhaps that was true for Holman, too. But he's above all a testament to what Tatel and Downey also illustrated, which is how keenly a physically diminished person can reorient and reacclimate, how potent that person can be at problem-solving.

I mean, a blind travel writer: It sounds like the start of a bad joke by a bad stand-up comic. How can you describe mountains without noting the greenness of their conifers or the grayness of their limestone, without marveling at their push toward the clouds? How can you hustle readers through an Italian piazza if you can't survey the riot of faces around you and the chaos of architectural fillips on the cathedral ahead?

You can share what you've gathered from other people, filtering it through a gift for expression every bit as valuable as the actual function of sight. You can rummage through the history of a city or a landscape rather than providing the prose equivalent of postcards. You can recount not what you are beholding, in a visual sense, but what you are experiencing, in a social one: the conversations that you trip across, the imbroglios that you tumble into. You can pay as much heed to the journey within as to the journey without. You can pivot from the cosmetic to the cosmic.

Holman, a British naval officer who was born in 1786 and lost his sight for undetermined reasons around the age of twenty-five, did some or much of that. He rejected the approach to travel as a pictorial experience. Yes, that rejection was a matter of necessity, but there was also a lesson in it. Those questions that I asked just a paragraph or so ago—about the mountains, about the piazza— betray a prejudice. I elevated the visual above all else. Holman couldn't, so he didn't. And he discovered a world of wonder that might have been invisible to him otherwise.

Here's how he himself put it, in the first chapter of *A Voyage Round the World: Volume I*:

> I am constantly asked, and I may as well answer the question here once and for all, what is the use of travelling to one who cannot see? I answer, Does every traveller see all that he describes?—and is not every traveller obliged to depend upon others for a great proportion of the information he collects?
>
> The picturesque in nature, it is true, is shut out from me . . . but perhaps this very circumstance affords a stronger zest to curiosity, which is thus impelled to a more close and searching examination of details than would be considered necessary to a traveller who might satisfy himself by the superficial view, and rest content with the first impressions conveyed through the eye. Deprived of that organ of information, I am compelled to adopt a more rigid and less suspicious course of inquiry, and to investigate analytically, by a train of patient examination, suggestions, and deductions, which other travellers dismiss at first sight; so that, freed from the hazard of being misled by appearances, I am the less likely to adopt hasty and erroneous conclusions.

Holman's journeys weren't the privilege of an affluent scion being escorted by a retinue of servants and using wads of bank notes, gold or other currency to smooth the way. He often traveled by himself and "entered each country not knowing a single word of the local language," Roberts wrote. "He had only enough money to travel in native fashion, in public carriages and peasant carts, on horseback and on foot." This was before anything resembling today's automobiles. This was obviously before airplanes, too.

Holman ascended Mount Vesuvius outside of Naples *while* it was erupting. He hunted elephants in Sri Lanka (then called Ceylon). He braved the cold in Siberia. He endured the heat in Zanzibar. He sailed to Brazil, where he entered the rain forest, and to Australia, where he explored the outback. All of this he did without eyesight and—this is where the "intermittently crippled" comes in—with a case of what was likely rheumatoid arthritis that sporadically left him immobile and in agony. He would wait out the pain or push through it. Roberts calculated that, all in all, Holman racked up about 250,000 miles as he journeyed to and through five continents. Next to Holman, Marco Polo was a shut-in.

Holman wrote in longhand, using a stringed device that helped to keep the lines of text tidy, parallel and distinct from one another. And he amassed so much knowledge on such an array of arcana that Charles Darwin, in *The Voyage of the Beagle*, mentions him as an authority on the fauna of the Indian Ocean.

When I first came across a mention of Roberts's book *A Sense of the World*, I immediately ordered it and, too keyed up to wait for it, tracked down Roberts in the meantime. He told me: "I thought I would write the typical uplifting, inspiring story." But no. Holman was less inspiration than revelation: of the multifarious ways in which life can be savored, of the potency of neglected senses, of all the information beyond our initial observations, of an unappreciated richness of detail in everything around us. "Nobody has ever experienced the world quite so vividly and completely" as Holman, Roberts told me. He added that he realized the sweep of that statement and stood by it. "For me to really understand how different the non-visual world is—how complex—was gobsmacking to me," he said.

He used the example of a wall of bricks. Those of us with eyesight, he explained, do an instant visual analysis of it that's not much of an analysis at all, and then we label it: *brick wall*. Maybe we note the color, too—*redbrick wall*—but we stop there, having tucked it into its category, having lumped it together with all the other redbrick walls we've seen. But Roberts said, "A person touching all those bricks will experience their individuality first." He or she will register all the rises and rough spots.

Or consider a table with four supposedly identical chairs. If they all look alike, those of us gazing at them are struck only or mostly by their sameness, because we prioritize visual appearance, and we regard them as interchangeable. But a blind person, attuned to other facets, might be struck by each chair's distinctiveness, by which one has a more or less yielding seat, which has the smoothest arm, which has the faintest of wobbles, which has the slightest of creaks. "For blind people, the individuality of things announces itself long before the unity," Roberts said. I wondered if that was more than a bit of a generalization and a tad too romantic, but I took his point, and was moved by it.

Holman indeed relied on and refined senses other than sight, becoming expert at human echolocation, which assesses where surrounding objects are by how much or how little they echo noise that you make—for instance, in his case, the tapping of a walking stick. Echolocation is how Downey appraised buildings after he lost his eyesight. "Others hear, but not as do the blind," Holman once said. "He concentrates his very soul while he listens, and can detect the slightest variations, the finest fractional point of tone."

One of the curiosities of Holman's prose, though, is that it's *not* primarily a celebration of sound and touch and feel and taste. I assumed it would be. But that wasn't the style of the era's travel writing, Roberts explained. And once Holman established his blindness near the beginning of whatever he was writing, he wanted the reader to forget it, so that he could serve as a more conventional, less obtrusive narrator. But that's not to say that he avoided those senses, as the following account of an ocean passage, also from *A Voyage Round the World: Volume I*, showed. It reflected the problem-solving that I referred to, the deployment and salience of certain observations when others can't be made:

> We did not long enjoy our easterly breeze, for in
> the evening the wind became variable, the rain
> fell in torrents, accompanied with lightning and
> thunder, and the night was dark and dismal, with
> an irregular sea, which made the ship very un-
> easy; then followed one of those scenes of confu-
> sion which can be witnessed only on shipboard;

the creaking of timbers as they were strained
by the conflict of the elements, the uproar of a
multitude of voices, the ludicrous accidents aris-
ing from the pitching and rolling of the vessel,
things breaking loose in all directions, chests
flying from side to side, crockery smashing,
people hallooing, others moaning and groaning,
accompanied with frequent evomitions, and occasionally a general scream, from some extraordinary crash.

He mentioned the "dark" of the night: a safe assumption,
but also a diversion of sorts. Dark and light had less bearing
on him than on others. The verb "witnessed," too, was almost a
head fake. But then, can't you witness something without seeing
it? Isn't there a surfeit of other evidence to tell you what's going
on? Whatever blanks are left, the people around you can fill in.
That's perhaps how Holman knew that the chunky projectiles
"flying from side to side" were chests.

Blindness, in and of itself, wasn't what most bedeviled Holman, what most stood in the way of his wanderlust. He had to
overcome the stigma attached to it. In England in those days,
blindness was often associated with syphilis, which could cause
it. So Holman, to make sure that people didn't recoil from him
and refuse him transportation, "had to get affidavits from his
pastor that he was of the highest character," Roberts said. He
also had to ride the crests and dips of his arthritis, which was
so severe, according to Roberts, that at one point he had to be
carried onto the ship that would take him to Africa.

Roberts explained to me: "I realized the only way he could withstand all of the pain was to make every single day a puzzle." That puzzle consumed Holman's mind with challenges and thoughts beyond his physical suffering. "He would wake up in entirely new circumstances, have to understand what was going on, and that process of deconstruction distracted him from his pain," Roberts said. "It's not that he overcame an obstacle. He lived a condition. And it gave him the courage to be original."

⁓

The starfish among us include Clif Magness, a songwriter and record producer whose career rocketed into the stratosphere in 2002, when he was in his midforties and the singer Avril Lavigne released her debut album, *Let Go*, which became one of the decade's bestsellers. Magness had produced and cowritten nearly half the tracks on the album. That put him on the radar of the folks at *American Idol*, who teamed him with some of its breakout stars, including Kelly Clarkson and Clay Aiken. He produced two of the tracks on Clarkson's debut album, *Thankful*, which came out in 2003. It was late that year that the right side of his face fell.

"It actually happened during a Clay Aiken recording session," he told me. "Very slowly, my eye started tearing while he was singing, and I thought I had an allergy or something." The next morning, he said, "I woke up with a slight droop on the right side of my face. It got progressively worse for the following week until I had complete facial paralysis on the right side of my face."

Was it a stroke? Bell's palsy? Doctors were stumped, and so began years of tests, including dozens of MRIs, along the way to the ultimate determination that a kind of skin cancer had spread near and wrapped around cranial nerves on his right side. It was strangling the nerve that controlled expression, and he soon lost the ability to smile and to blink fully. It went on to strangle the nerve involved in transmitting signals from his ear to his brain. Over the course of a year and a half, he lost all the hearing in his right ear. His business was sound, and now he was half-deaf.

Various surgeries—one in which doctors went into his head through the ear, another in which they drilled a small hole in his brow—relieved and repaired some of the damage: When Magness told me his story over a Zoom call in early 2021, I spotted no significant asymmetry or stillness in the right half of his face. The impact on his hearing, however, was permanent. He now gets all of his auditory information from his left ear alone.

But in his brain, he hears sounds from both sides of his head.

That wasn't so at the start. He remembers a night when he and his wife went out with friends to a restaurant in the Brentwood neighborhood of Los Angeles and, he said, "I became so panicked because I couldn't hear *anybody* on my right side." He couldn't hear *anything at all* from that direction. The world was aurally bisected, and the wash of sound around him utterly lopsided. He was completely disoriented, "a wreck," he confessed. He didn't know what to do.

And, it turned out, he didn't need to. Bit by bit, his lopsided world righted and balanced itself all on its own. He began to hear and be able to locate sounds coming from his right. That wasn't because that ear sprung back into action. It was because "our wonderful brain has the unimaginable gift of coping and rewiring itself to adapt to its new life," he said. His own wonderful brain figured out, from the volume and nature of the sounds coming into his left ear, which were really from the right side, and classified and flagged such distinctions so well that Magness experienced the result as if he were hearing from both ears again. He told me that in his late sixties, with only one working ear, his studio and musical skills were as good as ever,

The starfish among us include the blind photographers who exist in a large enough number, with plentiful enough output, that there are annual exhibitions devoted to them and there's a gorgeous coffee table book, *The Blind Photographer*, that was published in 2016 and is filled with their artful images. Some have learned to tell not just how close a human subject is but which way that subject's face is pointing by the nuances of the person's breathing. Some gauge the way the light is falling on an outdoor object by touching it to see where it's being warmed most and least by the sun.

The starfish among us include Stanley Wainapel, a doctor in his seventies who specializes in rehabilitation medicine in New York City and gradually went blind between his twenties and fifties, when, for a short time, he shut down, wondering about his ability to keep working and stay active. Once he got over that, he told me, "I took up a new hobby. Birding."

"Birding?" I said. "I associate that with someone looking through binoculars."

His wife, he said, does precisely that. But, he added, "A great deal of birding is done by ear. The best birders, in a thick jungle, *hear* the bird." He and his wife are a sort of sensory tag team, with her doing the intense looking and him doing the intense listening, which, he said, his blindness makes him better at. With one channel of stimuli turned off, he can tune more fixedly into another. He explained the dynamic by noting that "if a doctor is listening to a heart and they hear a very faint heart murmur, what do they do? They close their eyes."

The starfish among us include a young man I met not long after I'd disclosed and described my imperiled eyesight in the *Times*. His mother had read what I'd written and emailed me to ask if I'd talk with him. He was about to begin college at one of the country's most respected universities. Over coffee near my apartment one afternoon, he and his mother explained that from the time he was born, he had night blindness, double vision and other related problems with his eyes. But at first his parents didn't realize that anything was wrong because, even as a toddler, he did such an excellent job of compensation for these drawbacks that they weren't readily evident in his behavior. By the age of three, for example, he had memorized the physical layout and details of his home so well that at night, without light, he could navigate it as well as someone whose vision was perfect.

Despite serious deficiencies in spatial perception, he became a strong tennis player. He told me that it was hard to describe precisely how he surveyed the court and took in the action so well but that what he lacked he made up for by focusing intently on the contrast between the color of the ball and the color of its background—and between the size of the ball *against* its background—and by raptly reading his opponent's posture and tiny body movements to anticipate what he or she would do next. He could do those things better than many opponents.

I've done nothing in the league of the metamorphoses I've described, but there have been my own miniature versions of them.

I once couldn't—and I really do mean *couldn't*—listen to an audiobook, no matter how compelling it was, no matter how hard I tried, not when I was walking, not when I was driving, not when I was eating a meal, not when I was sitting on the couch with the aim of doing nothing *other* than listen to an audiobook. Within two sentences, two paragraphs or six paragraphs at most, my mind wandered. I'd become aware of a voice in my ear and realize that whatever it was saying, I'd missed much of what it had said in the minutes before, when my thoughts had drifted, even though I'd commanded them not to. This happened time and time and time again, so I accepted defeat.

But I made a fresh go of it after my stroke, figuring that if my left eye failed, audiobooks would be the only books I could manage. And maybe because I had extra motivation, or maybe because my brain had activated some emergency drill, it worked. It didn't work right away, and it didn't work for, say, Yuval Noah Harari's *Sapiens*, which was just a little too dense with anthropological arcana to be consumed by an aural amateur like me. But I read popular fiction and then literary novels with my ears, and within eighteen months, I read them at 1.3 or 1.4 or even 1.5 speeds.

I'm now resourceful and patient in ways I wasn't. I realized that on a night when I lost my iPhone in the middle of a thicket. I was out in the suburbs, visiting and caring for Dad, and I was on one of my nightly walks, when I'd catch up with friends by calling them and chatting while I wandered around. I'd use earbuds so that I could tuck the phone into my pocket.

One night, as I chatted with my friend Kerry, I decided to walk through rather than around a dense, dark cluster of trees between the path I was on and the road I wanted to get to. I hadn't noticed the cat's cradle of vines and bramble and roots on the ground and I tripped over them, falling down hard and nearly hitting my head on a huge rock. Somehow the earbuds stayed in, and I was expressing my relief about that to Kerry when I realized that with each subsequent step I took toward and then along the road, our connection grew scratchier in the exact manner that suggested a stressed-out Bluetooth link and a growing distance between earbuds and the source of the sound they were receiving.

My phone!

I felt for it in my pockets. It was gone. It had obviously fallen into the blackness of the thicket floor. How would I ever find it? That it was black and in a black case definitely wasn't going to help.

I told Kerry to hang up and call me back a few times, so I could look for the glow of the phone's face and listen for its ring as his call came in. But I saw no glow, heard no ring, maybe because I had left it on Do Not Disturb, maybe because its battery had been close to spent and now was.

Meanwhile, I walked around the thicket saying, "Hey, Siri!" over and over in the hope that *this* would prompt the phone to light up.

Nothing.

I couldn't be sure that I was walking anywhere near where the phone had fell. Until I'd noticed that it was missing, I was paying almost no attention to my precise route. I was just moving through vegetation. That was the extent of my consciousness.

I thought about returning the next morning, in daylight, but the weather forecast was for heavy rain that night and the chances, a day later, that I'd home in on the correct spot would diminish further. I thought about giving up, and I'm ashamed to say that the prior Frank—so often lazy, so frequently heedless—might have done so.

But I was mad at my sloppiness. I was even madder at my feeling of helplessness. Helplessness was what, when my stroke occurred, I feared and rebelled against. I would rebel against it now, too. I could find this phone, dammit. I *would* find this phone.

What if I retraced my steps? I didn't remember where I'd come out of the thicket, but I could probably find where I'd gone in because it was right where the path I'd been on petered out. And I knew where that path was. I circled back to it, walked to the end and told myself to relax and to follow my instincts and natural inclinations in terms of how I, traversing the thicket afresh, would get to the road just visible on the other side. Those instincts and inclinations would likely be unchanged from before.

Then I traversed. All the while, I kept my eyes—the useless one, the useful one—glued to the ground for a dark shape that, in its perfect rectangularity, couldn't be anything natural and must be my phone. I moved very, very slowly. And as I drew closer to the road, I spotted it—not the phone, not at first, but the big rock I'd noticed after I'd fallen, when I'd said a silent thanks that my head hadn't smacked against it.

The phone had to be near the rock. I surveyed the ground around it square inch by square inch, squinting, concentrating. There was something with a suspiciously even-toned darkness beneath a clump of branches or straw or whatever—I'm no ranger or botanist. But I'd found my phone. I was sure of it, and it was confirmed when I reached down and put my fingers around it.

My success probably didn't have to do with any discretely heightened brain activity, any specifically discovered talent. But there was definitely some link between my elevator soothsaying, my divot-vigilant nighttime runs in Central Park and the retrieval of my iPhone, and it was an attunement to detail that I hadn't exercised before. Maybe that was about stubborn insistence. Even so, *that* spoke to our capacity for change when change is our greatest consolation. Or our salvation.

Chapter Nine
KING LEAR HAD NOTHING TO DO WITH IT

I've been keeping something from you. I've let my story lurch ahead of a crucial development. Among the reasons that I was running in Central Park long after the sun had fallen is one that I haven't mentioned, and it also explains those nightly walks in the suburbs and why I'd head toward and through a thicket rather than stick sensibly to a trusty old sidewalk. You see, I'd fallen in love.

I suppose you could say that I *decided* to fall in love. There's a whole other book on that: whether we're genuinely swept away or essentially set ourselves up to be; whether love finds us or we stand there ready to be found, arms wide open, heart beating a welcome, a summons. I was an example of both—of someone taken aback by the swell of feeling that I experienced even as I willed that very swell. My heart needed more bounce in it. My head needed less Frank in it.

So, on a frigid night in the middle of March 2019, I paced outside a terminal at Newark Liberty International Airport and waited for my new companion to arrive. Her name was Regan, she was five years old and she weighed about fifty pounds, which I knew because the airline required various measurements and medical information, along with a kennel that met exacting specifications. I provided all of it and followed the airline's instructions and a veterinarian's advice, wanting Regan to reach me as safely, calmly and contentedly as possible. I was taking responsibility for another being and felt a profound duty to do right by her. As I'd learned in the eighteen months before her, I didn't have control over big chunks of my life. But I could determine a whole lot about her welfare. I was its *chief* determinant, a deity in flawed human form, her cyclops god. I resolved to fill her days with exercise, with adventure, with chew toys. That was my pitch to my younger brother, Harry, from whom I pried her.

Harry had adopted Regan from a border collie rescue group in suburban Los Angeles, where he lived, when she was just twelve weeks old. I'd first met her perhaps six months later. And I'd seen her about twice a year since then, when I visited L.A. for work or pleasure and stayed with him. I adored her—the completeness of her trust, the promptness of her affection, the pureness of her delight. When she first saw someone who was familiar to her but hadn't been around in a while, she grew so deliriously excited that she morphed from vertebrate to invertebrate, her body a mass of quivering gelatin, and she emitted these sounds—not quite squeaks, not quite squeals—that were the aural essence of ecstasy. People were always holding their emotions in, lest they give away too much and render themselves vulnerable. Not dogs. Not Regan. She was unguarded. Guileless.

And so pretty! Her thick, feathered fur was mostly black but had splashes of white so perfectly and symmetrically placed that a painter might well have applied them. The white on all four of her paws rose at least six inches up her legs: stockings. The white on the tip of her snout matched the white on the far plumes of her tail: parentheses. The blaze of white on her chest called to mind a medieval breastplate, while the white that fanned across her belly was the shape of a butterfly. The butterfly became visible only when she rolled over to present that belly for rubbing. She presented it often. I rubbed lots.

She had a spaniel's long snout, a lupine silhouette and a regal bearing when standing at full alert, by which I mean sizing up a squirrel. But when she was lazily shuffling or playfully squiggling around the house, her aspect was downright goofy. Part monarch, part jester: That was my Regan, a whole court in one canine.

A well-behaved court at that. Harry's wife, Sylvia, had surrendered to their four children's pleas for a puppy—in addition to the two cats already in residence—on the condition that this newcomer be trained properly, under the supervision of a professional. So Regan had been trained that way, more or less. Almost unfailingly, she sat or lay down on command. With few exceptions, she stayed put when told to and came when called. She wasn't a destructive chewer. Part of her training had been not to bite down hard and fast on people's hands, the way so many dogs do when they're being given a treat, so you sometimes had to place a bone in her mouth two or three times before she secured it tightly enough to carry it back to her doggie bed, which was her preferred domain for laying waste to it. She'd often bury it in a crease before she was done. You'd find it there days or weeks later, after she'd forgotten all about it.

She knew me as the periodic visitor to her California home who took her on long hikes. To a northeasterner like me, the trails through the canyons near Harry's neighborhood were a revelation, with unfamiliar vegetation in unusual shades of green and flashes of the mighty Pacific, so I'd choose routes that went for miles, and I'd bring along Regan and enough water for the two of us. Impossibly sure-footed, boundlessly curious, her ears swiveling like radio telescopes toward sounds I couldn't even begin to hear, her quivering nostrils reading the braille of the air, she was as riveting as the landscape. When I'd leave Harry's to head back to New York after a few days, my goodbye to her weighed heaviest of all my goodbyes because it was the realest. With her there could be no emails, no text messages, no phone calls to bridge the distance to our next time together. There was no way to say I miss you and can't wait to see you again.

I'm a dog person through and through. When I was growing up, we had a succession of dogs—a Brittany followed by two Alaskan malamutes and then a springer spaniel mix—and I doted on each of them more than any of my three siblings did. In my late twenties, for the last of the five years that I lived in the Detroit area, my romantic partner and I had a magnificent German shepherd, but when he and I broke up and I moved to Manhattan to take a job with the *Times*, I granted him his wish to keep her: I cared too much for her to insist that she trade a big suburban house and fenced backyard for a small one-bedroom apartment with no garden, no terrace, nothing. Ever since, I'd been dogless, but I'd never stopped wanting a dog.

That wanting intensified as the years passed and I gained more and more control over my schedule at the *Times*, doing the bulk of my work from home. I glanced at all the happy city dogs around me on the Upper West Side and realized how inadequately I'd appreciated the expanse of the parks, the number and nearness of dog runs, the proximity of so many canine playmates. At night, in bed, when I was too tired to continue reading anything demanding but not yet exhausted enough to fall asleep, I'd browse pet adoption listings and websites that went through the pros and cons of various breeds. I'd imagine a vizsla curled at the foot of my bed. No, a whippet. Make that a Shiba Inu—or a mix of all three! Instead of counting sheep, I'd count retrievers.

But I balked. I wavered. What would I do with the dog when I traveled? When I went out to eat, did I want to come home and, instead of melting into the couch, spring into action, leash in hand? Did I have the patience and fortitude to trudge out for walks in the dead of winter? Did Tom? He and I had this conversation frequently, almost talking ourselves into pressing the button, then talking ourselves out of it, as we resolved to get our dog at a more convenient time, a time that made more sense. It was never, ever the right time, and that's because we were being spoiled and foolish and cavalier about time itself, which is neither predictable nor elastic nor infinite. Putting off experiences often means never having them. As I moved on from my stroke with my new awareness of the future's uncertainty and the physical toll of age, I didn't want to be passive or lazy. I didn't want to put anything off.

I suppose I also wanted to fill the hole that Tom left. The apartment was too still when I had my morning coffee; the bed was too wide when I crawled under the covers at night. But his absence meant that all dog care would fall on me, or on me and whatever supplemental dog walking I could afford, and that raised the stakes of trying to find a dog that wouldn't be a significant hassle: no puppy that needed housebreaking, no older dog that was up for adoption because of behavioral issues. I'd have to be strategic, and just as I was saying that to myself, Harry mentioned that with three of his four children away at college and his tether to a job with regular office hours cut, he and Sylvia were flying around the country, and even out of the country, more than ever before. They were boarding Regan as often as every third or fourth week and sometimes for several weeks.

"Which is why," I told him, coming up with the idea only as I said it, "you should give her to me."

I compiled a list of reasons in addition to my less frequent travel. I made a case: I was a frequent runner, and Regan could come with me, burning off her energy that way. She liked to sleep on a bed, with one of her humans, and I'd let her, while Harry and Sylvia consigned her to a nook nearby. She had a cold-weather coat, and theirs was a hot-weather corner of the continent. She knew me already, so the change wouldn't be traumatic. Plus, I'd smother her in affection. They knew that about me.

They also knew that I was in need, though I didn't say that part, at least not with words, not out loud. But I'm sure it was in my voice, my eyes. In my life just then, there was a premium on comfort that didn't exist in nearly the same measure in their lives. They knew that. In the end, I think, they pitied me.

That was just fine. I could work with pity. Pity could deliver the goods as effectively as anything else. Pity delivered me Regan.

⁓

Here, again, I was a cliché, just as Danny, with Wee Man, was. Dogs were prophylactics against loneliness. Dogs were guaranteed affection. But the conventional read on dog owners like Danny and me is off, because it stresses the bid to get unconditional love. Speaking for myself—and, I'd wager, for Danny—I felt a stronger urge to give unconditional love. Although I don't think I could have sized up the dynamics accurately in real time, I'm certain in retrospect that I was looking to be the subject, not the object, of this transaction. With my physical powers in question, I wanted to flex my emotional might.

I might have flexed that through an extra, bighearted professional project with a special goal. I might have flexed it through teaching or some kind of volunteer work. Any or all of that would have been a wise response to where I was in life, because any or all of that would potentially have done for me what a pet did, what a dog did, what Regan did, which was to counter or blunt the panic and pain that a tough turn of events gave rise to. Regan took me outside of myself. I could be only so concerned with my own welfare when I had to lavish thought and energy on hers. She was the catalyst for a generosity that was at odds with, and offset, any sense of enfeeblement.

But take all of that off the table and I was still left with the gift of negotiating a new relationship with a creature whose full range of tics and talents was a revelation to me. I had plenty to learn about Regan. I was fascinated by every last bit of it.

She was so much smarter than I realized, and that became clear in two ways in particular. The first involved dog runs. She hadn't been with me even a week when I realized that every time we approached a closed gate into one of these runs, she veered toward and positioned herself at the seam where the gate opened, not where the hinges were. Every time. It wasn't that one edge of the gate looked all that much different from the other. I wasn't telegraphing the right place with my own physical movements, because she'd do this when the leash was amply extended and she was a good six feet ahead of me.

She'd do this as reliably with gates that she hadn't previously encountered as with ones that she'd gone through once or twice before. She'd do this when no other dog had entered just ahead of us, when there was no chance that she was simply mimicking its movements. She'd do this with gates that looked nothing like one another. The first five times she did this, I chalked it up to luck. But when it happened ten and then fifteen and then twenty times in a row? There was only one conclusion: She had figured out, at least visually, the fundamental architecture and mechanics of these swiveling portals and, looking at them, could predict the swivel.

My Regan: part engineer, part fashion critic. The latter was the second clue to her cleverness. Also in her first week with me, she realized that she could read her fate in my manner of dress. If she saw me putting on running shorts or sweatpants, she grew visibly excited and, with a spring in her step, followed me around, even harrumphing if I were dawdling. There was practically a dialogue balloon above her head: "We're going on a walk! A walk, a walk, a walk! Hurry up, Dad!"

But if she saw me putting on a dress shirt, slacks and a jacket, it was a different story. A dark one. She understood that I was about to commit treason—I was going to *leave her alone*—and she responded accordingly. She took a position in or just outside my bedroom, where I dressed. She stood there rigidly and glared at me, her amber eyes beacons of accusation and desperation. Then she disappeared, and where I invariably found her, minutes later, as I attempted to make my exit, was stretched on the floor across the breadth of the front door and pressed tight against it, a canine barricade.

Maybe this was her last-ditch pitch: "Take me with you." Maybe a guilt trip: "If you're going to hurt me this way, you're going to have to step over me to do it." I never did have to step over her, because her desire to make me feel bad ended at the possibility of making me mad. In the final seconds, as I drew closer to the door and reached for the knob, she moved out of the way.

But what an actress she was! In California she had lived with two cats, and while neither had shown her much affection, she had apparently grown accustomed to them, and missed them, so whenever we came near a cat on the street in Manhattan or in Central Park, she put on a performance that turned heads, stopped passersby in their tracks and mortified me. I should pause here to assure any baffled or doubting reader that, yes, there *are* cats out and about in the city, and I don't mean strays. I mean pets. You don't see a lot of them, but you do see a few: cats being carried by owners who are perhaps taking them to the pet store or the vet but are probably just showing them off; cats in the laps of people chilling on the front stoops of brownstones; cats on leashes, which the cats in question seem to find as bizarre as I did; cats being wheeled through the park in those baby strollers with zipped mesh covers over them. Regan crossed paths with enough of the latter group that, for a while, she associated *all* strollers—and, for that matter, all large wheeled luggage with the approximate dimensions of strollers—with cats, which meant that she strained hard on her leash to try to inspect the cargo for feline treasure.

But the straining was nothing next to the whimpering, the crying, the *keening* when she had a verified cat sighting. She wanted contact with that cat, and as it became clearer and clearer to her that I wasn't going to allow that, the sounds she made rose in volume and changed in nature to those that you associate not with emotional distress but with physical agony. They were screeches in the end.

What would happen if I let her at a cat? I nervously tested this in a pet store in my neighborhood that she tugged me toward because of its resident feline, Parker. I let her nearer and nearer and nearer Parker, until their noses were touching, at which point Regan, who'd fallen silent, was apparently so overcome with emotion that she jerked backward several inches and began crying anew. Then she turned away and trotted down an aisle of specialty dog food, doing an olfactory appraisal of each fancy package in her path. She glanced backward but forged onward. She wanted something from Parker—from all these cats—that she couldn't get or define.

Or maybe she just enjoyed her own histrionics. That was my thought after an unrelated episode in Central Park when one of three dogs with whom she was playing turned violent and there was snarling and yelping all around. Regan limped away from the tangle, seemingly unable to use or put any pressure on her left front leg, which she held several inches above the ground. By the time I got to her, two other dog parents had rushed over as well, alarmed by the sight of her and eager to help. She crumpled to the pavement, rolled onto her back and whimpered pitiably as the three of us stroked her and inspected and reinspected the leg for this awful injury that was causing such pain. We were still in search of the fugitive wound when her ears twitched, her head popped up and—*woosh!*—she darted toward a nearby fence, leapt over it and nearly caught the squirrel on the other side before it scampered up a tree. The crying was over. The limp was gone, never to return. Give Regan an Oscar.

Pretty much every one of Regan's days began and ended in Central Park, where we typically spent seventy-five to ninety minutes before 9:00 a.m. and another sixty to seventy-five minutes after 9:00 p.m. Those were the times when reasonably well-behaved dogs could be off leash, so I tried to take advantage of them. Her behavior met the laxly monitored and loosely enforced criteria, though it wasn't without flaw. She never charged strangers, never jumped on them or nosed them or slobbered on them, the way many a friendly but overexuberant dog did.

But if someone had a furry charge under foot, deep pockets, a hand in one of them and a faintly meaty scent, she introduced herself, sitting by the person's side with her body still, her head tilted up and her eyes brimming with transactional regard. She saw park humans in baggy coats as PEZ dispensers, ejecting treats, and experience proved her right. She got treat after treat after treat, along with compliments along the lines of, "How can I resist such a pretty, patient girl?" Fortune smiles on the beautiful, and if a beauty has good manners to boot? Fortune beams.

Apart from the occasional squirrel chase, Regan never strayed more than about fifty feet from me and usually stayed closer than that. She had to make sure I didn't get away. If she did lose track of me, maybe because she'd been absorbed in a game of tug-of-war with an especially pulchritudinous pinscher, her eyes widened, her body jittered and her head twisted this way and that. When she spotted me at last, she raced toward and hurled herself at me with an expression that signaled the blessed restoration of all warmth and safety in a world that had gone briefly terrifying. She was a cartoon of gratitude, a lampoon of relief, and I somehow always imagined her bounding back to me in slow motion, to a soundtrack of the Peaches & Herb classic "Reunited." There was one perfect fit, and Regan and I were it.

OK, not perfect, but close enough. We didn't do so well with the running; she chafed at the forced pace and monotony of it, of not being able to stop and smell the hydrants and lampposts and tree trunks, which I came to understand as the doggie internet, each piddle deposited on them an email or a tweet.

Fetching, too, wasn't a strong suit of hers. Toward the beginning of an off-leash walk, I'd take a ball out of my pocket and she'd do a little jig, poised for me to throw it and her to chase it. But from that moment on, all bets were off. Maybe she just watched the ball sail into the distance. Maybe she shot like a bullet to it and brought it back. Maybe she got halfway there and rerouted to inspect the underside of a nearby German shepherd. Maybe she reached the ball and picked it up but then decided to carry it *forward*, away from me, to our next patch of park. Maybe she dropped it accidentally in some sewer or murky crevasse into which no human hand would dare reach. You just never, ever knew.

I learned that I could improve our fetching odds in two ways. One was to use a squeaky ball—the kind that made a sound somewhere between a chirp and a yowl when a dog's jaws pressed on it—and to throw it for her when other dogs were around and would also pursue it. She liked to beat them to it, or at least to try, and when she succeeded, she pranced in triumph, taunting the losers by biting into the ball harder and harder at ever-accelerating intervals: squeak, *squeak, SQUEAK, SQUEAK!* She was exultant. Obnoxious. Adorable.

The other fetching aid was to throw the ball over a two-foot or three-foot fence, which she then had to clear. She liked *that* challenge, too. If I threw the ball over a succession of such fences, so that she was essentially running hurdles, the fetching odds grew better still. She basked in her own athleticism. She enjoyed showing off.

But was I anthropomorphizing? Not just about her mind-set when it came to fetching but about all her moods? Possible. There's fierce debate about whether we give dogs too little credit or too much, whether our analyses of them are more projection than observation. But I was sure of a few things about Regan, including that she experienced pride or some four-legged facsimile of it.

That had to be why, even when she and I weren't playing fetch, she'd occasionally divert from our route simply to fly over the top of a nearby fence and then to soar back. She obviously enjoyed the feeling of being up in the air, and maybe there was a delicious tingle of transgression in defying the boundary that the fence represented to explore, if only for a few seconds, what was on the other side. But why did she usually catch my eye just before the jump and then look my way again just after? It was an invitation to marvel. A boast. "Look at me. Look at what I can do."

So I looked. And marveled—not just at her aerial feat and nutty disposition but at how happy this one stupid moment could make me, how totally and completely happy, how I could curl up within it and gather it around me and forget whatever miasma of frustration and fear existed outside of it, how this discreet space was there for the taking and always had been. It didn't require a dog. It didn't require a fence. It required attention, openness, humility. It required the recognition that something small could be enough, that something ordinary could be extraordinary. Without therapy or thought, Regan reveled in being alive. That helped me do the same.

In 2020, after the coronavirus pandemic hit, the number of dogs on the Upper West Side seemed to swell, an infusion of newcomers making up for the ones that had followed their owners out of the city. On every walk, Regan and I ran into a fresh face, by which I mean the furry one on her level, pressing its snout to some part of her. A golden retriever puppy from a fancy breeder here. A full-grown Labrador mix from a rescue organization there. "Sit!" "Stay!" "Come!" *"Come!"* All the city was an obedience school.

"Pet adoption became an obsession in the time of COVID," Nick Paumgarten wrote in a June 2021 article in the *New Yorker* titled "What Will Become of the Pandemic Pets?"

"Veterinarians were slammed," he added. "Petco's sales rose by 11 percent, Chewy's by 47 percent, and Morgan Stanley has predicted that the pet-care industry will almost triple in size in the next decade." Paumgarten reported that his canvas of rescue and adoption organizations actually challenged the notion that the *number* of pets being adopted had risen significantly, but there was no doubt, he wrote, that the fascination with pets had intensified, along with the attachment to them.

"The pandemic pet boom seems mainly to be one of increasing attention," he explained, noting that it had given rise to a new magnitude and pervasiveness of "helicopter petting," with pet owners fixating "on every lump or limp, to say nothing of the hour-to-hour mood swings." But why? What about a lethal contagion put people in mind of kennels and kibble and fur?

Some answers were obvious. Confined to their apartments by government edict or personal avoidance of risk, people wanted a legitimate excuse to venture outside, a motivation to stay there, a counter to isolation. A dog and all that was necessary to take care of it provided that. Plus, arguments against having a dog—it would grow lonely, bored, restless and maybe destructive when you were in the office; you'd have to spend a fortune on dog walkers so that it got a midday bathroom break—vaporized. Nobody was going into the office. Everyone was home midday. If you'd worried about the vigilance and constant presence required for speedy housebreaking, well, you were now in a position to be vigilant and present as never before.

A new dog was also an agent of connection: not just between you and it but between you and all the other dog owners on the sidewalk and in the dog run and on the most densely dog-populated slopes of the parks. Your dog trotted over to check out someone else's and you ended up in a conversation with that dog's owner that wouldn't have happened any other way. You could have that talk at a distance of six feet, through the fabric or paper of a mask, and feel safer than in a restaurant or shop because no interior space had ventilation comparable to Mother Nature's. You came closer to normalcy, and to courtesy, than the pandemic otherwise permitted you to. Dogs were bridges. Dogs *are* bridges.

Well before the pandemic, I was fascinated and amused by how I would use Regan or other people would use their dogs as icebreakers and alter egos, funneling our social desires through them, summoning a nonexistent extroversion by outsourcing it to them.

"Can he come over and say hello?" a woman with a goldendoodle would ask as her dog did or didn't show interest in Regan—the dog's interest was beside the point. That became clear when the woman advanced and began to talk about the lousy weather or the terrible mayor or how many hours she'd been working lately and didn't even notice that her dog and Regan had twisted around each other so that their entwined leashes were essentially immobilizing them and they looked like big fish trapped in a net.

I was just as bad. I'd talk to Regan as a way of really talking to some cute man in the vicinity, using my comments to her as advertisements about me.

"You're not sure what to make of *this* many dogs, are you, because you're usually in the park much earlier in the morning or later at night," I'd ostensibly say to Regan but really say to the guy playing with his beagle on a field where dogs clustered. It was my way of establishing—*declaring*—what a diligent dog dad I was. "It's OK, sweetie. Go make some friends." Was the beagle's owner taking adequate note of my nurturing nature? Was my use of Regan as a wingman paying off?

Beyond that kind of situation, was she a boost to my well-being? Are all dogs, in general? There has been some scientific research into this, and it's contradictory and inconclusive. Certainly, an aging person who takes charge of a dog that needs multiple walks a day is improving his or her cardiovascular health. But beyond that?

Harold Herzog, a psychology professor at Western Carolina University who has examined and written about people's relationships with their pets, avoids sweeping verdicts, but, in an article on CNN.com by Sandee LaMotte, said, "Studies have shown repeatedly that people's good mood increases and bad mood decreases around pets, and so we know that there's immediate short term benefits, physiological and psychological, with interacting with pets. I have no doubt about that." That's why dogs are brought into senior centers, children's hospitals and the like. They add a lilt. They provide a spark.

But it doesn't necessarily endure, not according to the science. In the same CNN.com article, Megan Mueller, the co-director of the Tufts Institute for Human-Animal Interaction, said: "A lot of us who have pets think, 'Oh, they must be sort of uniformly good for us.'" But, she added, the truth is "a little bit more complicated," so she rejects the question of whether pets are good for us. A better question, she said, is "Who are pets good for? Under what circumstances?"

The pandemic: That was the right circumstance, but not just because dogs lifted moods that needed lifting and promoted mingling when mingling was rationed and proscribed. Dogs suited locked-down, cut-off people who were riding out a public health crisis for the same reasons that Regan suited an aging, frightened man who might or might not go blind. They were an injection of color and an amplification of vitality in lives primed or yearning for both.

Sure, they were trouble—they got sick, they shed, they dragged dirt onto carpeting and furniture, they demanded all those walks—but even that trouble filled days that could otherwise be too empty, adding noise where there was too much silence, motion where there was too much stillness. And mess was a kind of bounty. A life entirely resistant to it was an overly timid, excessively controlled affair.

Besides, I learned from Regan. I did. I know how dopey and Disney that will sound to some of you, and I'm by no means saying that she taught me or reminded me of things that nothing or no one else could have. I'm saying that she taught me or reminded me of things that I needed to be taught and reminded of.

I already hinted at one, when I described her elation in the air as she leapt over a fence. Dogs have a talent for joy that most people, including me, don't. When they're feeling triumphant or having fun or basking in comfort, it's unalloyed. It's total. There's no competing thought about some potential stress looming an hour later, no complicating flashback to an annoyance an hour before. Yes, this falls at least partly if not fully into the category of ignorance being bliss, but it's an example nonetheless, and a terrific one at that. It's still worth emulating.

Dogs have a talent for minimalism, too. What did Regan need to be content? The proximity of another being who felt warmly toward her and communicated that. Occasional visits, for lack of a better word, with like-minded (by which I mean like-pawed) creatures. Basic meals that came along in rough sync with her hunger. Routine, because its antonym is chaos. The temperature, padding and peace necessary for many hours of deep, uninterrupted sleep.

We humans obviously need more than that—Netflix, a Nespresso machine and a good moisturizer come to mind—but we get carried away, and I'd watch Regan and feel myself pulled back toward a less extravagant menu of wants, toward a saner set of demands. Basic meals at hunger-staving intervals, visits with fellow members of our species and many hours of deep, uninterrupted sleep really do go a long way. Much else is gravy.

More than anything, dogs, at least some dogs, have a talent for making do. I'd throw Regan in the back seat of a rental car and she'd be slightly agitated for all of two minutes, no doubt questioning why she was suddenly in this unfamiliar vessel and where it was taking her. But then she'd accept her lot. She'd stretch her body into the most pleasurable position for a nap and let the car, like a cradle, rock her to sleep.

The first time we went outside after a full-scale blizzard and her legs sank eight inches into the snow, she froze for about twenty seconds, utterly baffled. Then she unfroze. Whatever madness this was, whatever confusion she felt, she had to get to the park, so she trudged forward as best possible, moving a bit faster with every few steps. Just minutes later, her disorientation had been supplanted entirely by her determination. Faced with an unexpected and unsettling situation, she dealt with it, because the alternative, unacceptable, was to be stuck in place forever. Dogs didn't get stuck. At that, people excelled.

Early in life I mastered the art of making and breaking resolutions, not just when the New Year started but every week if not every day. I abandoned diets, failed to crack open books that I'd sworn I'd read, didn't visit the out-of-town friend who'd gone much too long without my attention, minted excuses and kicked the can so far down the road that it ended up in a different time zone. It's not that I was cavalier. It's that I was weak. But I kept my promises to Regan, promises that she obviously didn't even know I'd made.

At least three hours of outdoor exercise a day: That was the bar, the goal, what I'd decided was the minimum diversion necessary for a dog spending most of her time in a two-bedroom apartment too high above street level for her to watch the passing parade. I outsourced forty-five minutes of that in the early afternoon to a dog-walking service, but the rest was on me, and to keep track and hold myself accountable, I put a gadget on her collar that primarily served as a GPS tracking device, in case she got lost, but also functioned as a Fitbit, logging the miles that Regan accrued and the minutes that she was in vigorous motion every day. I could see if she passed 180. Most days, she passed 200. And once that became her routine, that became her expectation. I noticed that she grew antsy on the rare day when, say, we barely passed 150.

But just two months after she arrived, my commitment ran smack up against my rickety body, to which something mysterious happened. My right shin swelled, reddened and turned so tender that it hurt, badly, when I put weight on it, which meant when I walked (or, for that matter, stood). Every step was a stab. Was it possible to sprain or break a bone without noticing the injury in real time? If not, what the hell was going on? I planned to wait it out, but my friend Elli hauled me to an urgent care center, where I was told that I probably had a bad skin infection, of unknown origin, that was inflaming everything around it. The doctor prescribed antibiotics, which, she said, should take care of the swelling and pain—in *three to seven days*. Meanwhile, Regan needed to be walked.

So I walked her. I winced as I did it. I figured out a pace and a manner of placing my right foot on the ground that lessened the pain, from which I forcefully diverted my thoughts. And I kept moving. There was no other choice, at least none acceptable to me. I couldn't reasonably afford the extravagance of having the dog-walking service pick up two or three walks every day, besides which, Regan's leashless walks with me at morning and night were our quality time. So, for about four days, I limped and winced, winced and limped, laughing inwardly at the joke and spectacle of me, a man whose left half functioned perfectly well but whose right half—bum eye, bum leg—was a disaster.

Like I said, I was resolved to do right by Regan. I was focused much more on how well I was loving her than on how well she was loving me, and I wouldn't have predicted that, couldn't have foreseen how satisfying, even sustaining, it would be to figure out the riddle of healthy food that suited her sometimes finicky appetite; to whisk her to the vet when her bowels were acting up and get her relief from the stress of that; to find a hiking trail that invigorated her more than others had; to see her sleeping peacefully for hours on end in a dog bed that I had clearly chosen well and put in the right place. Before Regan, I'd been puzzled by how gaga some owners could be about dogs who had all sorts of problems and unpleasantness, but that was because I was all wrong in the way I evaluated these relationships, which weren't about what ready-made bundles of joy the dogs were.

No, they were acts of devotion. I don't have any science on this, and I suspect that a study along these lines would be impossible or prohibitively expensive, what with the brain imaging and all, but I bet that we're flooded with more serotonin or dopamine or endorphins or all of the above when we say "I love you" than when we hear it. No words are more exhilarating, no declaration more ennobling.

In dog runs, Regan cavorted only briefly with her peers, then came to whichever bench I occupied and, like a car backing into a parking space, wedged her rear between my legs. She liked to survey the action from the safety of that clamp, head swiveling in an unrushed fashion to the left, then to the right, then back again. I could feel her calm. I could sense her contentment. I combed her fur with my fingers. "I love you," I whispered.

In the morning, at home, she stayed in the bedroom long after I got up to make myself coffee and hop online. She knew that there was nothing for her in the sound of my tap-tap-tapping on a computer keyboard, no reason to rouse herself until she heard the zipping of a coat or the jangle of keys. I went back into the bedroom to grab a book I'd left on the nightstand and saw that she'd moved herself upward—given herself a kind of promotion—from the foot of the bed to the pillows that I'd abandoned and had her head on one, her left paw draped over another. Noticing me noticing her, she wagged her tail extra fast, which she did whenever she was asking me, begging me, willing me, not to be upset with her. Silly girl. A few strands of dog fur on the sheets weren't worth worrying about. I leaned over. I kissed the top of her head. "You know how much I love you, don't you?" I said. Her eyes fluttered shut in response.

Just for fun, I did one of those doggie DNA tests. She didn't look to me like she was all border collie, and I wondered what else was in her. I swabbed the inside of her mouth, sent the sample to a laboratory and got the results a few weeks later: She had *no* border collie in her. Half of her was Australian shepherd, about a fifth of her was Siberian husky and the rest was little bits of boxer and old English sheep dog and Staffordshire terrier and pit bull and "super mutt," which means the laboratory couldn't tell. "You're a big genetic mess," I told her, as her ears perked and her head titled sideways. "But I love you."

People asked me: "Why the name 'Regan'? Are you a *King Lear* fan?" Yes, I answered, but if Shakespeare had been the inspiration, I'd hardly have gone with one of Lear's two faithless daughters. I'd have gone with the faithful Cordelia. Regan's name came from Harry's kids, who simply liked the sound of it. But that's not what I told people. I told them she was named for the little girl in *The Exorcist*, on account of the demonic sounds she made when tousling with other dogs. They were scary, ugly, otherworldly—and they made me and anyone else who heard them cringe. "I'm going to bathe you in holy water," I told her, "but only because I love you."

And it was because I loved her that, during another one of those extremely rare instances in the park when she fought with another dog, I instinctively reached in to separate the two and keep her safe. The other dog's teeth ended up in my right hand, which bled. That dog's owner blurted out "sorry!" upon "sorry!"—it was her dog that had started the fight—and was so thrown by the whole thing that she was on the verge of tears.

"It's OK," I reassured her. "You couldn't have known. You didn't mean for it to happen." I said that because it was almost certainly true, or probably true, or maybe true; because there wasn't that much blood; because I wasn't going to need stitches; and because the damage was done. Stewing over it, fuming about it and assigning blame would just prolong the awkwardness for both of us.

Also, I had no idea, none at all, what her sandwich board would say.

"It's OK," I again insisted as my hand throbbed and as I pondered, in that odd and tense moment, whether I was possibly a bigger person than I'd once been, a better one, and if Regan got some small share of the credit for that. "Really, it's going to be all right."

Chapter Ten
WHEN IT RAINED EGGSHELLS

My favorite spot in Central Park is Summit Rock. It's on the park's west side—between West Eighty-Third and West Eighty-Fourth Streets—and it's touted as the park's highest natural elevation, though I think that some of the crests in the North Woods, which are just below 110th Street, have legitimate quibble with that. Also, Belvedere Castle, between the Delacorte Theater and one edge of the Ramble, reaches higher into the sky, but it's man-made so apparently doesn't count. It's also crowded. I've never known Summit Rock to be.

I'd never known Summit Rock, period, before Regan entered my life. I'd known of Belvedere Castle—it's impossible to be anywhere near it without spotting it, the way it's impossible to bop around Athens and not get regular glimpses of the Parthenon—but I'd never taken the time to climb the stone staircase up to it and check out the views of the city from there.

I'd never walked into the Ramble, though it's smack-dab in the middle of the park, a quasi island whose forested slopes end at or near various curves of the park's main lake. And in all the years that I'd run the interior six-mile loop of the park, I'd never noticed that the North Woods, which that loop skirts, has walking trails into it, so I didn't realize that they lead in one place to a gurgling waterfall tucked into a ravine that takes you so far away from the scrum and steel of Manhattan that you forget the city is even there. With Regan I caught up on the castle and the Ramble and the waterfall. I luxuriated in all of it.

As for Summit Rock, well, on a clear day, in the right spot, you can look to the west and get a glimpse not just of the Hudson River but also of New Jersey on the other bank. You can watch the sun sink, in a blaze of reds and pinks and purples, below the horizon. Do a 180-degree turn and the lights in the buildings on the Upper East Side of Manhattan twinkle ever brighter in the gathering night, as the treetops at your feet turn from a green, undulating carpet to a formless blanket of darkness. It's a show that never goes on hiatus, a theater that never disappoints.

In autumn, that carpet of trees to the east is yellow, orange and crimson. In winter, it's gone, replaced by a lattice of leafless, skeletal branches, but there's a gift in this: The wall of trees that hugs the southern edge of Summit Rock now has enormous gaps in it, through which Midtown's mammoth skyscrapers—slender monoliths that soar over seventy stories, over eighty stories, over ninety stories—magically appear. It's as if a veil has dropped or a curtain parted to reveal a scene of urban majesty almost without rival.

All of this was just minutes on foot from my apartment. All of this was just there for the taking. And yet I hadn't taken it. I had zipped into the park for exercise and stayed on that one loop, amid the hordes of bicyclists and other runners, or I had walked in a straight line to and from the Delacorte for performances of Shakespeare in the Park, or I had peeked at a few patches of the park as a taxi sped me along one of the sunken transverse roads that connect the Upper West and Upper East Sides. But I hadn't explored the park, hadn't comprehended its bounty: all the thickets, all the meadows, all the rises, all the dips, all the plazas, all the monuments, all the nooks, all the crannies.

Within six months of welcoming Regan, that changed. Within a year, I knew Central Park exhaustively and intimately: You could have dropped me anywhere in those 843 acres, which form a half-mile-wide rectangle that stretches the two and a half miles from 59th to 110th Streets, and I would have been able to tell you where I was and to chart the course from there to any other spot in the park. I knew that the park, like a person, has moods, only it has more of them and almost all are good. They change with the season, the weather, the hour, the particular hue of light and the number of New Yorkers and tourists exercising, loafing, playing music or walking their own Regans. The park can speed your heartbeat or slow it. It can put energy into you or leach the stress out of you. It's a need-activated, mission-targeted medicine.

I knew all the best vantage points, not just Summit Rock and Belvedere Castle but also a tiny, easily missed dirt clearing in the southwestern corner of the Ramble with two wooden benches so spare and rough-hewn that they look like pretzeled reconfigurations of the smaller trees and larger shrubs around them. The clearing's far edge is the lake, and directly across the water, perfectly framed, are the ornate stone towers of the San Remo, built in 1930, one of Central Park West's most coveted addresses. To see it up close, from the sidewalk, is to see only pieces and patches of it because like so many of New York City's gems, it's wedged among all the buildings around it. But from the Ramble, all but its lowest floors are visible. In the early morning, when the sun rises just high enough in the east to clear the park's tallest trees and cast its rays on the San Remo, it turns from faint gray to light gold. It glows.

I knew that an especially broad stretch of Central Park West's most beautiful residences can be glimpsed from a lightly trafficked and (at night) unlit path that traces the southern border of Sheep Meadow, the improbably expansive lawn so popular in warm weather with picnickers and sunbathers. I knew that alongside the Central Park Zoo there's a broad walkway open to the public—no admission fee required—that allows you to peek at the seals doing laps in their doughnut-shaped pool and chilling out on the rocks in the hole of the doughnut. I knew that just north of the zoo, several hundred feet up a steep hill, is a gazebo-esque structure aptly identified on detailed park maps as "A Treehouse for Dreaming." Only partly detectable from below, it lifts you maybe a quarter of the way up the nearby skyscrapers, which seem almost within your fingers' touch.

But my point isn't the wondrousness of Central Park, amply chronicled by others. It's that there was a splendor in my immediate world that I'd been too preoccupied and distracted and even lazy to notice. Central Park was the perfect symbol of that: public by definition, free to all, overlooked by so many people precisely because it was too available to be eventful, too accessible to be precious, something to be enjoyed another day, a better fit for tomorrow's or next week's or next month's schedule.

How many of us really investigate our towns or neighborhoods for the most spirit-stirring patches of greenery or fillips of design? How many of us know where people regularly gather, what they do and whether it might be invigorating or reassuring or at least modestly diverting to be among them? How many of us tune into changes in weather and shifts in light not because we want to know whether to wear a jacket, put on sunglasses or carry an umbrella but because this infinite variety is fascinating and mesmerizing in and of itself?

How many of us pay heed? I started to, and so I observed, on one late-autumn night when I took Regan into the park, that there were as many leaves on the ground as on the trees, and that they formed a magic carpet: crackling underfoot, releasing a perfume like no other. The same gusts that had brought some of them tumbling down tickled those that remained tethered to their branches. They sounded as if they were giggling. I vaguely remembered this music from the past, when I had listened to it so much less closely, and it reassured me. There were phenomena a person could count on. The changing of the seasons was one of them.

I'm romanticizing Central Park. I concede that. I'm editing out the rats, populous on many summer nights, when trash from the swell of people who revel there on hot days spills over the garbage cans onto the asphalt around them. I'm editing out that refuse, collected less quickly than it should be. I'm editing out the color of all the water, which is black at its comeliest and an algae-slicked, sickly green at its scariest.

But none of that competes with the miraculous existence of the park in the first place, with its enduring defiance of the concrete pressing in on it from all four sides, with this burst of nature where nature doesn't seem to have any business. And nature, well, there's no greater source of inadequately noticed, insufficiently relished splendor. There's nothing that we smug and wayward humans more shamefully take for granted. And there's no better balm.

I thought about that whenever I ventured to Westchester County, just outside New York City, to visit Dad and, with Regan, began exploring the nature trails near his house. I thought about that when I went to stay with my friends Joel and Nicole in Sag Harbor, New York, on the eastern stretches of Long Island, and did a sampling of parks within a short drive. The forest in Cedar Point County Park ends at a meandering beach on a bay, so that after walking a mile or two through the woods, Regan and I could walk several more along the water, going all the way to the tip of a peninsula of dunes and tall sea grasses and then back.

Sometimes I had those internal dialogues that I described before, my versions of prayer, but the content was changing, evolving, a marker of my own movement and growth. I less often pleaded for strength and more often marveled at its presence in me and how I might honor and preserve it. These silent conversations made me feel rooted, grounded, less easily toppled by the whims and winds of circumstance. I would say as much to Regan, even out loud, and I'd convince myself that the Rorschach of her gaze was agreement.

Sometimes I sang as we walked. I'd always been a secret singer, belting out tunes when driving down the open highway, but with an emphasis on "secret": I stopped whenever someone pulled up next to me, as if I'd been doing something wicked. And even now, I sang only if, as best I could tell, there was no one within earshot. But I knew, obviously, that there might be someone just around the bend or on the other side of the trees. I occasionally got nabbed. So what? I would suffer much worse embarrassments in this life than having someone catch me mid-chorus in Amy Winehouse's "Back to Black."

Or having someone hear me belt out the climax of "Sisters of the Moon." One of Stevie Nicks's songs on the Fleetwood Mac album *Tusk*, it both nods and contributes to her witchy, mystical image, and it played on my iPhone, through my earbuds, one night in late winter when Regan and I went into the park around 10:00 p.m. and had it almost to ourselves. A patchy and wet mist had settled over Manhattan; I could feel it on my cheeks, even taste it on my tongue, and it obscured the middles of the Midtown skyscrapers, so that their upper stories floated in space, swimmy ribbons of light seemingly disconnected from anything below them. I sang along with Stevie but then hit pause, because apart from the music, there was near silence, so precious in this frenzied city, and I didn't want to miss it. No sirens. No shouting. Nothing. I could hear the fall of one of my feet in a shallow puddle. I could hear Regan's panting.

She was a few dozen feet ahead of me. Many other city dogs wore illuminated collars at night, but Regan didn't need one. She could be tracked by her white stockings, which moved like pistons in the darkness. She slalomed this way and that, and I restarted the music and resumed my singing, and there was no one, at least as far as I could tell, to cordon us off or rein us in.

"Sisters of the Moon" gave way to "Angel," another of Stevie's songs, with a recurring line that was characteristically cryptic but clear to me at that moment. Stevie and I sang it together: "So I close my eyes softly till I become that part of the wind that we all long for sometimes." This music. This park. This mist. This wind. Eyes closed or eyes open, I was indeed a part of it, and I wanted for nothing just then.

This fresh appreciation of the bounty in my life wasn't confined to the outdoors. I remember walking through my apartment one day, studying the bookshelves and roughly calculating how many of the hundreds, maybe thousands, of volumes I hadn't read or hadn't finished. The answer was at least a third of them. And they were books that I'd wanted to read, books that I *still* wanted to read; they just hadn't become urgent enough priorities before another book caught my eye, called my name and crowded them out. I could end my acquisition of books then and there and have more than enough to read, because if I managed to get through all that I hadn't, I could circle back to books

I'd finished and loved decades ago and could barely remember. My life wasn't just stuffed but overstuffed, at least if I took a proper inventory of it. The unread books were a metaphor.

Beyond the bounty, I experienced and refined a new ability to identify and amplify discrete moments that warranted a pause and were worth savoring. I ritualized the ones that could be ritualized, like cocktail hour. I didn't observe it every day or even every other day. It wasn't a specific and unchanging hour. And it wasn't necessarily devoted to cocktails; more often, I had white wine, and on occasion even an Aperol spritz, no matter how much derision this combination of prosecco, Aperol and club soda had come in for, because you know what? It's the color of a sunset and it's delicious.

Whenever I indulged in cocktail hour, whether it happened at seven thirty (p.m., *of course*) or six thirty (why not?) or five thirty (on *exceedingly* rare occasions), I tried to be unhurried about it—"mindful" would be the more fashionable word—and to ace the details: a wineglass whose contours delighted me; a highball glass that felt good in my grip; a bit of recreational reading I'd been looking forward to; a phone conversation I knew I'd enjoy; the actual company of someone whom I loved spending time with as opposed to someone whom I felt obliged to see. The drink, too, would be one that could be relied on, one that guaranteed me pleasure. Maybe once a week I'd allow myself a martini (or two) because I enjoyed the fetishistic making of it, the *shaking* of it, and few if any other cocktails delivered a first sip that crashed through me in one shivering wave. There was nothing like a martini to blunt the day and polish the night.

Bounty, moments: If not those words, those ideas came up

again and again when I communicated with people whose lives had taken an anxiety-making or confidence-shattering turn, who were visited by reminders of fragility or thoughts of mortality that hadn't been there before. I communicated with many of them: When you open yourself up the way I had by writing about the damage and threat to my eyesight, you find that the world opens up to you, your own admission of vulnerability teasing out similar confessions from others, your own journey validated by the ones being shared with you.

That was one of my friend Dorrie's formidable talents. My God, what Parkinson's had put her through: the shakes, the falls, the twisting of parts of her face and body, the brain surgery, the implanting of a version of jumper cables inside her, the fine-tuning of how much of a charge to have those cables deliver to her brain, the periodic changing of the cables' subcutaneous battery, the open frustration of family members who sometimes couldn't easily make out what she was saying with a voice whose volume had been muffled by the disease. And my God, how she clung to sunshine, with a strategy of tallying her blessings, not her slights.

I don't mean to make her into a saint or a rube whose bliss comes from ignorance about what she's confronting and what has been taken from her. She gets it. And she told me that in the early stages of Parkinson's, she went through episodes of pure rage, captured in a bizarre habit that she hid from her husband, Eric. "I secretly kept my 'banging pot' when we lived in Norfolk, Virginia," she explained in one of her long emails to me. "Whenever I felt self-pity or anger or just was overwhelmed in general, I would go into the backyard (Eric was never around when I did this) and I would pound the ground with that pot. It felt great. I think it made me a better wife and mother and person in general. Instead of burdening others with my issues or snapping at my husband, I had a piece of well-tenderized earth and a bent pot." When Dorrie and Eric relocated to a new city and new house at one point, they hired movers, who indiscriminately threw anything and everything into boxes. Eric later emptied the one with the strangely misshapen, almost mangled pot. He held it up, stared at it for a while and then groused to Dorrie: "The movers really did a number on that, huh?"

But banging was the exception for Dorrie. Banging made its opposite possible. And its opposite is what I get in most of the emails and Facebook messages she sends me. Here's spontaneous Dorrie, referring first to a trivia contest and then to Amazon's virtual assistant: "Funny things that happened today—I won HQ! Me and 2,500 (give or take) others split over $100,000 in prize money. Everyone won $40. It was definitely the thrill of the win. We have also been yelling at Alexa all day. I think the beginning of the AI revolution is nigh. I asked Alexa to play Marky Mark and the Funky Bunch. Response: 'I can't find anything on flatulence.' Either I was having a real Hal moment or Amazon pre-programmed commentary on my musical choices."

When she and Eric were passing through New York one weekend in 2019, I joined them for brunch about ten blocks from my apartment. Afterward, Dorrie, a dog lover, asked if she could come back to my apartment and meet Regan. She'd seen pictures of her and was smitten. Eric wasn't keen on the idea, and I quickly understood why. The walk was tough on

Dorrie, who wasn't having her easiest day and indeed fell hard on the street as we crossed one intersection. But she got up. She laughed. She kept going. And then she ran her hands through Regan's fur, a gesture that obviously gave her every bit as much pleasure as she expected it to. Dorrie knows where a day's slivers of happiness lie. And she moves, however arrhythmically, toward them.

She wrote to me at one point that she refuses to be "mired in what I don't have. My philosophy is live each day the best that you can. One day my meds might be off or I wake up super stiff or it just sucks in general for whatever reason. The day will pass. Everyone—diseased or not—has days that suck."

That's how Eric DeVos also talks. He's another member of my ad hoc community of post-stroke acquaintances who know or knew the fear of going blind, a retired New Jersey man who, a decade ago, around the age of sixty, experienced what I did: the sudden glazing of vision in his right eye. In his case, though, it wasn't NAION; it was meningioma, a benign tumor in his brain that was pressing on the optic nerve behind that eye. Doctors told him that he could leave the tumor alone—it wouldn't kill him—and that taking it out entailed the risks of any surgery in general and of brain surgery in particular. But the tumor would grow, eventually destroying the vision in both of his eyes. That wasn't a possibility. It was a certainty.

He told them to operate. To get at the tumor, they opened a flap of his skull above his right eye. The procedure lasted more than six hours. He woke up with a terrible headache. But the tumor's removal restored clear sight in his right eye and eliminated the threat to his left one.

He was different afterward. The uncertainty of the outcome and the precariousness of his situation heightened his appreciation of everything in his life, and a nonending sequence of other medical problems and operations—old age was bearing down on him—sustained his gratitude for all that had gone right and was still going right in his life. He had a comfortable home, no financial worries and a family he adored. He saw that more sharply than ever.

During one of our conversations, he listed some of the wonders in his everyday life. "My wife's face," he said. "My daughter's face. My three-week-old granddaughter's face—which looks just like my daughter's three-week-old face. To have her look me in the eye. To put her little nose against my nose. It's amazing."

A little more than two years after my stroke, shortly before the gravity of the coronavirus became clear and the lockdowns began, I rented a car to drive from Manhattan to central New Jersey, where my sister, Adelle, was living and where her daughter, Bella, then a senior in high school, was in a school play. A musical, to be precise. *Mamma Mia*, God help me.

I'm not in general a fan of musicals. I also feel that a little ABBA goes a long way. I actually walked out of the movie version of *Mamma Mia*—despite Meryl Streep, despite Christine Baranski—after about thirty minutes, and that's only because I had trouble persuading my three companions to walk out after twenty. So the thought of watching a version of *Mamma Mia* performed with significantly lower production values while sitting in a hard metal chair on a gymnasium floor didn't thrill me. But being there for my niece did. I'd never heard Bella sing before—I'd never known that she had any interest in singing—and she blew me away. Her voice was clear, strong, lovely. Her movements were sure, without a trace of the overwhelming nervousness that she'd copped to in our exchange of text messages earlier that day. Tears welled in my eyes as I listened. What unplumbed talents the people whom I loved—and people in general—possessed. What unheralded pluck.

But as moving as that Saturday night performance was, the moment that meant even more to me and stayed with me longer came the next day. I'd rented the car not only so that I could get to Bella's show but also so that, the morning after, I could drive my father, who got there separately, back to his house in Westchester County, where I was going to take care of him during that period, the one I mentioned earlier, when he and his wife were apart. As I also mentioned, he was too confused to fend for himself. So at about 11:00 a.m. Sunday, we left Princeton, New Jersey, and set out on our ninety-minute trek, much of it up a famously ugly stretch of the New Jersey Turnpike.

My father, once so extroverted and charming, was no longer much of a conversationalist. I wasn't sure what to expect. Those ninety minutes might well feel like nine hours. But I was saved by modern technology and unmodern song. The car I'd rented was up-to-date enough that I could connect my iPhone to its sound system and play music that way. Dad was fascinated. Such innovations amazed him, even if he'd encountered them a dozen times before.

"Watch this," I said to Dad. Then I told Siri to "play Frank Sinatra." Thus began a stream of Sinatra's greatest hits, one after the other, each a surprise because it was chosen for us, not by us. Dad hummed along, and even sang a few bars of several of the songs. I did likewise. And I was no longer thinking about how much of the drive we had ahead of us and how quickly or slowly it would go. I was in no rush.

I was absurdly happy. Happy to discover how easy it can sometimes be to bring someone amusement and comfort. Happy to be reminded that what's ordinary to one person can be a revelation to another and that sharing that can turn life into a never-ending exchange of gifts. Happy above all to have this moment of connection. Dad and I were separated by nearly thirty years in age and by even more in terms of our sensibilities, our political leanings, the adventures we'd chosen and the lives we'd fashioned. His cognitive fade had widened those divides. But we agreed on Sinatra. We reveled together in "Summer Wind."

"It's my favorite," I said to him when it came on, right after "Fly Me to the Moon (In Other Words)."

"Mine too!" he said, astonishment in his voice.

Then the drive got even better. "Summer Wind" ended and what began, at the *precise second* that the skyline of Manhattan came into view, was "New York, New York." We weren't in a car; we were in a movie. "Start spreading the news," Sinatra sang, and there it was, far to the right of the Jersey Turnpike, the object of his ardor, the end point of his odyssey, a city that churned and yearned and glittered like few others. *My* city, I thought as I once again took in the height and heft of it. I had made a home deep in that jumble of steel, stone, brick and concrete. There was a mailbox with my name on it, a room with my reading chair, a cupboard with my smoked Spanish paprika and my dill.

As "New York, New York" ended, Dad said that he'd always loved Sinatra's duets with a female singer whose name he groped for and didn't come up with.

I struggled myself, but then: "Ella Fitzgerald?"

"Yes!" he said.

I smiled. "OK, Dad, watch *this*." And I told Siri to play Ella Fitzgerald. So it was Ella, not Frank, who got the two Franks— Senior and Junior—the rest of the way home. Ella's "My Funny Valentine." Ella's "I Get a Kick Out of You." I hadn't listened to her—to that velvety voice with its perfect pitch—in years. Why? Because there was so much beauty in this life, so much accumulated treasure, that a huge chunk of it could go missing: eclipsed, buried, forgotten. You needed to remind yourself of it.

And you needed to hold tight to moments like the one Dad and I were having just then when they bloomed. The glory of that ride wasn't just that I was happy but that I recognized that happiness, properly labeled it, lingered over it and committed it to memory, so that it was a kind of keepsake that I could dust off and ponder anew when necessary.

I stayed with Dad for two weeks then and another five weeks later, when the pandemic had really taken hold and the lockdowns were firmly in place. I ventured from the house to get groceries and other essentials, but Dad, at eighty-four, was much more vulnerable and had to be careful to stay inside, without visitors. I felt awful about the monotony of his days, during which he moved only between his bedroom, the kitchen and the family room, where he watched hour upon hour of television. I baked chicken. I broiled lamb chops. We played cards—games that he'd known so well for so long that his confusion was lessened. His eighty-fifth birthday came and went. Easter neared. For neither occasion could my siblings and I organize the kind of celebration he was accustomed to, the kind he deserved. The universe was depriving him—and me—of the moments I'd at last come to value sufficiently.

So I thought hard about how to contrive one. Then I thought even harder: What could we do that would give him some diversion and might have some meaning but wouldn't pose any or much risk of infection? Something came to me, and on Easter Sunday, after serving him a rack of lamb that I'd made for just the two of us, I tucked him into the passenger seat of his big tan Cadillac, I let Regan sprawl across the buttery leather in back and the three of us set off for a tour of his past.

Although Dad had at times ventured far from his birthplace in Westchester County, he had spent most of his life, including this current chapter, within about a ten-mile radius of his childhood home, and his peace with that—his contentment, even—was a powerful argument for maintaining a center of gravity. He knew the particular and special solace of traveling down streets, pulling into parks and slipping into restaurants that compose a living, breathing photo album of your path to the present.

On that Easter Sunday, we drove by the frumpy two-family dwelling where his parents raised him and his two younger brothers and where, every Christmas, they assembled a gargantuan crèche on the front lawn: a wood shack in and around which Mary, Joseph and the rest of their entourage hung out from late November through early January. (The plaster-of-paris baby Jesus didn't join them until midnight on Christmas Eve, when, in a pantomime of his birth, Grandma Bruni carried him from a drawer of her bedroom dresser to the straw-cushioned cradle in the wood shack.) Then we drove by the first house that he and my mother had bought, a humble Cape Cod where I spent the first seven or so years of my life.

Next we checked out the second house that he and Mom owned, triple the size of the first, an emblem of his determined rise in the world. "We thought we would live there forever," he reminded me. But a sequence of promotions took him away from New York for nearly a decade and a half, and cancer took Mom away long, long before he should have had to let her go. Our little tour on Easter Sunday brought back all of that. He smiled and shook his head as the memories washed over him.

He had one last request: Could we swing by the house where Mom lived as a teenager and where he would pick her up to take her out when they were high school sweethearts? I somehow doubted that he'd locate the right street, let alone the right house, but like many people with dementia, he had better access to information stored decades earlier than to what he read or was told just a half hour ago. He found the address. Then he requested that we park along the curb just opposite it, so he could stare at it for a while.

Being with him, looking at him, I saw that over the two decades since Mom's death, his weakened mind had nonetheless done him an extraordinary kindness, taking a good marriage with a normal allotment of highs and lows and turning it into the grandest of romances, a fairy tale whose chapters and big scenes he could replay at will, as an answer and a ballast to his grief. I saw that he was replaying one of those as we sat together. I saw that he was, at this late stage of the game, comfortable enough with me—and comfortable enough with himself—to do that. And I saw that what he felt as he did it wasn't sorrow. It was gratitude.

I took that in, hoping to learn from it and never forget it. *This* was a moment, intimate and exquisite. Into the storehouse of keepsakes it went. Put enough of them there and you build a powerful shield against despair.

When I took that trip to the Greek island of Chios—garden of mastic and cradle of neurological hope—I had a revelation that had nothing to do with the medicine I was injecting. It came about in a conversation over lunch one day with the freelance photographer from Athens, Maria Mavropoulou, whom the *Times* had hired to shoot the pictures for my column.

We were between stops on our tour of the island, at a beach-front taverna, the two of us plus an assistant who traveled with her and a representative of Chios's mastic industry who was guiding us. He had chosen the place and was choosing the seafood, based on what the proprietor said was freshest: shrimp, red mullet, something else I can't recall. Not a bad gig, this job of mine. Not bad at all.

Maria and I were still getting to know each other, and she asked me about places I'd traveled for work and then about places I'd traveled in general. I asked her the same. It was as if each of us unfurled a black-and-white map of the world and began crossing off countries by coloring them in. I'd never done an exercise like this before and was impressed with my tally: Brazil and Botswana, Iceland and Israel, Norway and the Netherlands, Portugal and Poland, Saudi Arabia and South Africa, Tunisia and Turkey. I colored and colored.

"So you've never been to Russia?" Maria asked.

"No, no, I have!" I immediately said. I just hadn't gotten around to mentioning it yet. "To Saint Petersburg." I told her about a Baltic cruise I'd taken a month before my stroke, at the *Times*'s behest, to be a part of a lineup of speakers, most of them *Times* writers, who mingled with a particular cluster of cruisers between stops in Stockholm, Copenhagen, Helsinki and, the crowning jewel of the itinerary, Saint Petersburg.

"But not to Moscow?"

I'd been there, too. But until Maria mentioned it, it had slipped my mind, not only during this conversation but also for a long time beforehand. And that was crazy, because I'd not only been to Moscow, I'd been there for a wild adventure. More than a decade earlier, a friend who was a senior editor at *Men's Vogue* for the magazine's brief and well-funded existence decided that he wanted a writer to go through—and then recount—a few of the paces of preparation for space travel, the prospect of which was drawing the interest of more private companies and more private citizens. He chose me. I booked passage on a "zero-gravity flight," a hollowed-out plane that flew from LaGuardia Airport in New York City out over the ocean and did "parabolas" that, for thirty-second periods of steep descent, created weightlessness, permitting the dozen or so passengers to float. Then I traveled to Star City, a grim campus in the woods outside Moscow where Russian cosmonauts trained. The centerpiece of Star City was an enormous contraption billed as the world's largest centrifuge, into which a person—in this case, me—could be inserted and spun around so that he or she experienced and became accustomed to the crushing multiples of gravity that an astronaut endures.

I was strapped tight to a vertical board, like Hannibal Lecter being transported in *The Silence of the Lambs*. Then a bunch of Russians I'd just met wheeled the board and me into this capsule. I marveled and then quivered at my volitional vulnerability: What if they left me there? What if they spun me too fast and too long? The centrifuge whirred to life and I felt movement and then the physical pressure of 2 Gs and 3 Gs and then 3.55 Gs. I was reminded of that awful tightening in your cheeks and forehead when your sinuses are severely congested, only this tightening affected my whole face along with my neck and chest.

As I related all of this to Maria, a sense of shame shot through me. What kind of ingrate has an experience this exotic, this kooky, and nearly forgets it, letting years go by without mentally revisiting and reliving it? I thought about that, and then I thought about the Ferragamo neckties.

In my late thirties, when I lived in Washington, DC, there was a period of years when I gained and then failed to lose dozens of extra pounds. My waist expanded by about six inches. My cheeks ballooned. I stopped having sex. And, for the most part, I stopped buying any clothes other than what I needed to

accommodate my expansion. I wanted to avoid the mortifica-
tion of trying anything on. And I didn't want to invest in anything that was going to be so temporary. I'd convinced myself
that any day, any week, the weight was coming off. No sense in
acquiring clothes that would soon be obsolete.

Neckties, though: You didn't have to try them on, and they'd
fit just as well after you lost weight. Buying a few every so often
was a way of staying in the game while out of the game—of saying that I hadn't given up on, or stopped caring about, looking
good even though I didn't look good at all. They were a way
of investing in the future without discomfort in the present.
They were a distraction. And while I didn't wear them often, so
I didn't need many, they'd last, right? I'd be wearing the ones I
bought today fifteen and even twenty years forward.

A men's clothing store near my town house had an especially big selection of Ferragamo neckties, the soft colors and
swirling designs of which I liked, and always had several that
were discounted, so I watched for those and bought them in
twos and threes every few months. Soon I had six, then twelve,
then maybe fifteen. I stopped there, even though I told myself
that I wasn't being wasteful: I was collecting and storing these
up to be used later. I wouldn't have to buy nice neckties then
because I'd bought these nice neckties now.

On Chios, as I talked to Maria about Moscow and Saint
Petersburg, I realized that all of those countries colored in on
my map were, or could be, like the neckties: a hoarded stash to
sustain me across time. Half consciously or maybe one-quarter
consciously, I'd done with travel what I'd done with neckwear,
only I'd subsequently done a bad job of going to the closets

and drawers in my mind and retrieving my treasure. But it was there. It was available to me. I could do a better job of it from now on. And that was powerful consolation.

I had no plans to slow down significantly, not just yet. I could tell—in my own life, but even more so in the lives around me, which I now examined more thoughtfully—that the best way to press on was to *press on*, to stay engaged. But fate could slow you down nonetheless. Hadn't that been one of the many lessons of the pandemic? People weren't coloring in their maps much then. They were left, for a while, with the coloring they had already done.

Someone who "lives in the past" is generally an object of pity or disapproval. Reality, I think, is more complicated than that. Our pasts can be troves and balms. But taking advantage of those troves and taking comfort from those balms hinges on gratitude, which lay at the root of my awakening. No journey pays greater dividends than the one from assumptive to appreciative.

In the 2020 movie *Nomadland*, about a band of people who have been displaced from the American dream, there's a hauntingly lovely scene in which a nomad named Swankie—who's not a fictional character but a real person playing herself—talks about why and how she has made peace with old age and her terminal brain cancer. "I'm going to be seventy-five this year, and I think I've lived a pretty good life," she says, noting the vistas and wildlife in the American West that she has seen from "kayaking all those places." She recalls one stretch of one river in particular, and how she came around the bend to "find hundreds of hundreds of swallow nests on the wall of the cliff and the swallows flying all around and reflecting in the water so it looks like I'm flying with the swallows, and they're under me and over me and all around me, and the little babies are hatching out and eggshells are falling out of the nest and landing on the water and floating on the water, these little white shells. It was just so awesome. I felt like I'd done enough. My life was complete. If I died right then, in that moment, it'd be perfectly fine."

She was so alive to those swallows, and they were so alive in her.

Chapter Eleven
THE TRICK BEHIND ALL THE OTHER TRICKS

In the late spring of 2020, maybe two months into the pandemic, I called a longtime friend of mine who lives by herself in a state far away. I wanted to know how she was holding up. This was when there were long lines outside many grocery stores and empty shelves inside them, and what I meant was: Did she have enough toilet paper? Was her job safe? Was she lonely or sad or bingeing on a good miniseries that solved both of those problems?

She talked about flirting with men near the mozzarella at Whole Foods.

She was over sixty, and while she had always cast that as a drag—on her professional marketability, on her metabolism, on her dating life—it had an upside at this particular moment: It qualified her to shop in the first hour after Whole Foods opened, when it was reserved for older customers more vulnerable to illness from the coronavirus and thus in greater need of un-crowded spaces that allowed for six-foot social distancing.

"Frank," she told me with a chirp in her voice, "I've finally figured out where and how to meet men my age!"

Bars had never been her thing. Same for internet dating sites. But the cheese aisle? That was so totally her.

"And there are no younger women for the men to look at," she said. "None of that competition. My face mask hides wrin-kles. I don't have to worry much about makeup. I can pour all my energy into my hair." She has great hair.

"The other day," she continued, "when it was just me and this fit guy over six feet tall, I dropped a wedge of Jarlsberg, thinking maybe he'd pick it up." He didn't. Didn't even seem to notice.

"I guess I've got to work on my technique," she sighed.

That, I said, or try Gruyère.

I told her that I had my doubts about cheese dropping as a viable mating ritual. I noted that masks worked both ways and she couldn't see whether the men were worth the Man-chego. But I was only half-serious, because I knew that she was only one-third so. She wasn't really betting on high-lactose love (though if it had come her way, she would have milked it for all it was worth). She was finding some comic relief—and, sure, a seed of genuine possibility—during a trying time. She was in-jecting mischief into a passage that needed it.

When I hung up the phone, I flashed back more than five years, to an afternoon in the waiting room of a surgeon who was about to carve a crimson hillock from my back. I was nearing fifty and already learning that one of the rites of aging was that your body started generating superfluous things that you wished it wouldn't—hairs, moles, pounds—and that the removal of some was a matter not of vanity but of survival. In this instance, I had a baby cancer between my shoulder blades, and it threatened, if unattended, to mature into a nasty adolescence.

Seated across from me were a man and a woman, neither of whom looked a day under seventy. I could tell from their conversation that they'd just met and that they'd both been in this place and through this drill many times before. When it came to carcinoma, they were frequent fliers.

"Too much tennis," the woman said to the man as she pointed to a subtle divot on her neck, where the sun had done its cruel handiwork.

"Golf," said the man, touching a similar dent on his brow. "Should have worn a hat."

She gently pulled up the hem of her skirt to reveal a jagged, angry red line just below her knee. It gave her an excuse to show some leg.

Then she reached over to touch a patch on one of his forearms, which had also clearly gone under the knife.

"Yard work," he said, sounding all virile. Her fingers lingered on the spot. He let them.

It reminded me of that scene in *Jaws* when the shark hunters compare scars, except that the battles that my fellow patients had waged weren't with the deep's monsters. They were with the body's betrayals.

Cosmetically, these two had been diminished. But by other yardsticks? As I watched them turn rogue cells into compatible memories, affliction into flirtation, I couldn't help feeling that they'd actually been amplified, and that there was a mercy and a kind of miracle in how we're constructed. That feeling returned as I listened to my lactose-exuberant friend. As our physical muscles grow weaker, our emotional muscles grow stronger, and we're better at seeing the comedy in the tragedy, the advance in the setback, the good in the bad.

We become grand masters at perspective, which is the tweak of all tweaks, the trick of all tricks, the cornerstone of all coping. What Barbara was doing in Whole Foods and what those elderly patients were doing at Carcinoma Central was changing their perspective on the woes that they'd been through, the challenges they still faced, the supposed ravages of time. A positive perspective is what Dorrie and Juan Jose and Miguel Neri all aced, the umbrella under which their varied, individual adaptations fell. It's what I was exercising when I imagined all those sandwich boards. It's the feat of subjecting circumstances to a new light, sizing them up from a different angle, realizing that you can put a more flattering frame around them and that when you do, the picture is no longer grim. It's sometimes more interesting.

This tweak and trick happen earlier, I think, for people who've navigated certain hardships. But it's a tool at all of our disposals, one that's usually more important in the later stages of life, and it's so wickedly sharp that it can turn the procession of vulnerable, masked seniors through a supermarket into a Roquefort rom-com.

As best I can tell, there are three overlapping pillars of perspective. One is the capacity to put what you're going through in context: to be alert to those sandwich boards and understand that the words on other people's boards are anagrams of the words on your own. The other two pillars are the abilities to recast limits, which aren't merely limits, and to reconceptualize loss, the arithmetic of which isn't a simple act of subtraction.

Donna Von Bargen, a retired psychologist in North Carolina, learned that. As a child, she had terrible asthma. As an adult, she suffered chronic exhaustion that, she said, was probably related to the immune-suppressing side effects of her asthma treatments. Doctors often weren't certain what was going on with her, but she tired if she tried to do too much, caught anything contagious if she mingled with too many people and had periods of grave gastrointestinal distress.

A tale of hardship, no? She doesn't tell it quite that way. She described most of these challenges not so much as burdens, which they indeed were, but as influences, as the determinants of how she spent her time, how she shaped her life and who she became. She liked that shape just fine. It agreed with her. So she framed, and regarded, her path less as difficult than as distinctive.

"It became really clear to me that, for example, coming from the family and the background that I did, there's no way I would have become a psychologist if I had not had asthma as a child," she told me, referring to her years growing up in a working-class community in the Ontario province of Canada. "My mom worked at a Safeway, as a cashier. Dad was a chemical technician at a paper mill. While other kids were running and playing, I was sitting and reading—comic books, anything I could get my hands on. I really did well at reading."

Because she did well at reading, she did well in school. Because she did well in school, she stuck with it long enough to get a PhD in psychology. With that credential she established a counseling practice, and much of her work was with people overcoming trauma. Her own challenges made her better at understanding theirs, and her own challenges were persistent. There were periods, she told me, during which she had to take a midday nap to be sufficiently attentive to the patients she saw before and after it.

Also, she said, "I had to work very hard to accept that I really couldn't have much of a social life, once I was working and raising a family—that's about all there was. There just wasn't extra time and energy." She let her husband take their two daughters to church; she needed Sunday mornings to recuperate.

She skipped big gatherings at night as well. "I found one or two really good friends," she said, adding that she also found that such intimacy suited her. "Chitchat doesn't really rock my boat. Never has. Never will." If her health didn't create that sensibility, it speeded her to that assessment. Either way, she was satisfied.

Her limited store of energy and her need to be discriminating about when, where and how she deployed it compelled her to define her priorities across all aspects of life, including relatively superficial ones. "Makeup," she said. "I don't wear makeup." Its importance to her isn't commensurate with whatever small effort is required to put it on correctly. At some point she stopped styling her hair, though she *does* dye it because that's the part that matters to her. "I got good at saying that there's a certain level of involvement in fashion and appearance that I care about and I decided that I'm going to find the lowest level that I'm comfortable with."

She presented that as an arrangement born of flawed health. I think it's also born of age. That sentiment—I need only this much, really, to be content, and can be quite content with it— is one that I've heard older friends and older relatives express. They speak of letting the nonessential things, the trivial stuff, slide.

It's what most of us had to do when the pandemic descended, and many people I know were as surprised by how many activities they *didn't* miss as by how many they did. If they were fortunate enough not to lose jobs, loved ones and substantial amounts of money, they discovered that at least a few of the ways in which life was collapsed, constrained and cloistered had upsides. In terms of some of those new logistical realities, their lives weren't getting worse. They were being reconfigured. Less time with a big circle of people meant more time with a small bubble of them. The office was out of the picture, but so was the commute. Zoom conferences weren't ideal, but neither were conferences that required airplanes, airports, suitcases and such.

There are so many different angles from which to come at work, love, life. There are so many roads and means of transportation. To be denied one is to reach for another, and even when that's an indisputable sacrifice, it can also be an endurable swerve. Sometimes an ending is a new beginning. Sometimes a limit or a loss is, as I mentioned in an earlier chapter, a gateway to experiments that you wouldn't have sought, skills that you wouldn't have acquired, insights that you wouldn't have gleaned. You just have to allow for that prospect and finesse that perspective.

Devin Person exemplifies that. I happened across an article about him in the *Times* in 2019, with the headline: "'I'm Weird, but I Get Results': Have You Met This Wizard on the Subway?" He was then thirty-three and living in Brooklyn, and he often dressed in a long green robe, with a matching conical hat, and considered himself a professional wizard. As such he held group meditation sessions, including one called the Wizarding Hour. "He speaks to companies," the article, by Mary Pilon, explained. "He officiates weddings. He reads tarot and performs hypnosis. He hosts a podcast."

All of which was plenty interesting and amusing. But the detail of his story that piqued my interest concerned how he came by his cosmetic calling card: a long white beard that, while perfect for a wizard, was odd for a man as young as he. The beard, it turned out, was the legacy of a joint disease for which he was prescribed a medication that, as a side effect, turned many patients' dark hair white. He told Pilon that when the doctor warned him about that, "I started a tap dance in his office." Person was then developing his wizardly vocation and decided to regard the medication's toll as a gift: a potential bit of costuming courtesy of nature. His joint disease was a bad turn. But his white beard was propitious branding.

Kim Chambers, too, alchemized misfortune. I suppose I should have known about her before, in early 2020, I picked up the journalist Bonnie Tsui's just-published book *Why We*

Swim, which attracted me because, from ages nine to seventeen, I spent between twelve and twenty-five hours a week in a pool and was an excellent competitive swimmer. Chambers is "one of the best marathon swimmers in the world," Tsui wrote in a chapter devoted to her, noting that Chambers "holds multiple world records for distance swimming, including one she set in 2015 by becoming the first woman to swim solo from the Farallon Islands to the Golden Gate Bridge, a thirty-mile journey that began with her slipping into pitch-dark waters just before midnight in the notorious Red Triangle of great white sharks." Chambers was also "only the sixth person in history to complete the Oceans Seven, the open-water equivalent of the Seven Summits."

That's remarkable in and of itself, but it's even more so when you consider that she "began swimming as an adult, in 2009, to rehab a leg she almost lost to amputation." Wearing high heels, she teetered and then tumbled down the stairs outside her San Francisco apartment. Doctors told her that, functionally speaking, the leg was almost surely a lost cause. "It took her two years to learn how to walk again," Tsui wrote. "It took much less time to discover that she is freakishly gifted at long-distance swimming." Freakishly fulfilled by it, too. And she might never have discovered that otherwise. But when she was shut down on one front, she looked for and pivoted to another front where she wasn't. She didn't stew in her deprivations. She took robust advantage of her remaining gifts.

Granted, Chambers was about thirty when she took to the ocean, and the swerves doable at that age aren't quite the same as the swerves doable in your fifties, when my right eye went on strike, or in your sixties, seventies and eighties, when aging invariably erodes your physical might. But there's no age limit on the idea—the reality—that we have second selves and probably third and fourth selves to rescue us when our first selves are compromised or killed off. Or that life is such a cornucopia of choices and possibilities that to be denied some is to be nudged toward others.

I had some practice in that, though I'd lost sight of it until I lost sight. I'm referring to how, when I was young, I handled being gay. As prone as I was in general to self-pity, as gifted as I was at melodrama, I didn't rail against my lot, curse the heavens or resign myself to a lifetime of opprobrium and ostracism. I drew myself a new map. I figured I wouldn't have kids—back then, most gay men and women didn't—and decided to treat that as a kind of liberation. It made the size of my income less important because there would be fewer people depending on it. I could ignore the siren's call of the suburbs, with their low crime rates and good schools, and be a cosmopolitan denizen of the city. The city is where I'd be welcomed, so the city is where I'd go. That was settled, and it was good to have things settled.

Choices had to be made in accordance with some criteria. Homosexuality was my criterion. It was clarifying. I'd point myself toward a profession rife with nonconformists, so that I wouldn't have to worry too much about being judged and penalized for being different, and I regarded that necessity not as a punishment but as a helpful sorting and collapsing of options, as an agent of self-definition. Complete freedom can be its own tyranny. By being less free, I was more directed. It wasn't fair in the least. It was out-and-out unjust, and I've devoted chunks of my career and no small amount of my writing to exploring the wages of hatred toward and discrimination against gay people—wages that include not just shattered dreams but broken bones—and to arguing what shouldn't even need arguing, which is that we deserve access to the same spectrum of opportunities that straight people do. But as I argued, as I fought, I also made the most of the part of the spectrum available to me, because I wanted not just to be angry but also to be happy.

That past and that thinking came back to me after my stroke, not right away but as I wrestled control of my emotions and tamped down my fears. *When one eye closes another opens.* That's not a fact. It's a perspective, which makes it no less true. And it manifests itself in the smallest, stupidest ways, which are emblematic of bigger, wiser dynamics. During one of those many nighttime walks through Central Park with Regan, I toted a new iPhone, which I'd set up incompletely or improperly, and I couldn't make the audiobook that I wanted to listen to come through my earbuds. I couldn't make music do so, either: no "Sisters of the Moon" that night, no "Angel." For reasons that stumped me, only podcasts would work. But "only" was the wrong word, because there were podcasts galore—from NPR, from CNN, from the *Times*, from TED Talks, not to mention all the serial audio documentaries that were there, for free, by the graces of digital data and with the tapping of my fingers in the rights spots on my tiny screen. They were available to me on Summit Rock, and they were available to me by Sheep Meadow.

We folks on the far side of fifty like to talk about how the world is deteriorating, how we'll be lucky to get out while the getting is good, and there's reason for that. There's vicious political polarization, the stubborn allure of autocracy, environmental disaster, climate change. But that's one attitude. Here's another: Advancing technologies have sped education and entertainment to us as never before. Diversion has never been more abundant or accessible. During the pandemic, movie theaters shut down, but we still had movies. Music concerts ceased, but we still had music. We had books in multiple formats: physical, digital, aural. And we were cut off from one another only physically. We otherwise remained deeply and constantly connected.

I feel that way—or, rather, have learned to feel that way—despite not using technology all that well. I'm terrible with it. And because I'm terrible with it, I'm routinely smacking up against walls. The Apple Play that was working through my rental car's dashboard before the rest stop suddenly works no more. My iPad reboots and I can't access Netflix or figure out why. So instead of using Apple Play, I use the good old-fashioned radio, and what do you know? There's a right-wing talk show that's sociologically and anthropologically fascinating—more fascinating in its fashion than any podcast I would have carefully curated and more professionally useful, too. Instead of bingeing on a Netflix series, I finally read that Colin Harrison thriller that I'd downloaded and then neglected, and it's a pulse-quickening lark. In both cases, I win. I win because I've allowed myself to. Or willed myself to. Either way, it's a victory.

Todd Blenkhorn used that filter or one much like it. When we corresponded by email and then talked on the phone in early 2020, he was forty-two, living in Toronto with his wife and children and doing information technology work for the Canadian National Institute for the Blind. His place of employment was no accident. Todd had begun having trouble with his eyesight when he was a child, though that trouble worsened and improved in a manner that stumped doctors, who have never affixed a definitive diagnosis to it. "Optic neuropathy of unknown origin" is a phrase that he has become familiar with, and that's a medically fancy scratching of the head, a semantic shrug. His affliction, like mine, is nerve-related, but in his case, the nerves' nemesis can't be named. Through college, he had enough central vision to read and do computer work without any special assistance, but flawed peripheral vision and a missing chunk of vision below the center of the frame made certain activities difficult or impossible.

His sight deteriorated progressively until, around 2013, when he was in his midthirties, he could no longer make out words on a page or computer screen. By then he was married and the father of two boys, the youngest of whom wasn't yet six months old. It depresses Todd, who grew up in a household that revered books, that he has never been able to read to his second-born son and that he had to stop reading to his first-born when the boy was just three. "It doesn't sound like a big thing," he told me. "But it is. It's probably the biggest and most difficult thing I've faced."

He got a cane, then a guide dog. Both announced to anyone who spotted him that he was blind. And that elicited responses that fascinated and amused him—and that he turned into riffs and punch lines in an amateur stand-up set. Todd has always loved comedians. So, in late 2019, he signed up for stand-up comedy class at Second City in Toronto. It began in January 2020 and ended two months later with a comedy-club performance of a five-minute set.

When he started the class, he told me, he hadn't intended for his jokes to be about blindness. But those were the ones that came to him most naturally. That's where his mind kept going. He thought about all the silly, stupid things that people say to someone who's blind. He realized, in dwelling on those things, that they must bother him more than he usually admitted to himself. But he also realized that he could repurpose those annoyances and frustrations. He could treat them as clay. So he molded his clay, the liberating effect of which was obvious in the joy on his face when he did his set and the audience laughed and laughed.

I saw the set because he sent me a video link to it, and I couldn't hear all of his jokes because the audience's laughter was so frequent and loud. He was terrific. He began by exaggerating the use of his cane as he walked toward the microphone, and he folded the cane along its hinges very, *very* slowly, to bring yet more attention to it and to his blindness. That was the clever windup for him to say, hilariously, with his face turned toward the audience: "It's a good-looking crowd."

He then shared his bafflement at some of the language that attends his disability: "Legally blind? I don't know—I've never done any paperwork or anything." Instead of being called "visually impaired," he asked, should he and others like him be called "visually inconvenienced?" No, that didn't quite work. "Visually inconvenienced—I picture a sighted person on the beach when I walk through their line of sight with no shirt on," he said. "*That* person has been visually inconvenienced. Possibly visually traumatized."

He talked about what he'd like to tell parents who answer their children's questions about why that man over there has a cane with a *whispered* "he can't see": "It's OK—I already know!" And he marveled at the nuttiness of people who ask him how he manages to shave. "Just a little test," he instructed the audience. "Everyone, close your eyes. Can you find your face?"

What Todd found was a voice and a point of view. Being robbed of his eyesight and having to navigate parenthood, work and everything else without it involved extra effort, a period of sorrow and instances of fear. But there was absurdity to it as well. There was a perspective from which it was riveting and funny, whether he was shaping it into punch lines or making peace with it away from the microphone.

⁓

Someone somewhere has probably floated the proposition that for every loss there's a commensurate gain, but that's not what I'm peddling here. I don't believe that at all—not the grand sweep of that statement, not the *commensurate* part, not the tidiness of that arithmetic. And there are limits that press down on our spirits no matter what fancy mental footwork we're capable of and no matter how much energy we put into it. But I do believe we have a say in whether those limits crush and immobilize us. We can divine, in our losses, not just a robbery but a repositioning.

Marge Feder and her husband, Bob, were the couple with whom my parents were friendliest during the last five years of my mother's life, and after Mom was gone and then after Bob died, I'd get emails from her, not just checking in on Dad but also sharing thoughts on the news or responding to columns that I'd written in the *Times*. I loved hearing from Marge, who had such palpable intelligence, such a positive outlook, such a glow. I loved seeing her on those rare occasions when some event involving Dad brought us together. She made me feel connected to Mom, to Dad before his Alzheimer's, to Mom-and-Dad when there was still a Mom-and-Dad. She turned back time.

Marge, who is eighty-nine and taught English as a second language before retiring and doing volunteer work, has known loss. One of her five children died at the age of fifty-three. One of her nine grandchildren died at the age of two. And then, in early 2017, Bob died. They had been married for more than sixty-five years and everything about their lives was entwined; in many contexts, she wasn't Marge but half of Bob-and-Marge or Marge-and-Bob. They were a team. And then they weren't, except in memory.

Marge told me that she'd never thought much about what old age would be like. She'd never counted on getting there. "My mother died at fifty-four," she said. "I had no expectation, frankly, of living to be this age. I had no role model. Bob's father died at fifty-seven, and both of them talked about what they were going to do when they retired, and how they were going to travel, and neither lived to retire, which was a lesson for us not to postpone things—to do the things we wanted to do when we could."

As she spoke, I remembered something that I hadn't in a long while: In 2003 or 2004, when I was living in Rome and working as the *Times*'s Rome bureau chief, she and Bob had come through the city and invited me to join them for dinner at their favorite trattoria in Trastevere, a neighborhood of especially narrow, roughly cobbled streets on the Vatican side of the Tiber River. Marge and Bob had been to Rome often enough over the years to *have* their own special spot there. "It's quite a marvelous thing to look back on, that there was nothing that we really wanted that we left undone."

One secret, then, was to go full blast while you *could* go full blast, so that all that territory was covered, all that road traveled, to be savored in reminiscence when your pace invariably slackened, when time ran out. That's what I realized that I'd wisely but half inadvertently done when I tallied my travels for the Greek photographer in Chios. But reminiscing isn't enough, and it wasn't the full or even main source of Marge's contentment. Marge diverted her attention from what had been subtracted from her life to what remained and what could still be added to it. This was the arithmetic that she preferred, the perspective on which she insisted.

She was a docent at the Jewish Museum in Manhattan, and she loved the education she got every time she had to bone up on a new exhibit. She had maintained her and Bob's subscription to the Metropolitan Opera in Lincoln Center and, at the beginning of each season, she'd send her grandchildren the schedule so each could pick a performance to accompany her to. Her grandchildren and children got regular use out of the pool in her backyard and the grill on her spacious terrace and, she told me, "As soon as the weather gets a little warmer, there'll be a crowd back there every weekend." She loved that, too. And she loved the two vacations she took every year, neither of them long trips, neither of them extravagant. One was to a lake just an hour away. She loved its water and the mountains around it. The other was to the Niagara Falls area because she loved the flowers there at the right time of year.

She told me that on her most recent trip to the lake, "I kayaked. I kayaked for the first time."

"Really?" I said. "At the age of eighty-six?!"

"At the age of eighty-six," Marge said.

"Did you like it?"

"Oh, I loved it. I'm a strong swimmer. I swim regularly. And so I thought, 'What's the worst thing that's going to happen? Is it that I'm going to capsize and I'm going to be in the water, and I'll either get back to shore or they'll come and rescue me?' And everything was fine until I got back to the dock and I couldn't get out of the kayak. I could not lift myself up. And I'm getting advice from all these teenagers on the dock. Finally, I realized the only way I was going to get out was to capsize the boat there at the dock, so I just turned it upside down." Then she wriggled out of it underwater and resurfaced beside it.

"There's always *some* way, right?" I said.

"There's always some way—yes."

There was so much Marge loved, enough to take up the space once occupied by loves lost. And there were discoveries beyond loss. She told me that when it became clear to her that Bob was dying, she realized that she had no idea how or whether she'd manage on her own. She didn't mean in terms of taking care of

herself and her house and the bills and such—she knew how
to do all of that. She meant socially. The Marge-and-Bob/Bob-
and-Marge calendar happened on autopilot, and there were
many events that stemmed from Bob's leading role in a prominent local law firm that bore his name. She realized that some,
perhaps most, of those invitations would dry up. Some people
would stop reaching out. Did Marge have it in her to be the ini-
tiator, to go alone into situations that had always included Bob?

What she learned was that she could let any anxiety about
that go. She could do what she needed to do, which was to make
overtures to people who weren't making their own overtures. "I
can't sit back and wait," she said. So she doesn't, and she takes
satisfaction from taking control.

She added, "I'm proud."

I told her that she was proof that even in one's eighties, and
maybe beyond, a person can develop what I referred to as "new
muscles."

"I think that's a very good way to put it, yes."

I reminded her of one of my grandma Bruni's favorite ad-
ages, the first two words of which I used as the title of a 2009
memoir about family and food. "Born round, you don't die
square," I said. "Like so many things, it's true and not true at
the same time. I think you can die square. You can develop new
muscles."

To become infirmed or to grow old is to lose things, absolutely,
but also, ideally, to let things go: self-consciousness, or at least

the acute version and undermining dimensions of it; gaudy expectations, which are often cruelties and not catalysts; anger, because it takes more out of you than it puts back into you. I could tell that Marge had let many things go.

So had that couple in the office of the doctor who was doing minor surgery on my back. I wish I could go back in time, get their phone numbers, follow up, find out more about each of them before that moment and about each of them after. I wish I could hear how their conversation ended—I didn't, probably because I was summoned to see the doctor in the middle of it. Maybe they never exchanged another word after the last one I heard.

Or maybe they swapped telephone numbers and, within weeks, were off on vacation together somewhere. And maybe it was the best vacation either of them had ever had, not for the blueness of the water—and not, dare I say, for the intensity of the sun—but because it came at a point where they savored every pleasure as robustly as possible.

Chapter Twelve
HEARTS BROKEN OPEN

When my stroke happened, I had been friends with Bob Kerrey for about five years, during which I'd had many dinners with him, many drinks. He liked tequila, and it visibly loosened him up, though he really didn't need the loosening in the first place. On the far side of his political career, he was blunt, unguarded and voluble, happy to answer any question I threw at him, like how in the world he ended up dating Debra Winger decades earlier, when she was a big movie star. That was how Bob first came on my radar, in the mid 1980s, when I was in college and paid as much attention to Hollywood as to politics. Bob was then the governor of Nebraska and Winger's surprising romantic partner. He explained to me that much of *Terms of Endearment* was shot in Nebraska, and that he met its cast, including Winger, at a local news conference to announce the movie's in-state production. The rest was pheromones.

He was unblushing about that and unhesitant with insider accounts about his subsequent campaign for the Democratic presidential nomination in 1992, when Bill Clinton took the prize. Bob always gave me the sense that I could ask him anything, and yet, until my stroke, I'd never asked him about one of the most transformative and profound experiences in his life, which was the loss of the lowest stretch of his right leg from a horrible injury during combat in Vietnam.

The way I met Bob says something remarkable about his character and his candor. It was 2012, and the national debate about marriage equality was at peak intensity. The state of New York had legalized same-sex marriage with legislation the previous year, and the states of Washington, Maryland, Maine and Minnesota were putting it on the ballot, so voters could weigh in directly, in November. Bob had returned part-time to Nebraska from New York to campaign for the US Senate. He was the Democratic nominee and, the party felt, its best hope in a state that had turned redder and redder over recent years.

Republicans did all they could to squelch that hope, audaciously portraying him as a carpetbagger and a bohemian from the famously lefty enclave of Greenwich Village. Bob, mind you, was born in Nebraska. He grew up in Nebraska. He graduated from the University of Nebraska, came home to Nebraska after receiving the Medal of Honor for his service in Vietnam and has a bridge named after him in Omaha. He spent, in aggregate, sixteen years as the state's governor or one of its two US senators, up until leaving the Senate in early 2001. Only then, in his late fifties, did he move to Manhattan and take a new job as president of the New School.

But that nonetheless meant that it was most definitely *not* in his political interests, during his 2012 campaign, to emphasize progressive positions or dwell on anything that fed into his opponents' caricature of him as someone out of touch with the heartland. So I was surprised when I heard, from a friend who was keeping tabs on Bob's campaign, that Bob was routinely volunteering his support for same-sex marriage in the remarks he made as he stumped across Nebraska. My friend gave me Bob's contact information, I reached him directly and I told him that I wanted to write a column about his stance and his emphasis on it, preferably by flying to Nebraska soon and interviewing him there. He said an immediate yes and added that someone from his staff would get back to me to schedule a time.

Someone did get back to me, only to inform me that Bob had misspoken and couldn't accommodate this interview. Sorry.

My gut told me that Bob's staff was intervening to protect him by discouraging attention to his advocacy of marriage equality. I got back in touch with Bob directly to express my disappointment. The interview, he said, *would* happen; he'd fix it. A week or so later, I flew to Omaha and had drinks with him one night in a restaurant downtown. Although an aide showed up to chaperone us, Bob shooed the aide away.

He articulated his conviction that gay people were made that way, saying, "Do you think anyone in his right mind would choose to be gay in Nebraska?" He said that they deserved a full complement of rights, most certainly including the right to marry. He had long believed that, and back in 1996, in the Senate, he voted against the Defense of Marriage Act, which defined marriage as the union of a man and a woman. Most of his fellow Democrats in the chamber, including Joe Biden, voted in favor of that legislation. Bill Clinton signed it. But Bob, representing Nebraska, which was hardly any hotbed of gay rights, opposed it. He told me that he believed then and believed now that his position was the humane, just, correct one.

I went through all of this in the column. Bob proceeded, as expected, to lose that Senate race.

And we've been friends ever since.

When I told him in late 2017 about the damage to my right eye, he said that it would challenge and change me, in ways that I'd find more endurable and probably more meaningful than I expected. He was among the friends who brought up my compromised vision with some regularity, asking if there was any news and how I was doing all in all. He was more cognizant of it—and more alert to the possibility that it was perniciously rattling around my thoughts—than most other people. But it wasn't until several years after my stroke that I probed his own early experience with much, much greater hardship and asked him what he'd learned from it. For the first time, we talked about the injury he suffered in Vietnam and the aftermath.

—

It happened in mid-March 1969. He and a team of fellow Navy SEALs, closing in on a Viet Cong encampment, found themselves under intense enemy fire. A grenade thrown in Bob's direction exploded near his feet. He was knocked out, after which, he said, his main feeling was "almost relief that I was alive." But he understood quickly that he'd suffered devastating damage to his right leg, where "the heel was gone, a couple of toes were gone." He was pumped full of morphine and evacuated first to a field hospital in Japan, then to a hospital in Philadelphia. During that journey he watched his remaining toes, which stuck out from a cast on his right leg, become blacker and blacker, deprived of blood because the arteries feeding the lower part of that leg were no good. He knew what that meant.

"I was smart enough," he said. He told the surgeon who was about to operate on him in Philadelphia: "Just leave as much as you possibly can."

The surgeon had to amputate Bob's right foot and ankle. Bob was fitted with a prosthetic to take their place, and, he said, "It hurt like shit. The first time you step into that hard socket, and you've got soft tissue and scarring, you realize this is not going to be easy. Flying back to Nebraska, going through O'Hare airport, geezers are walking past me. Two weeks earlier, I was on a SEAL team."

There was more pain to come—a lot of it, over a long period— and there were many medical adjustments, but overarching all of that was the impact that the missing part of him had on his self-image. "It made me feel like I'm a freak," he told me.

"How long did that feeling follow you around?" I asked him.

"It's still there," he answered, and it's why, though wearing a prosthetic continues to hurt a bit most of the time, he is loath to take it off, even at home. "I have a little bit of discomfort right now," he said from the opposite side of a booth at a favorite Greenwich Village lunch spot of his. "I would be a lot more comfortable with this leg off—like *ten times* more comfortable."

"So how often do you take it off?"

"At night, when I sleep."

"But not when you get home?"

He said he didn't like sitting around that way. "I still have some residual self-consciousness," he said, "even with my wife and son." He shared with me anew something that he'd mentioned to me before: His relationship with Winger—whom he dated before he met his wife, when he was single—had been so powerful because this major celebrity, someone who'd played the love interests of John Travolta and Richard Gere, was not put off by his glaring physical imperfection. He described that as "a gift."

It's not just mild pain or discomfort that keeps him ever aware of his imperfection. It's logistics. He can't get the prosthetic he usually wears wet, so he has a second for showering. But it's bulkier, as is the case that carries it. Whenever he travels, he has to decide whether to leave it at home and be forced to balance precariously in the shower, with the support of just his left leg, or whether to bring it with him despite the extra burden.

In the years and then decades after Vietnam, he frequently visited amputees in military hospitals. He told them, "The big lie is that you'll be able to do everything you did before. So don't get disappointed. And if you want to know what you're not going to be able to do, I'll give you a list. It's not the end of the world. On the other hand, there are things you *are* going to be able to do, because you're a changed person."

Explaining the change in him, he told me, "I can see somebody hurting because I know what pain is and I know what I need to do to adjust so I can see it. We all muscle through it.

And I can see it. I can see it in their face." He can spot when they've gone deep into a tunnel and need to be pulled out. He can spot when they're at the mouth of that tunnel, trying to resist it. He can do that because the tunnel is familiar. Sometimes he'll meet or be talking with someone and ask, "Are you OK?" And the person will say, "No. How did you know that?"

There's a simple answer.

"I get that way myself," Bob said to me, later adding: "It's not a bad thing to have more compassion."

As I listened to him in real time and then, later, thought more about what he'd said, I wondered if hardship could be an invitation to a deeper kind of living, a prompt for fresh connections and new kinships, a force multiplier for a humanity that too often gets buried under the jumble of a life untouched by significant turmoil. I wondered about vulnerability. Whether it came early in life, because of affliction, or later, because of age, was it perhaps a portal and a bridge?

In the 1997 memoir *The Diving Bell and the Butterfly*, which was turned into a gorgeous and haunting 2007 movie by the director Julian Schnabel, Jean-Dominique Bauby explored that idea. Bauby, a magazine editor, suffered a stroke that left him with what's known as "locked-in syndrome," which prevented him from moving or speaking even though his mind was intact. He did have control over his left eyelid, so he communicated with blinks. That's how he wrote his memoir. He could also read, and he started getting letters from acquaintances who, in those missives, wrestled in personal ways with the nature of suffering and the meaning of life. "By a curious reversal," Bauby observed, "the people who focus most closely on these fundamental questions tend to be people I had known only superficially. Their small talk had masked hidden depths. Had I been blind and deaf, or does it take the glare of disaster to show a person's true nature?"

The title of the writer Reynolds Price's 1994 memoir, *A Whole New Life*, refers at least in part to a kind of awakening he experienced after he began to have trouble walking in 1984 and doctors discovered a tumor braided around the core of his spinal cord. Surgery and radiation saved him, but he endured a long rehabilitation and persistent pain and never walked normally again, needing to use a wheelchair. In *A Whole New Life*, Price described cancer, the fear of dying and the work of healing as humbling and clarifying, and he pronounced the years since the tumor better in many ways than the ones before. "They've brought more in and sent more out—more love and care, more knowledge and patience, more work in less time," he wrote. Indeed, he was as prolific in the final stretch of his life as he'd ever been.

My friend Dorrie is sure that her Parkinson's has made her more empathetic, not just the fact of it but the nature of it and how the world receives her as a result of it. I've witnessed that reception myself: servers in restaurants paying more attention to other people at the table than to her, as if her ailment, visible in her movements, robbed her of a voice; servers not trying very hard to hear that voice, which can be soft. She told me that she has grown accustomed to people posing questions about her to her companions, as if she lacks not only a voice but also a working brain.

Being Dorrie, she has converted that into something positive. "Parkinson's has given me greater understanding of what being Black or Muslim or Hispanic or gay must feel like in this country, the feeling of not knowing how you will be treated, how someone will react to you because of your color—or, in this case, my handicap," she wrote to me, adding that it's "the closest I've felt to being marginalized because of the way I sound or look."

She questions all the time whether she's been altruistic enough, considerate enough, and while that was part of her constitution all the way back in college—I remember being touched by it and sometimes even shamed by it—it's an undeniably greater force in her now. Something bad happens to her and her first reaction, or at least her strongest one, is to wonder about its impact on the people around her. In the spring of 2021, she and her husband moved from Madison, Wisconsin, to Sacramento, California, where he'd found an exciting new job, and in response to an email that I sent her in late June 2021 to ask how things were going, she wrote: "So I was carrying a box out our back door and I froze. What that means is that my feet stop moving but my body continues in motion. Anyway, I've learned to take my scrapes, scars and bruises as par for the course. I've got about an eight-inch abrasion down my forearm and both my shins have two-inch scrapes. I try to do too much. That's what my family has told me for years. I've ignored their pleas, thinking that I'm fighting the good fight. Until today. I realized that I could have actually killed myself or at least been really hurt if I had hit my head."

"I have not taken into account how my actions affect my loved ones," she added. "So although Parkinson's has made me a better person to the world, it has created a selfish blind spot when it comes to my family and some friends. I've assumed that if I 'soldier on,' they will be proud of me and not call attention to my disease. Instead, I've created worries and frustration that I will injure myself beyond repair." She's not wrong. Her grit is their terror, and there's some foolish pride in it, even some arrogance. But for that to be her takeaway? For that to be her commentary, when she could have been weeping about her hurdles and hurts? It's beyond generous. As hard as I always struggled to find the right words for Dorrie's college smile, I struggle harder to find the right words for her radiance now.

I became aware of Cyrus Habib in early 2020. Just thirty-eight, he was nearing the end of his first term as the lieutenant governor of the state of Washington. He was also blind. But neither of those details was why he caught my attention and why, once he did, I was so eager to speak with him. I wanted to ask him about his announcement that, despite a potentially huge political career ahead of him, he would be stepping down before the end of the year to become . . . a Jesuit priest.

In the first minutes of my first long telephone conversation with Habib, he described what it would take to become ordained in accordance with the Jesuit script: a decade, if not more, of service to the needy, theological education and more. The checklist was longer and the requirements more arduous than those for basic ordination. He would take vows of not only chastity but also poverty and obedience. For the first two years

he'd live humbly, even ascetically, in a community of other novitiates, or Jesuits-in-training, in Los Angeles and do volunteer
work in soup kitchens, nursing homes or such. And all of that,
he knew, would be a seismic shock after his years as lieutenant
governor, during which there was no shortage of people around
him who sought his advice, deferred to his judgment and followed his commands.

"I've developed a type of entitlement where I'll just walk
into a situation and I'll say, 'Why don't we do it this way?' That
comes with the position and the title and having your own
staff." And that was about to change radically. He was reminded
of that when, during a visit to the house in Los Angeles where
he'd initially live, he wondered at their housecleaning exertions
and suggested a possible relief in the form of a robot vacuum
cleaner: "I said, 'Can my family donate a Roomba to the whole
society so we can use that vacuuming time to do other things?'
And the other novitiates were like, 'Dude, it's not about that.
This is going to be an interesting transition for you.'"

He braced for that. But he told me, "I don't see it as a shrinking of my world. I see it as a shrinking of myself. When the
focus is not as much on *my* brand, *my* messaging, *my* reelection, *my* fundraising process, *my* legislative agenda, when you
take those things and shrink them down, you create more space
for God to operate on you."

And in his case, Habib said, the *my* was encouraged by the
extra attention and acclaim that outsiders lavished on him as
the overachiever, the trailblazer, the man who managed to do x,
y and z *despite having lost his sight at the age of eight.* He was the
first Iranian-American elected to statewide office in America.

He became Washington's lieutenant governor when he was thirty-five. And he was the exceedingly rare blind person at such a pinnacle in politics. All of that came after a sequence of prior distinctions, including a Rhodes scholarship.

He was born in America to parents who'd immigrated from Iran. Their only child, he was still an infant when he received a diagnosis of retinoblastoma, an uncommon cancer that most often afflicts children. His left retina was removed before his third birthday. To preserve the right one—and his vision—for as long as possible, he went through radiation and chemotherapy. When he filled me in on all of that, he focused on his parents' ordeal. "Hell is probably not dissimilar to walking into a pediatric cancer ward and seeing, as my parents had to, beds of kids lined up, each connected to an IV pump, and knowing your kid is going to be joining that," he said. He also called himself lucky. Being able to see until he was eight, he said, let him amass a thick catalog of visual memories to rummage through later.

He learned braille and went to public schools in the Seattle suburbs. His parents insisted that he not be treated differently than other children were. Habib has often told the story of how his mother, Susan Amini, responded when she learned that he was being kept on the sidelines of the school playground because he was blind and administrators worried that he'd hurt himself: She marched to the principal's office, declared that she herself would teach him the layout of the playground and demanded that he be given full access to it from then on. A broken arm, she said, could be fixed more easily than a broken spirit.

Habib devoured popular fiction, serious literature and history, reading in braille or listening to recordings. "Books allowed me to see—through the eyes of the author, the eyes of the narrator," he said. He excelled academically. Outperforming his peers was his insurance against being belittled or marginalized. He took up the piano, karate, downhill skiing.

He gained admission to Columbia University, where he focused on comparative literature and Middle Eastern studies, then won the Rhodes, then went to Yale for law school. "From braille to Yale" is how he distilled all of that in the public remarks he subsequently made as a politician. Politics was another way to prove himself, another arena in which to surprise anyone skeptical of how high someone like him could rise, another ladder on which there were always rungs to reach for—or so he came to understand as he ascended that ladder but didn't find the peace and joy he sought.

That wasn't all that politics was to him. It afforded him an opportunity, through what he used his soapbox to advocate and through the changes he championed as a government official, to extend to other underdogs the opportunities from which he had benefited.

But politics was also a race, a rush. He didn't merely win his first bid for the Washington House of Representatives in 2012 and then his first bid for the state's Senate in 2014 and then his first bid for lieutenant governor in 2016. He established himself as a preternaturally effective fundraiser. His admirers assumed there'd be even higher offices for him. They tagged him as a likely future governor.

But the more frequently they mentioned that, the more awkward he felt. His friend Lee Jason Goldberg, who went to

Columbia with him, told me that Habib watched other pols sprint to the television cameras and meticulously plot their careers and was turned off. "Every step that you're taking, it seems like there's another one you need to take," Goldberg said.

Habib recalled: "I was in talks with a top literary agent in New York about a book deal, and it was all predicated on *my* biography, *my* identity." He could feel himself being sucked into "a celebrity culture" in American politics that had nothing to do with public service. He could feel himself being swallowed by pride.

"How many ways," he said, "can you be called a rising star?" And how attached to being a star had he become? How dependent on what others were saying and writing about him?

He climbed to the peak of Mount Kilimanjaro in the summer of 2019. It was another of those accomplishments that he loved to rack up, he said. But on the final stretch of the march to the top, he became ill and had to pause every ten steps. "I was thinking to myself, 'If I don't summit, people will never believe that it was because of the bronchitis or altitude sickness—they'll think it's because I'm blind,'" he said. "I never told that story publicly, because it shows my vanity—that the only thing I feared more than death was public humiliation."

Something additional forced Habib to reevaluate who he had become and where he was headed. In late 2016, at the age of sixty-four, his father died, and Habib's grief consumed him, filling him with a sadness that no conventional badges of excellence—no higher rungs on the ladder—could alleviate. It also reminded him that there was indeed a limit that was non-negotiable: mortality.

"Someone once said, 'To say that your heart is broken is very close to saying that your heart is broken open,'" he recalled. And his broken-open heart, he added, put these questions at the forefront of his thoughts: "Am I experiencing real joy? Is this the path I want to travel?"

Although he hadn't been particularly religious as a child or in college, he was now drawn to Catholic teaching and faith, and one of his spiritual advisers in the church recommended that he read *The Jesuit Guide to (Almost) Everything*, by the Reverend James Martin, a nationally renowned Jesuit priest and bestselling author. Habib did—and it pointed him toward a different method of helping people and an even more different perch in the world, one where *my* wasn't the beginning of so many phrases on his lips and in his brain, where the rungs disappeared and the climb wasn't toward greater glory but toward greater generosity.

He thought long and hard about that perch, decided it was where he needed to be and announced, in March 2020, that instead of running for reelection to a second term as lieutenant governor in November, he would soon leave office to become a Roman Catholic priest. As part of that announcement, he wrote a first-person essay for the Jesuit magazine *America* in which he explained his decision. "I have come to believe that the best way to deepen my commitment to social justice is to reduce the complexity in my own life and dedicate it to serving others," he explained in the essay. "And I also know that, in this time of consumerism, distrust and polarization, many Americans are longing for an encounter with the transcendent, the joyful, the loving." Those many Americans included him.

I asked him if he was really going to be OK with the vow of chastity. He said that while he'd had romances, he'd never had an urge to be married with kids, so that part of the priesthood wasn't so daunting.

I asked his mother whether he was wired to take orders from others. She told me: "I actually joked with him that I wanted to see how that vow of obedience was going to work for him. More power to the Jesuits, I have to say."

I asked his friends what they made of this and whether they were blown away by it.

They weren't. One of them is Ronan Farrow, who was a classmate of his at Yale Law. Farrow said that Habib had always had "a tremendous degree of self-reflection. Maybe that goes hand in hand with his faith. He's a person on a journey, and he has developed a stillness and a centered-ness that I wouldn't have necessarily expected, because he was this bright, shining, super-ambitious leader. There's an extraordinary arc to Cyrus."

—

I talked with Habib, his mother and his friends in late March and early April 2020, for a column published in the *Times* on Easter weekend. A year later, on the cusp of another Easter, I reached out to him anew to get an update on his life since moving to Los Angeles to join the other novitiates the previous August.

He told me that he was actually just outside Tacoma, Washington, where he'd been sent "on assignment" for three months to live in a community belonging to L'Arche, an international group that helps people with intellectual disabilities. It was the kind of service work that he'd do much of in the course of his Jesuit training, which, in November, had included thirty days of silent reflection. For that period he cut himself off from the news and social media, so he had no idea what happened on Election Day until the following Sunday, when the priest celebrating the Mass that he attended wished President-elect Joe Biden strength and luck. Even then Habib didn't learn of the recounts and recriminations. He'd gone from political operator to political ostrich. And that seemed to suit him just fine.

He'd lost twenty-seven pounds, he said, adding that they were pounds he'd needed to lose. He was sleeping better than ever—an uninterrupted eight hours many nights. "I'm really happy," he told me. "I feel calmer and more at peace than I have since middle school. And that's a frightening thought, because that was thirty years ago." He chose that marker, he said, because it was after middle school that the worry about standing out enough in high school to get into a selective college began. Then he had to stand out in college to get to wherever he was going next, and so on, ad infinitum. Life became so busy with ambition. Life became so busy, period. Only after entering the novitiate, he said, did he realize that he'd lost "the ability to really be thinking about the thing that you're doing right then and not be thinking of other things." Even on vacation, he said, he'd be taking mental stock of his career progress, fretting about his social or romantic life, plotting the next month of work. He couldn't separate himself from all those concerns long enough to concentrate on the here, on the now, on what was right in front of him. But his new religious life was teaching him to do that.

It was also making him realize "how much of my answer to the question of am I happy was outsourced to other people— how much, instinctively, I'd think about how *other* people would perceive my experience. I'd say, 'Yeah, I'm having fun climbing Kilimanjaro,' because everyone would look at that and think it should be fun." His reports on his own state of mind "wouldn't follow a true inventory of my own feelings," he said. He couldn't ever forget "what Frank Bruni thinks of me or the readers of the *New York Times* think or the people of the state of Washington think or my mom thinks. The monologue in my head was not what was in my heart. It was the voices of imaginary interlocutors, imaginary spectators."

But not anymore. He was learning to tune out those voices. He *had* tuned out those voices. "I am done," he said, "trying to mold my heart into the shape that others would have for it."

It doesn't necessarily take membership in a religious order or thirty days of silence to get there. The most broadly relevant part of Habib's arc isn't that it bended toward the clergy. It's that he took a sledgehammer to his ego along the way. Did his disability factor into that? I believe so. I believe that it was a nudge and possibly a shove toward contemplation—of his place in the world, of his obligation to others, of the point of it all—that had more than a bit in common with Bob Kerrey's injury and Dorrie's Parkinson's. There are devastations that break a heart open. And there can be beauty in the rupture. In the shards.

Chapter Thirteen
SHOWBOATS AND TUGBOATS

Before Joe Biden announced his 2020 presidential bid, I didn't just write a column saying that he was too old to run. I wrote two of them.

Oh, I gave reasons beyond his age. I mentioned his indiscipline during his two prior presidential campaigns and the fact that both of them, mismanaged and characterized by missteps, suggested that he didn't have a successful campaign in him. I asserted that voters, especially Democratic ones, tended to prefer forward-looking candidates to backward-looking ones, and I discussed how it was impossible for Biden not to present himself and be cast as a restoration of the Barack Obama administration, a return to the past. But some of those points were just anagrams of my lament about how long he'd kicked around, how much less vigorous he seemed, how fully any youthful glow was gone. They boiled down to: He's past his prime.

Except, it turned out, he wasn't, at least depending on how you defined prime. And it can be defined in any number of ways. "Prime" is in the perspective of the beholder. Past-prime Biden, who was seventy-seven on Election Day in November 2020 and seventy-eight at his inauguration the following January, had a lot going for him that in-his-prime Biden didn't.

Past-prime Biden defied the naysayers. He did that in the Democratic primaries, when his response to a fourth-place finish in the Iowa caucuses and a *fifth*-place finish in New Hampshire a week later wasn't some freak-out. His confidence didn't crumple. His campaign organization didn't implode in a storm of recriminations and finger-pointing. He didn't look beaten down or scared. He soldiered on—to Nevada, where he did better than he had in Iowa and New Hampshire, and to South Carolina, which he won handily. That was the beginning of the end—for his rivals. He kept winning from then on.

Biden again defied the naysayers at the Democratic National Convention the following summer. Before his big speech on the convention's climactic fourth night, many trained observers—present company included—wondered whether he still had enough gas and enough grip to get to the end of it without losing velocity or swerving this way and that. He did.

He wasn't in the fleetest, shiniest, nimblest form of his protracted career, a fact that Donald Trump, then seventy-four and no Ferrari himself, tried to exploit. But what Biden lacked in zip, he made up for in zen, and he was wise enough to present himself in a fashion that invited a more appreciative appraisal of what an unusually long road he'd traveled to his party's presidential nomination. He was a paragon of stamina and optimism for a country suffering through a pandemic and reeling from the melodrama of Trump's unsteady stewardship. In a period of great pain, he personified perseverance.

He had survived personal tragedies. When he was in his late twenties, his young wife and daughter were killed in a car accident. He outlived another of his children, Beau, who had been the attorney general of Delaware and a rising Democratic star shortly before he died of brain cancer at the age of forty-six. Biden had also suffered political humiliations and been given ample reason in the last of his eight years as Obama's vice president to believe that his career in politics was over. Obama and his aides saw Biden as too chatty, too goofy, too corny to shoulder the Democratic Party's ambitions in 2016. They threw their support behind Hillary Clinton. And that was supposed to be that.

But the tumult of Trump's presidency created an opening and appetite for Biden, who maximized that opportunity with a composure on the campaign trail, a patience, a steadiness and a succinctness that had always eluded his younger self. Those traits contradicted the timeworn notion that our habits and orientations become more fixed, not less, when we reach the age that he had, and that you can't teach an old dog new tricks. Biden had learned new tricks.

He had once been a windbag, famous for sucking the oxygen out of a room. I recall a lunch that several of my fellow *Times* columnists and I had with him in Charlotte, North Carolina, in 2012, during that year's Democratic convention. The meal went well beyond its supposed time limit because Biden could never keep to any time limit, not when he was doing the talking and basking in attention from a rapt audience. We came away from that meeting marveling not just at his accessibility and his warmth but at his verbosity, which was wholly intact when he visited the *Times* building the following year and met with a small group of editors and writers, including me. A single answer to one of our questions could sprawl across five to ten minutes. He went on and on.

I watched him on the campaign trail in 2020 and in Washington in the first months of his presidency and kept marveling at what felt to me like one of the most remarkable personality transplants in modern American political history. The quasiclownish exuberance was gone and, with it, many of the gaffes. Where he'd once been a braggart, he was now modest, diverting attention from his own aspirations and accomplishments to Americans' hopes and needs. He was less showboat than tugboat, humbly poised to pull us out of perilous waters. Each day, each week, he tugged and tugged, his head down, his comments circumspect, his focus precise.

His approach to the presidency was entirely about lessons learned. In so much of what he did and said (or didn't say), the invaluable benefit of experience—of age—came into play. For example, many officials in the Obama administration had come to believe, in retrospect, that the enormous 2009 stimulus was too restrained and that its mechanism for delivering relief to Americans in need was neither obvious enough to its recipients nor adequately touted. So Biden, with his $1.9 trillion American Rescue Plan and a sequence of public events around the country to celebrate it, addressed that concern. Some officials in the Obama administration felt that they squandered too much time seeking at least some Republican support for Obamacare when it was never destined to come. Biden enacted the American Rescue Plan without a single Republican vote in the Senate or the House.

That arithmetic didn't fit the way he'd often described himself, as someone bent on bipartisanship and open to compromise. But he'd decided that a fraught passage in American history and Republican obstructionism called for something different. So he did something different, and suddenly there was talk of a progressive watershed, of a turning point in Americans' relationship with their government, of a transformative moment. That moment came courtesy of a president who was the oldest ever when he took office, which he did after—and almost surely because of—his own late-in-the-game metamorphosis.

During the chapter of my life when I began to contemplate and experience aging as I never had before, there was so much vivid proof of its upsides in the subject that I wrote about most frequently, American politics, which is a veritable gerontocracy. The runner-up to Biden in the Democratic primaries, Bernie Sanders, was more than a year *older* than he was. Sanders, in turn, was a year and a half *younger* than Nancy Pelosi, who reached the zenith of her public regard during Trump's presidency, which began when she was seventy-six and ended when she was eighty.

She jousted with Trump more effectively than perhaps any other politician, and the reasons included her poise and steel, the kind forged by many battles over many years. She made clear that they accrue as wrinkles do, with prolonged exposure to the elements. Like Biden, she carried the moral authority of someone who had done so much loving, so much losing, so much regrouping, so much figuring out how to press on. She knew how systems worked and she knew how to work them.

Pelosi was arguably more powerful than ever on the far side of seventy-five. Ruth Bader Ginsburg was arguably more popular than ever on the far side of *eighty-five*. When she died in September 2020, at eighty-seven, after more than a quarter century on the Supreme Court, a friend wrote to me, "Isn't it incredible that R.G.B. reached the pinnacle of her profession at sixty and became an icon in her eighties?"

Incredible? No. Interesting and worth thinking about? Definitely, and it was an aspect of her life—of its arc—that got somewhat short shrift in the appraisals and analyses of her. I think that's mostly because there were so many *other* aspects to appraise and analyze. But I think it's partly because we're a country in thrall to youth and sometimes incapable of considering the triumphs of older people as a function of their age rather than a contradiction of it. Sometimes people's best opportunities don't come along for a good long while: Opportunity is kin to serendipity, and you can't plan for that.

Youth has its indisputable advantages, cerebral as well as epidermal. "Our rapid synaptic processing speed and working memory peak in our twenties," Rich Karlgaard, the author of the book *Late Bloomers*, told National Public Radio in 2019. He cited a respected 2015 study that examined what people did best during each decade of life. And while there were trophies for the twentysomethings, there were medals for their elders, too. "In our 30s, 40s, and 50s," Karlgaard explained, "we begin to develop a whole range of skills we didn't have before: executive functioning, management skills, compassion, equanimity. All of those things."

And in our sixties and seventies? "Wisdom really begins to kick in," Karlgaard said.

Of course, none of that's neat and clean. It doesn't apply to everyone. But what I saw in Biden, in Pelosi and in Ginsburg looked a whole lot like wisdom. I saw such varied but overlapping talents as taking the long view, taking a breath when necessary, taking the measure of a person or an event in a context large enough to get the assessment right, taking comfort where it's readiest and most reliable, taking courage from the fact that you've made it this far and are likely to make it at least a tad further still. Wisdom was what I heard and felt in Marge Feder's words. It's also what I read in an essay in the *Times*, written by someone in his late sixties, that spoke so precisely to how I was beginning to feel in my late fifties.

Its title was "Why It's Good to Be Old, Even in a Pandemic." Its author was Bob Brody. He resists the belief that people over sixty-five cower in fear because of their greater vulnerability, statistically, to life-threatening cases of Covid-19. He didn't question that vulnerability or dismiss those fears. But he articulated what he believed to be a truth larger than one perilous period and undiminished by it. He called that truth "the biggest dirty little secret of all time" and defined it this way: "Aging can in so many respects make us better than ever."

He explained that he was "now old enough to know that our

lives, like all of nature itself, go in cycles." A bad week or day no longer sent him into a tailspin because he had enough experience to understand that "tomorrow is all the more likely to be fine." "The older I get," he added, "the more comfortable I feel in my own skin, too—it's at once thinner and thicker now. I've come to accept myself as I am, limitations and all. The umpteen uncertainties that afflict us while young—about our identities, our role in the community, our philosophy of life—have largely evaporated. By now I know with absolute certainty what I like (quiet, solitude, reading, movies, basketball) and what I dislike (noise, crowds, ice hockey)." He could have been writing for Biden. For Pelosi. For me—or me in a few years, at my current rate of progress. I was getting better and better at both the compassion and the equanimity that Karlgaard associated with people in their forties and fifties. Once I nailed those, wisdom would be right around the corner.

He didn't mention Jonathan Rauch's 2018 book, *The Happiness Curve: Why Life Gets Better After 50*, but he was condensing many of the same dynamics that it explored. Through profiles of people in their fifties and older, through extensive interviews with experts and through personal reflections of his own, Rauch showed how something remarkable happens to most people as they leave their forties behind and approach old age. A contentment settles in, not because they've finally devised a formula for it or belatedly adhered to a golden script but because, well, maturity works that way. It's predictable. It's mappable. "Stress declines after about age fifty," Rauch wrote. "Emotional regulation improves."

Citing the work of one scholar, Rauch ticked off the psychological and emotional habits at which people over fifty excel: "Living in the present. Taking each day as it comes. Savoring the positive. Dwelling less on the negative. Accepting. Not overreacting. Setting realistic goals. Prioritizing the really important people and relationships in life." Those are the building blocks of the happiness that older people report in surveys that probe how individuals of different ages feel about themselves and their circumstances. "Asked to rate their life satisfaction with a number, respondents score their sixties and seventies highest, with only a slight decline in the eighties," Rauch wrote.

An excellent article by Susan Bell on a website operated by the University of Southern California referred to some of the same surveys that Rauch consulted, name-checked some of the same researchers and reached the same conclusions. Bell noted that a landmark longitudinal study by Susan Charles, a psychology professor at University of California, Irvine, and Margaret Gatz, a psychology professor at USC, "showed that negative emotions such as anger, anxiety, stress and frustration, far from increasing as we get older, actually decrease with age. Positive emotions, such as excitement, pride, calm and elation, remain stable across the life span. Only the very oldest group registered a very slight decline in positive emotions." By that she meant people in their eighties and above, not in their sixties and seventies.

Another study that Bell mentioned showed that older people seemed better able, or at least more inclined, to notice and concentrate on positive scenes and stimuli, just as Rauch flagged. These people edited the world so that an image of a smiling baby took up more of their brain space than one of, say, a graveyard.

"This also affects memory," Bell wrote, "with older people remembering the positive images more often than younger people, who are more likely to remember the negative." Bell at one point focused on people who are physically frail or ill, reporting that these conditions seem not to translate into discontent, whether you're a young person to whom those developments aren't supposed to happen or an older person to whom they are.

"We believe that if we're sick or in a wheelchair," Bell wrote, "life would be miserable, and yet study after study shows that is not the case."

Norbert Schwarz, a professor of psychology and marketing at USC, explained that what determined people's happiness wasn't their physical conditions or capabilities but what they paid attention to, what they emphasized, what they accomplished within the possibilities available to them. He told her: "It's important to realize that no matter what your illness is, you're not a patient twenty-four hours a day. Much of your day is still pleasant. The sun still shines, you spend time with friends, food still tastes good. All of these things are just as enjoyable as before."

Rauch's book, Bell's article and other writing on the topic underscore how much contentment has to do with what we accept, what we expect and what we measure our current situations against. Many younger people are still anxiously in search of themselves, in the manner that Bob Brody described in his essay in the *Times*. They don't know what to accept, what to expect. Many are still busily amassing accomplishments, a process that can be as exhausting as it is exhilarating, and haven't yet found their financial footing in the world, something that's more likely to come with age. Many are suffused with dread about the future they're creating for themselves: Will it be at least minimally secure? Will the shape it takes be a workable one?

Older people know that the answer to the latter question is yes, because they've reached that future. They're living it. The amassing is over. The anxiety is pointless. There are incidental frustrations. But they're not mistaken for existential ones, and they don't shake the fundamental confidence forged by sheer endurance.

Anthony Fauci is part of the American gerontocracy, someone who reached his maximum exposure and tallest public profile deep into his career and life. He was seventy-nine when he appeared at the daily news conferences that President Trump held toward the start of the pandemic. He was eighty when Trump left office and the right wing's demonization of him only intensified, casting him as a bespectacled Beelzebub intent on crushing liberties rather than saving lives. He was attacked by deeply conservative, grandstanding lawmakers at congressional hearings. He was savaged by conservative media. He received death threats. So did his family.

I spoke with him in July 2021, at what seemed to be the peak of the anti-Fauci fervor. He was smiling and his voice was steady, and I asked him if that calm would have been as easy to maintain if all of this had happened to him in his thirties or forties or even his sixties for that matter.

"I don't know, but I don't think so," he told me. "I don't want to make analogies that are not appropriate, but I think this might be appropriate: Look at soldiers in the middle of battle. Those who have been through it know there is a risk but also know that there's an end—there's victory." By the time Trump and the pandemic came along, Fauci had been through the AIDS epidemic, during which he learned from early mistakes and many of the activists who initially denounced him as uncaring came to respect him mightily. He had been through SARS and Ebola and knew what it meant to make the best judgment calls that you could on agonizingly incomplete evidence, to have those calls questioned, to have your motives and your methods picked apart. He had learned the temperaments and handled the demands of many presidents, if none remotely like Trump. So he had faith—in science, in himself, in the healing of wounds with the passage of time. That kind of faith comes only with experience, which multiplies with age.

He also knew that he was where he should be, where he must be, because he knew himself—what brings him peace, what doesn't—better than he had as a young man. That, too, was a source of comfort. He understood that, at his age, retirement would be reasonable and, for most people, preferable to sixty-hour workweeks and furious public opposition. But, he said, "I'm not a lying-on-the-beach-with-a-piña-colada kind of guy. I'm just not. I've never been." He was, instead, someone who had to see things through, to finish the job, to tie up all the loose ends, to provide guidance when he had some and it was sorely needed.

He was also someone who could survive the fury and the ugly name calling because, thanks to his age, he was less sensitive to insult, less fixated on his moment-to-moment reputation.

He asks himself not how he's mentioned in headlines but how Americans "get this outbreak ended as quickly as we possibly can," he told me. He obsesses not on what kind of important paper about the pandemic he can write for some lofty medical journal but on how an entire country successfully turns the page. Being praised pales next to doing right, doing good. His vanity ebbs or at least takes a more constructive form. "The older you get, the less and less it is about you," he said. "The less important it is to strive to advance, and the more important it is to look at what's going on around you and try to have a positive impact." And that's more and better than liberating. It's happiness-making.

⁓

Celebrity interviews have been a thread throughout my journalism career, beginning at the *Detroit Free Press* in the early 1990s, when, as a late twentysomething, I became the newspaper's chief movie critic, the last job I held there before moving in 1995 to the *Times*. At the *Free Press*, which was Michigan's big morning newspaper of record, the movie critic wrote not just reviews but also long articles about the people in them, and I spent time with Mel Gibson when he was promoting *Braveheart*, Sandra Bullock on the set of *While You Were Sleeping*, Robert Redford when *Quiz Show*, which he directed, was released. I also did a long interview with Sigourney Weaver about her role in Roman Polanski's *Death and the Maiden*. She remembered it a quarter century later, in the summer of 2020, when I interviewed her several times for a different reason and we became friendly.

What she remembered—or, perhaps more accurately, re-freshed her memory of—was what a jumble of insecurities she had been that first time around. She hadn't jabbered or cried or anything like that, but she'd opened up about, and splashed around in, her long struggle to get to a place of confidence, even in spite of *Aliens* and Oscar nominations. She was forty-five then.

"I always felt a little bit illegitimate," she told me then. "I did these action pictures. I did *Ghostbusters*. Whenever they talked about serious actresses, I always felt that I had one foot in the land of Arnold Schwarzenegger, one foot in the land of Ivan Reitman and maybe a toe in the land of Meryl Streep and Glenn Close." She added that her agent, Sam Cohn, was also Streep's and that she "used to go into Sam and stand there crying, say-ing, 'But, Sam, I want an *Out of Africa*. I want a *Sophie's Choice*.' I used to say this, but I never did anything about it. I never had the confidence to go after those roles. Roman had to come after me." She meant for the movie version of *Death and the Maiden*, which, as a play on Broadway, had starred . . . Glenn Close.

She said that when the Streep-like role in *Gorillas in the Mist* of the doomed primatologist Dian Fossey *did* come her way, she at first tried to convince the director, Michael Apted, that she was wrong for it. "I sat there telling him whom he should interview," Weaver said. "I mentioned Diane Keaton, Vanessa Redgrave, Judy Davis. I'm a good caster. I can always come up with someone better than myself."

My reunion with Weaver twenty-five years later came about because the *Times*'s fashion and style magazine, *T*, had asked me to profile her for its annual issue of "The Greats," five people being enshrined in a sort of cultural-relevance hall of fame. I had profiled Alessandro Michele, the fashion designer who had spectacularly resuscitated the Gucci brand, for a "Greats" package. Because of the pandemic, Weaver and I did only one of our three interviews in person, at her apartment on Manhattan's east side, and the other two on Zoom. She brought up the fact that we'd met before and told me that she'd gone back to reread my article, noticed that she'd also talked about being in therapy and cringed. She said that I'd presented an accurate portrait of that version of herself, but that version was distant from the current one. She was so much calmer now, she said, so much more at peace, so much more content. She was seventy.

And I could sense that this wasn't some sort of airbrushing or sales job. Her posture was relaxed; her smiles, frequent. While her remarks in 1995 were distinguished by self-criticism and regret, her comments in 2020 suggested a detached fascination with her past and present quirks, a bemusement at the unanticipated turns that her life had taken, a thankfulness that so much of it had gone well and a resignation to any upsets that came along. A minor upset came courtesy of me: Because of the dictates of social distancing, I seated myself so far from her in her living room that my iPhone's "voice memos" program failed to record audibly the bulk of our nearly two-hour interview that evening. When I tried to listen to it the next day, I realized it was useless. I had to ask Weaver to do the whole damned thing all over again on Zoom. No problem, she said, and there was no edge in the response, no prickle. Just the making-do of someone who understood that making a fuss often magnified inconveniences without erasing them.

Weaver's equanimity wasn't about some retreat to a rocking chair. Over the years just before our 2020 interviews, she'd done work on a bunch of movies, most of which were in the can but all of which had yet to be released, thanks in part to the pandemic. A few of those movies had asked as much of her as any in the past.

Playing the lead in *The Good House*, about a small-town real estate agent whose denial about her alcoholism catches up with her, she carried the movie from its gently comedic opening scenes to its tear-filled closing ones. She was magnificent. (I was given an advance viewing of it.) To reprise her *Avatar* role for *Avatar 2*, she had to learn to "free dive," which requires holding your breath and steeling yourself so you can plunge and linger deep underwater without a scuba diver's oxygen tank. Many of her scenes were to be shot on the bottom of a gigantic tank.

So she practiced in Key West, Florida, and in Hawaii. Over hour after hour with a coach who had trained elite military divers, she built up the length of time she could go without breathing. She got to a point where, after a big gulp of supplemental oxygen, she could last for more than six minutes. She also had to learn not to squint or clamp her mouth shut—both natural reactions when you're submerged—during take after take in the tank. She had weights around her waist and professional divers who sped her back to the surface for air at brief, regular intervals.

Her age, she told me, was a major motivation: She wanted to show all the younger cast members what an older person could still do. Besides, she said, "My hope is that what I receive from the universe is even more outrageous than anything I can think of. I don't really say to myself, 'Well, you can't do this.' Or, 'You can't do that.' Let me at it! And we'll see."

Let me at it! And we'll see. It brought to mind Marion Sheppard's motto: *As long as we're alive, we have to keep moving.* Not a shabby pair of directives to tuck into your pocket and carry into your late fifties, your sixties, your seventies and beyond. Not a bad way to look at every challenge, every day.

Weaver also made me think of Nancy Root, whom I'd met in September 2017, about a month before my stroke, on that Baltic cruise, and whom I saw again that December, when I took my first long post-stroke flight so I could visit her in her home outside Phoenix. At the time of the cruise, Nancy was eighty-two, and she was confined for the most part to a wheelchair: When she introduced herself to me at a cocktail party at which I and the other speakers from the *Times* mingled with the passengers who'd signed up for our lectures, she did so from her chair, flanked by a young couple whom she'd brought with her on the cruise so that they could help her navigate the ship's narrow corridors and get offboard and back on board when it docked in its various ports of call. I adored her immediately.

She also fed my vanity. "How's Adelle?" she asked me, about my sister. From *Born Round* and my columns, she knew all of my siblings by name.

After that cocktail party and maybe one other, I didn't see Nancy much. She came to my lectures, which occurred every three days or so. But the other social gatherings for our group, which happened pretty much daily? She skipped them. I never had a chance to ask her why or to say goodbye on the last day of the cruise, so I got her email address from one of the group organizers and followed up with her when I arrived home in New York.

"On our cruise," she wrote to me, "I *again* experienced the uneasiness of people toward us 'physically challenged' types. Even among our educated group, people ignored me." So she parceled out her exposure to them. Rather than stew or mope, she did her own thing with her two traveling companions.

I asked her if I could talk with her more about this, potentially for a column, if I came to Phoenix. Yes, she said, and so I went there, dropping by her apartment and then taking her out to dinner two nights in a row. She jettisoned her wheelchair for those dinners; she could do that occasionally, by taking a Percocet just beforehand, using a cane and moving slowly. I allowed extra time to get to the restaurants. From my end, it was no big deal. It was a privilege, really, because Nancy had such a positive outlook, such a generous spirit, such engagement with the political news of the day and the books, fiction as well as nonfiction, that she compulsively read. She loved words. Nothing about her condition got in the way of that.

That condition stemmed from a childhood bout with polio and was called post-polio syndrome, which afflicts many polio survivors much later in life, degrading their muscles. The degradation of hers had necessitated a wheelchair, which she'd begun using a few years before the cruise, and she'd noticed that whenever she was in it, she disappeared. People looked over her, around her, through her. They assumed that questions about her should be directed to whoever was accompanying her, as if her compromised mobility equaled idiocy.

That's what I spoke with her about and then wrote about, a

kind of bigotry that flourished even at a time when Americans were increasingly examining and acknowledging their prejudices. She was angry about that disrespect. But her anger paled next to her determination not to be dissuaded by other people's dismissals of, and condescension toward, her. No matter what they thought or said, she would go where she wanted to go, do what she could still do, relish the pastimes that gave her such pleasure.

She had traveled, wheelchair and all, to Singapore not long before the Baltic cruise. Back in her Phoenix suburb, she had her favorite places for eating out and she ate regularly at them, even if it could be a bit of a production to get there. She also had ready access to robust memories of a rich life that included college at Oberlin, marriage, motherhood and important, fulfilling jobs at the National Science Foundation and the Department of Agriculture. "I have my mind," she told me, "and I see where others are losing theirs." While her husband was no longer alive, her daughter lived nearby.

Toward the end of our second dinner, after two glasses of wine apiece, we mulled the vocabulary of her lot. She'd been calling herself "crippled," a reflection of the premium she placed on directness and of the streak of mischief in her. She was being naughty. Even so, I told her, the word made me cringe.

"Well, 'handicapped' isn't supposed to be OK," she said, "and I'm *not* going to call myself 'differently abled.' You're a writer. Give me a word."

"What about 'limited'?" I said. "We're all limited in ways. You're limited in a particular way."

I was satisfied with that solution at the time. We both were.

But I grew less and less so, not because it was untrue in the abstract but because it was untrue to her perspective. "Crippled" for her was a kind of joke, a way of laughing in the face of physical indignity, not a harsh reckoning with diminished potencies and truncated possibilities, and she didn't emphasize the truncations, the limitations. So "limited" didn't work for her— or for me. We were . . . recalibrated. Reoriented. I could cycle through a thesaurus of options and not find the right one. She was a human being in a challenging situation, which meant that she was more like than unlike everyone else. She was a human being in flux.

Deep into the pandemic, I realized that I hadn't heard from her in a while. I sent an email. A day passed. Then two days. Then a week. By dint of her medical condition and age, Nancy was the kind of person for whom the coronavirus could be disastrous. I grew worried.

Then, nine days after my email, a response: "I've just emerged from giving over the month of December to cataract surgeries on both eyes. I never realized, in my first eighty-five years, how nearsighted I was—even with contacts. How I wish there was such a surgery for you! But, Frank, how well the brain compensates, at least for me."

She went on to say that a few months earlier, she'd had "a spinal cord stimulator surgically implanted permanently in my back." It communicated with an iPod in her living room, which gave it signals to stop her brain's experience of pain. "It won't let me walk again, but I now can put weight on my polio leg and sleep through the night." She sounded amazed at scientific ingenuity. She sounded upbeat. Which is to say that she sounded, after so many months in which the pandemic's hardships added to her others, like herself.

She inquired about Regan—whom she'd come to know as she had Adelle, through my gratuitously autobiographical writing—and sent "much love" to both of us. I promised myself that I'd check in with her again in a few months, to make sure she knew that I was sending much love back. But before I could, I received an email from one of the two people who'd traveled with and helped her on the Baltic cruise. Nancy had died.

I didn't ask how. I didn't want details. I had the one that mattered most, which was the spirit she'd shown—and the experiences she'd insisted on—before it was all over.

I went to Iowa when Biden did. I spent the week before the Democratic caucuses in 2020 doing what I'd done in 2016 and in 2012, following various presidential candidates around the state so that I could hear them give their speeches, assess their connection with their audiences and ask those voters what they were looking for at this particular juncture in the American story. It was the usual drill, the same old same old. Except it was different.

On election-year trips to Iowa past, I'd been conscious of what all my journalistic peers were doing, of whether they'd chosen to attend the same rally that I'd picked or gone to some other candidate's competing event. I'd question my own decisions, even reverse them. I'd fill my evenings with work-related dinners, convinced that if I didn't debrief this fellow reporter or that campaign operative, I'd miss out on something crucial. I'd overstuff my schedule from dawn on, not because I brimmed with energy but because I swam in insecurity. I'd doubt myself. And I'd hobble myself by doing so.

Not this time. I'd been around long enough to figure out that there was an overabundance of material at hand, that I was just one person reaching for a few pieces of it, and that to collect too much was to create waste and court exhaustion. I figured out, too, that my obsession with what colleagues were thinking and what campaign hands were saying often muffled my own instincts and voice.

Just as I'd always become so nervous before calling someone famous on the phone, I'd become even more so when approaching strangers to ask them questions. It made me feel so conspicuous, so intrusive. I hated anything that fell into the category of what were known in the business as "man-on-the-street" interviews, and talking to the people at a candidate's rallies fell squarely into that category. I'd lose minute after minute to dallying, to dread, to mentally girding myself.

But at the first rally in Iowa that I attended this time, which happened to be a Biden rally, I just dove in. I was going to have to do that eventually, so why not do it sooner? That was an obvious deduction, but it seldom persuaded me before. It persuaded me now. I had less patience for complications of my own doing and traps of my own making. Amid all the stuff beyond our control or prediction, how and why wouldn't we control what we could?

I approached and quizzed a voter just inside the front door of the school where Biden was holding his rally. Then I approached and quizzed another voter maybe a dozen feet beyond her. Then another in the gymnasium where Biden would deliver his remarks. I steered clear of the gymnasium seats where members of the media were supposed to cluster and deposited myself in a nearby set of bleachers, among yet more voters. I could turn to my left, to my right, to my front, to my rear and interview whoever was there. I did just that. I scribbled and scribbled, filling the pages of my spiral-ring notebook. I wasn't going to make each day in Iowa as long as I'd made the days in 2012 and 2016, but I was going to make each hour count. If ambition is the province of the young, efficiency belongs to their elders.

Once the gymnasium had filled with voters, Biden and his entourage arrived. He took a seat in a row of folding chairs set up right in front of the bleachers where I sat, no more than fifteen feet in front of me. I had an unobstructed view of the back of his head, where the white wisps of his remaining hair didn't cover the scalp beneath, mottled with damage from decades of sun. It wasn't one of the parts of him that faced the television cameras and received the attention of foundation and concealer. It was a more honest patch of skin.

And what it honestly said was that there's no predicting which stretch of life will bring people their greatest emotional riches and get them to the place where they've long been trying to go, but they're more likely to feel comfortable in their own skin, to use the hoary locution that Bob Brody did, when it has spots and it sags than when it's even-toned and taut.

Biden listened to several tributes to him by Iowa supporters and then bounded to the microphone, where he spoke at shorter length, but with greater conviction, than was his custom in the garrulous old days. I listened to him then and again at another event a few days later and wrote a column that took issue with the gathering consensus that he'd do poorly in Iowa and maybe overall in the contest for the Democratic nomination. That consensus was right about Iowa and wrong about the big picture, but Biden didn't seem to be paying any attention to it anyway. He was heeding an inner voice. He heard it almost perfectly.

Chapter Fourteen
LEVITATION

You should see me fly.

It's a whole watery production. It's a big, bloated joke. Because a fear of flying was instilled in me almost from the moment my right eye malfunctioned, because I was warned off high altitudes and dehydration, I became convinced, even after further fact-finding should have calmed me, that the only sure way to remove the risk of going blind from air travel was to do it with a body as pumped full of water as a body could be. To be *super* hydrated, a human water balloon. I reasoned that if thin oxygen *or* dehydration was the possible nemesis of my one good optic nerve, then thin oxygen *plus* dehydration equaled ocular Armageddon.

So I would drink a bottle of water en route to the airport. Then I would get and drink another bottle once I'd passed through security. Then I'd buy and bring *another* two bottles on the plane, so I could continue saturating myself with water. My belly would swell. My bladder, too, even though I was wise enough to make the restroom nearest my departure gate my last stop before boarding. I'd be itching to tear off my seat belt and sprint to one of the plane's toilets the minute that we reached cruising altitude and I could do so without a censorious look and stern verbal reprimand from a flight attendant. And the rest of my flight would be a periodic pinballing to and from the toilet as I hydrated myself to a fare-thee-well and relieved myself accordingly. I made sure to get an aisle seat, always, no matter how far back in the plane I had to go to do so, because a window or middle would have been cruel to fellow passengers in my row.

Was I overdoing it? For sure. There was as much superstition as science in *this* level of liquidity, but there was a soupcon of science in the mix, and I felt safer this way, so it became my habit. My commitment, really. I went incrementally lighter on the number of bottles and frequency of sips over time, but I stuck to the principle. It was costly: The markup on water from airport newsstands is criminal. It was inconvenient, as I surrendered too much potential reading or laptop time on every flight to the toilet.

And it was, on occasion, painful. The layouts of some small airplanes prevented ready access to a restroom. The turbulence on some flights trapped me in my seat. I'd fight the need to relieve myself for periods twice as long as I thought I could last, not sure whether the pressure on my bladder or the panic in my brain was worse. I'd count each second of the plane's descent. I'd resolve to sprint faster than Usain Bolt from the jetway to the terminal's nearest toilet. I'd curse my predicament, certain that it would end in grave humiliation. And then I'd survive it.

In my late fifties, in the aftermath of my stroke, I had discomforts that hadn't been there before. Worries, too. And there were surely additional worries barreling toward me, thanks to the nature of aging. (Stay tuned!) I wished I were moving through the world more gracefully—I'd say "fluidly," except I've established that fluids were a culprit in my gracelessness. I wished that my body weren't a vessel of so many unpleasant surprises and sensations.

But it was a sturdy body regardless. And it did move. I made peace with its imperfection. I hatched contingency plans. And no matter how awkwardly or achingly, it got me where I needed it to get me. It carried me through.

⁓

I've tried to be honest about everything that I've shared in these pages, but I did tell a lie, and I told it repeatedly. What I mean is that I mischaracterized and minimized something, though that wasn't my intent. It was my coping mechanism, and while I want to come clean now, before I'm done, about this deception, I have every intention of going back to it. Deception—at least the right kind—is our friend. It's my friend. I'm hurting nobody with this one. I'm helping me.

Anyway, my confession: There are many days, even after all these years, even after all this practice, despite this ever-plastic brain, when my vision does a number on me. I downplay that in part because I still have trouble describing the experience. I'll be typing or reading and instead of my sight being trained on one cluster of words or one line of text, it's swimming over and under and around all the words and all the text. This isn't consistent with any commonplace symptom of NAION. It's not a phenomenon that my eye doctors mentioned and warned me about. It's the idiosyncratic offshoot of the particular damage done to my partially defunct optic nerve.

It was harder to write this book than it was to write any of the half dozen books I produced before it. It's harder to write columns and other articles. Some of them I toss off as easily as ever, or more easily than ever, because when my eyes aren't misbehaving, my decades of professional experience can kick in. But my eyes do misbehave. Not on most days. Not with most articles. But with many articles. I do a few hours of work, I think I've done well, and then I circle back and notice not only that there are missing words and mangled words but a mangled rhythm and mangled conceptualization. The gumbo of my vision has made a soup of my thoughts.

I start over. I fix what needs fixing. That it's fixable is what matters—that there's an action to take, an adjustment to make. And I'm more than my work. I know: duh. But it can be easy to forget that.

I'm a son who has done and continues to do his imperfect best, under difficult circumstances. A degree of respect for my father's privacy compels me to skimp on details, but Dad's deepening confusion opened and then widened a gulf between him and me and, equally, between him and my siblings. It was as sorrowful a situation as any I've encountered, all the more so because it *wasn't* fixable. There was nothing to do but grieve it, and to remember that it was just one late and discrete chapter of his life and of our relationship. It didn't erase all the other, better chapters before it.

I'm a brother who drew even closer to his siblings because of that situation, who takes a joy in them and a comfort from them that have nothing to do with the acuity of his eyesight or the physical toll of aging. Our bond stems from forces independent of those—from the ease and volubility of our conversations, from the vividness of our overlapping memories, from the compatibility of our senses of humor, from their intimate understanding of what's distinctive in me and my grasp of the specialness in each of them.

I'm an uncle with the privilege of watching nine nieces and nephews figure out who they are and where they belong in this confusing and chaotic world. They're full of surprises because life is. The oldest of them, Leslie, my goddaughter, was married in June 2021, in a ceremony in Hilton Head, South Carolina, a place chosen in part because it was a frequent vacation spot of my family's when Mom was still alive, when Dad was still sharp, when there were no nieces and nephews and then Leslie and then another and another.

On a trip to Hilton Head when Leslie was around two, I asked her parents—my brother Harry and his wife, Sylvia—a big favor: Could I be the one to escort her from our rental house to the beach and show her, for the first time, the Atlantic Ocean? They generously said yes. I led her by the hand for part of the way, then carried her in my arms for the rest. She was then learning to speak not only English but also a bit of

Spanish, including the word for "water." When I asked her what she thought about the gray-blue expanse of the Atlantic, she answered, "So many aguas in there!" I kept hearing that as she walked down the aisle, as she said her vows, as she and her husband, Charlie, danced, and as the music of the past blended with the music of the present to become something even more beautiful, something that I'll always hear and always have.

I'm a teacher. A *professor!* In late 2020, I was approached by Duke University about an appointment there, an endowed position teaching journalism to undergraduates under the auspices of the school of public policy. At that point I'd been working at the *Times* for more than twenty-five years and, for the last sixteen of them, been living in the same apartment building on the Upper West Side (though I'd changed apartments nine years in). Enough. I itched for change, for a new adventure, and a new adventure was not only an affirmation of all the ability still within me but also a vote of confidence in what I could manage if true disability struck. Because I'd looked for it, because I'd looked hard *at* it, I'd seen that disability was navigable, taking people down different roads but not to dead ends. If Juan Jose could conduct diplomacy, if David Tatel could decide complicated legal matters, if Todd Blenkhorn could get up on a stage and make an audience roar with laughter, well, I could write and teach without sharp eyesight. If necessary, I'd do so.

The position at Duke not only permitted but also created time for outside work, so while I ceased to be a full-fledged columnist at the *Times*, I continued to write for it in a regular-but-reduced capacity from North Carolina's Research Triangle, the three points of which are Raleigh (the state capital), Durham

(Duke's location) and Chapel Hill, where I'd gone to college at the University of North Carolina and where, in the summer of 2021, I moved into a large house on a wooded lot near the end of a quiet road. In Chapel Hill the rhythm of my life was gentler than it had been in Manhattan. That was intentional. That was the point, and so was a redirection of my exertions from my own ambitions and my own achievements to the ambitions and achievements of the next generation. Cyrus Habib was right: *My* and *me* are prisons. I just staged a less dramatic, more qualified jailbreak than his.

I liked having new vistas, new rituals. I missed Central Park. I'm sure that Regan did, too. But I got her a big backyard with plenty of greenery to sniff and dozens of trees for shade. And a screened porch! Leading to a deck! What was ordinary for many veteran suburbanites was a revelation to me, and on my and Regan's second night in our new house, I poured myself a tall glass of chardonnay, lit a three-wick citronella candle and, despite the heat, sat on one of the deck's built-in wooden benches as the sky darkened. I sipped and sipped as crickets fiddled and fiddled. I grew woozy, maybe from the wine, maybe from the heat. It was precisely the sensation that I'd been looking for.

The next morning, I drove eight minutes to the edge of the UNC campus, found a place to park, put Regan on her leash and took a winding two-mile walk past the residence hall where I'd lived freshman year, nursing so many insecurities and battling so many anxieties that I wasn't confident I'd make it all the way to May; across the quadrangle where I'd sat on a blanket with the teaching assistant for my art history class, mooning over him but never letting him know; through the campus arboretum, where I'd snuck a few joints on a few nights; to a storefront that had been a bar where I'd traded so many confidences with so many friends. We'd confessed our fears that we'd never amount to anything. We'd admitted to doubts that we'd find true love. Would we have pretty homes? Would we live in interesting places? So many unknowns, so many apprehensions. But I don't recall any of us asking if we'd go blind.

We have no control over what happens to us; we have enormous control over what happens to us. I'll spend the rest of my life better understanding and better accepting that paradox, which I understand and accept better today than I did before October 2017, before that first day of incomprehensible blur, before an education in neuro-ophthalmology that became an education in so much more.

Will I spend the rest of my life alone, by which I mean without a husband or such? After Tom and I broke up, I had a short series of casual sexual encounters, and I wondered—as did several of my friends, who asked me about it—if the specter of lost sight would raise the premium on touch, making me more eager for it and more receptive to it. It didn't, not for me. It made me less patient with romantic ambiguity, with situations in which signals were unclear, gestures were contradictory and time was possibly being wasted. When I did end up dating one man on and off for about eight months, it wasn't just because he was considerate, intelligent and handsome; it was because his ardor was emphatic and he didn't play any guessing games. But he was more than twenty years younger than I was, and I'd never had that in me and still didn't. He was in the aspiration phase of his life. I recognized it and knew it well. But that was no longer the phase of mine. We're friends now, and for now, my friends give me all I really need. I prefer going to bed by myself. I like being able to binge-watch whatever I want—no negotiations, no compromises—until sleep claims me. If I'm sloppy with the popcorn, so what? I can clean up the stray kernels the next morning.

And I needn't make conversation when I take long, meditative walks. I took too few of them in my twenties, my thirties, my forties. In my fifties, I remedied that, connected as never before to that basic, fundamental pleasure. Regan motivated me, sure. But that wasn't the whole of it. Plus, I'd summoned her, not the other way around. I created that motivation. And I think, in retrospect, I knew exactly what I was doing.

In my strolls through Central Park with her after my stroke, I noticed something that I hadn't back when I'd used the park solely for exercise. It was something that must have been there all along because I now noticed it all the time, not just in Central Park but also in Riverside Park. It was clearly common, ongoing.

What I noticed were old men and old women in wheelchairs. I don't mean phalanxes of them or all that many, really, but a woman here, a man there, almost always near one of the park's entrances, close to a perimeter street—they hadn't been wheeled all that far. A caretaker of some kind, perhaps a relative, just as likely a health aide, accompanied each of them. The duo would sit together quietly, positioned for a good look at a patch of pond, a sliver of river, a grouping of trees, a gaggle of geese.

When I first noticed them, it made me a little sad. I focused on the wheelchair and all that it connoted. I registered the hunch or stoop in most of these old people's postures. I thought about their dependency—there was no way to spin that as a positive or even neutral development. I felt sorry for them.

But after more observation and more reflection, I didn't. I focused on the big, fluffy, cozy-looking blankets unfurled across their laps in fall, winter and spring. I focused on the sense of calm around them, on their rootedness in this one prime spot on this one overabundant Earth. They couldn't traverse as much ground as they once had, couldn't travel far on their own. But they still had the outdoors, at least a piece of it, and that piece wasn't such a shabby one. Reading their expressions, I suspected that many of them appreciated that. How many of them had trouble with their own eyesight? How many were blind or nearly blind?

I thought about that, about the question mark of my own future and about what an unexpected truce with that question mark I'd made. Maybe I'd drawn strength from Bob Kerrey, from Dorrie, from Cyrus Habib. Maybe I benefited from the fact that my particular condition—my individual challenge—involved a long pause between a period of being moderately compromised and a period, if it even arrived, of being much more so.

I thought about how crazy and potentially cruel it was that some of the bounty in the world that I appreciated more than

ever was visual—and would be taken from me in a worst-case
scenario. The shifting light and changing colors of Central
Park: Those would be gone. So would the views of the midtown
Manhattan skyscrapers standing guard over the park's southern edge. So would Regan's sudden levitation above a fence, her
split-second suspension in the air, where she briefly broke free
of gravity and existed in a perishable bubble of contentment all
her own. So would the stars.

With my untrustworthy eyes, I gazed up at the night sky all
the time. I rediscovered the heavens, wondering why I hadn't
angled my face and my wonderment in that direction before.
I couldn't get enough of the stars, and when I found myself on
a field or beach or street where the fewness and dimness of
the lights brought the stars into relief, I stopped and I stared. I
stretched out the moment as far as I could. I breathed it in and
made it permanent, emblazoning that tapestry of twinkles on
my mind, the way Swankie had emblazoned those eggshells
on hers.

Then I closed my eyes. I did this more and more. It was a
dare, an experiment, a girding. I did it in Central Park when
reveling in the foliage, on a porch beyond which the sun was
setting, on a beach pummeled by angry surf. What happened
when these images were stolen from me? How thoroughly was
I impoverished?

I refused to do any careful accounting. I did a looser, la-
zier tally of all that remained. I had the sound of that foliage—
because it *did* make a sound—along with the caress of the wind
that orchestrated it on my skin. I had the birdcall at dusk; in
time, I might be as expert in its music as Stanley Wainapel

was. I had the faint spray of those waves, palpable if you drew close and concentrated hard enough. And I had an imagination that, like Juan Jose's and David Tatel's, could fill in the blanks. It could also take me places I'd never been, fill me with feelings I'd never felt.

There was this one long, quiet, dead-end street in Sag Harbor, where my friends Joel and Nicole live, that I'd take Regan down when the last vestiges of the sun were gone and nightfall was complete. She'd scout for deer and sometimes chase one or two for ten to fifteen seconds before boomeranging back to my side. I'd scout for the Big Dipper, the Little Dipper, other celestial configurations for which I could invent my own names. I'd do the stopping I mentioned, the staring I mentioned. I'd also do that thing with my eyes I mentioned, shutting them tight, as if they were out of business, never to resume operation again.

And when I did, I'd levitate. Not like Regan—not just a few feet. I'd go up, up, up. I'd be riding the breeze, I'd be rocketing into the cosmos. I was powered by my profound appreciation of the riot of experiences, more of them thrilling than gutting, that had delivered me to this place in this frame of mind. I was buoyant with the determination to keep clinging to the highs and sloughing off the lows. I swayed and soared on my belief in the beauty of every stage of the precious day, from the near side of dawn to the far side of dusk. On those gusts of feeling, I didn't need to see the stars because I hovered among them.

You should see me fly.

Acknowledgments

There are many too many people to name. But still:

Elinor Burkett, Kerry Lauerman, Jennifer Steinhauer, Honor Jones, Maureen Dowd, Alessandra Stanley, Gail Collins, Trish Hall, Tom de Kay, Sarah Rosenberg, Cassandra Harvin, Marysue Rucci, Anne Kornblut, Dan Senor, Campbell Brown, Bret Stephens, Jim Rutenberg, Ondine Karady, Barbara Laing, Vivian Toy, Liriel Higa, Anna Marks, Mike Valerio and Lee Jason Goldberg: all of you have shown me such extraordinary kindness over the last few years. I'm grateful for, and honored by, your friendship.

Joel Klein and Nicole Seligman: "Grateful" and "honored" don't begin to cover it. This book wouldn't have been finished without you. In my thoughts, we're always at the American, heaters blasting, a white first and then a red.

I'm indebted to all of the people interviewed for and

profiled in this book, but must single out two. Dr. Rudrani Banik, you were so very generous to me at a moment when I needed that more than you knew. And Dorrie Pence Sundquist, meeting you almost four decades ago was a blessing; knowing you ever since, a privilege.

I'm indebted as well to Eric Johnson and Eliza Grace Martin for their research help, counsel and good cheer.

Across more than a quarter century, the *New York Times* has provided me with wonderful opportunities, for which I thank everyone there. Duke University has given me the warmest of new homes, whose denizens have my enormous gratitude and affection.

At Avid Reader Press, everyone has been a consummate professional and joy, no one more so than Ben Loehnen, whose patience, grace and sound editorial judgment kept my spirits as high as the spirits of an author stumbling toward a (repeatedly renegotiated) deadline can be.

And Amanda (Binky) Urban: I relish you—and our walks, with Regan, across fairways dappled with deer.

Finally, I thank my father, Frank Sr., for all that he tried to teach me, during an era I miss so much. I thank my uncles, aunts, cousins, nieces and nephews for demonstrating, every day, what family, at its best, can be. Above all, I thank my siblings and their spouses: Mark and Lisa, Harry and Sylvia, Adelle and Dan. What a team we have. What a gift you are.

About the Author

Frank Bruni is the author of four *New York Times* bestsellers, including the memoir *Born Round*, and spent more than twenty-five years on the staff of the *New York Times*, in positions as varied as op-ed columnist, restaurant critic, Rome bureau chief and White House correspondent. In April 2021, he was named Eugene C. Patterson Professor of the Practice of Journalism and Public Policy at Duke University's Sanford School of Public Policy. His work continues to appear in the *Times*, where he is a contributing opinion writer. He lives in Chapel Hill, North Carolina.

The Beauty of Dusk

Frank Bruni

This reading group guide for The Beauty of Dusk *includes an introduction, discussion questions, and ideas for enhancing your book club. The suggested questions are intended to help your reading group find new and interesting angles and topics for your discussion. We hope that these ideas will enrich your conversation and increase your enjoyment of the book.*

Introduction

One morning in late 2017, *New York Times* columnist Frank Bruni woke up with strangely blurred vision. Overnight, a rare stroke had cut off blood to one of his optic nerves, rendering him functionally blind in that eye—forever. In *The Beauty of Dusk*, Bruni recounts a medical and spiritual odyssey that involved not only reappraising his own priorities but also reaching out to, and gathering wisdom from, longtime friends and new acquaintances who had navigated their own traumas and afflictions. The result is a poignant, probing and, ultimately, uplifting examination of the limits that all of us inevitably encounter, the lenses through which we choose to evaluate them and the tools we have for perseverance.

Topics & Questions for Discussion

1. Why do you think Bruni chose the title *The Beauty of Dusk* for this memoir?

2. Bruni writes about sincerely embracing the familiar sayings that emphasize the bright side of human resilience when faced with hardship: "When you're given lemons, you can indeed make lemonade, and that was a big part of my education, which included the confirmation . . . that clouds have silver linings and that the night is darkest before dawn." After reading the book, do you agree with Bruni's perspective? Do you feel the same way about your own experiences?

3. When Bruni was in college, he absorbed the refrain of a psychology professor: "Life is about adjusting to loss." What do you think the professor meant? Do you agree with this statement?

4. After Bruni loses partial vision, he grows more aware of other people's hidden pain. He imagines a world where everybody walked through life with a sandwich board advertising their invisible struggles. "If each of us had just a glimpse of the burdens that people were shouldering," he says, "we'd all be a whole lot less consumed with our own misfortunes and slights—and a whole lot more understanding of other people's moods and misdeeds." What are some ways in which we could make this world a reality without adopting literal sandwich boards?

5. What's one thing that your sandwich board would say?

6. Are you open about difficulties? Why or why not?

7. *The Beauty of Dusk* is a memoir of one man's life-altering experience, yet Bruni looks for wisdom in the stories of other individuals who live with physical limitations or emotional pain such as grief. Which of the other stories in the book spoke to you most profoundly, and why?

8. How has this book changed the way that you think about aging?

9. Living through the Covid-19 pandemic prompted many of us to reevaluate our lives. Bruni writes, "Many people I know were as surprised by how many activities they *didn't* miss as by how many they did. . . . They discovered that at least a few of the ways in which life was collapsed, con-

strained and cloistered had upsides." Did you find yourself evolving as Bruni described? Or did you experience different revelations?

10. Becoming the owner of a dog, Regan, helped Bruni's well-being by motivating him to exercise and experience nature, giving him companionship, and showing him how to get the most joy out of life's simple pleasures. What lifestyle changes can we do for physical or mental health with a pet or by ourselves?

11. Bruni's friend Dorrie, who lives with Parkinson's disease, turns to a physical outlet for her frustrations when she feels overwhelmed: beating a cooking pot on the ground. Dorrie tells Bruni, "It felt great. I think it made me a better wife and mother and person in general." Why is it important to recognize and process our negative feelings? What tactics do you find effective?

12. What does Bruni gain when he loses vision in one eye?

13. Bruni writes, "I went to bed with more grievances than I could count. I woke up with more gratitude than I can measure." What is one grievance you can let go of right now? What is one thing you can be extra grateful for?

Enhance Your Book Club

1. Reflecting on the title of the book, go around in a circle and have each member think of a different title for Bruni's memoir. Then go around and ask each member to think of the title they would give their own memoir.

2. If you could ask Bruni one question about his life or his book, what would you ask?

3. Bruni reminds us that we never know how much time we have in prime physical health. Go around the group and commit to fulfilling one resolution for a trip, a dream goal, any bucket list item to complete this year.